The Institutionalization of Indoctrination

The Institutionalization of Indoctrination

An Exploratory Investigation Based on the Romanian Case Study

Paul Dragos Aligica and Simona Preda

LEXINGTON BOOKS
Lanham • Boulder • New York • London

Published by Lexington Books

An imprint of The Rowman & Littlefield Publishing Group, Inc.
4501 Forbes Boulevard, Suite 200, Lanham, Maryland 20706
www.rowman.com

86-90 Paul Street, London EC2A 4NE

Copyright © 2022 by The Rowman & Littlefield Publishing Group, Inc.

All rights reserved. No part of this book may be reproduced in any form or by any electronic or mechanical means, including information storage and retrieval systems, without written permission from the publisher, except by a reviewer who may quote passages in a review.

British Library Cataloguing in Publication Information Available

Library of Congress Cataloging-in-Publication Data

Names: Aligică, Paul Dragoș, author. | Preda, Simona, 1978- author.
Title: The institutionalization of indoctrination : an exploratory investigation based on the Romanian case study / Paul Dragos Aligica and Simona Preda.
Description: Lanham : Lexington Books, [2022] | Includes bibliographical references and index.
Identifiers: LCCN 2021053137 (print) | LCCN 2021053138 (ebook) | ISBN 9781793635495 (cloth ; alk. paper) | ISBN 9781793635501 (ebook) | ISBN 9781793635518 (paperback)
Subjects: LCSH: Propaganda, Communist--Romania--History--20th century. | Communism--Romania--History--20th century. | Romania--Politics and government--1944-1989. | Romania--Social conditions--1945-1989.
Classification: LCC JN9632.Z13 P8525 2022 (print) | LCC JN9632.Z13 (ebook) | DDC 303.3/75094980904--dc23/eng/20211201
LC record available at https://lccn.loc.gov/2021053137
LC ebook record available at https://lccn.loc.gov/2021053138

∞ The paper used in this publication meets the minimum requirements of American National Standard for Information Sciences—Permanence of Paper for Printed Library Materials, ANSI/NISO Z39.48-1992.

Contents

Acknowledgments vii

Introduction ix

PART I: THE INSTITUTIONALIZATION OF PROPAGANDA AND INDOCTRINATION: THE PHENOMENON THROUGH CONCEPTUAL AND THEORETICAL LENSES 1

Chapter 1: Ideocracy, Totalitarianism, and the "New Man" 3

Chapter 2: The Functions and Logic of the Indoctrination and Propaganda Institutions 19

PART II: THE ROMANIAN CASE (1948–1989): DESCRIPTIVE AND NARRATIVE FACETS 41

Chapter 3: Indoctrination and Propaganda in Communist Romania: An Overview of the General Patterns of Organization and Evolution over Time 45

Chapter 4: The Ideological Worker: An Overview of Its Profiles and Functions in the Context of the Romanian System 67

Chapter 5: The Ideological Turn in Higher Education: Further Insights from the Romanian Case 99

PART III: EVOLVING FRAMEWORKS OF ANALYSIS AND EMERGING RESEARCH AGENDAS 123

Chapter 6: A Failure of Institutionalization: A Key Insight from the Case Study and the Challenges of its External Validity 125

Chapter 7: Research Directions in the Study of Indoctrination and
    Its Institutionalization   147

Bibliography   157

Index   171

About the Authors   175

Acknowledgments

This book was made possible by the support offered by the Institute for Humane Studies at George Mason University and the Center for Governance and Markets at the University of Pittsburgh. We acknowledge with gratitude the tremendous contribution of these two organizations. Jennifer Brick Murtazashvilli deserves special thanks for her belief in this project, which in fact started as a result of a series of conversations between her and Paul Dragos Aligica regarding their parallel institutional experiences in the context of contemporary academia. Her constant support, over the entire duration of the project, is most sincerely and gratefully acknowledged. The investigation reflected in one chapter of the work was supported by a grant of the Romanian Ministry of Education and Research, CNCS-UEFISCDI, project number PN-III-P4-ID-PCE-2020–1076, within PNCDI III. Paul Dragos Aligica expresses his gratitude for the spillovers generated by that grant, allowing a research investigation into the nature and resilience of a very peculiar institutional structure.

This book also owes immensely to the advice and encouragement we have received over the years from our colleagues at the University of Bucharest and George Mason University. Special thanks to Richard Wagner, Peter Boettke, Virgil Storr, and Dan Rothschild for creating a hospitable and productive setting at Mercatus Center at George Mason University for an entire research program, out of which this book is just a small contribution. Individual chapters of the book or ideas and arguments now presented in sections and fragments of various chapters were read, discussed, and most helpfully commented on by Richard Wagner, Robert Whaples, Eileen Norcross, Marian Zulean, Marian Preda, and Eleanor Ealy. We thank them for their generous feedback, criticism, and encouragement.

The book includes material published in Paul Dragos Aligica, "The Ideological Commissar and the Institutionalization of Indoctrination," *Independent Review*, vol. 25, 2021. We thank the *Independent Review* for permission to reprint this material.

The invaluable help of Logan Hansen is gratefully acknowledged. Logan's help in revising and editing the first draft of the manuscript was decisive. His competence, dedication, and professionalism are most highly and gratefully appreciated. We also want to thank Miruna Voiculescu for her assistance in translating from Romanian some parts of the text, and to Jonathan Plante for reviewing them.

A different sort of debt is owed to three people at Lexington: Joseph Parry, whose interest in and support of the project in the initial stages were crucial, Sara Noakes, and Melissa McClellan. They supervised the project with professionalism and dedication, easing the progress of the manuscript from submission to its publication. We remain responsible for any errors or omissions.

Introduction

This book is an exploratory contribution to the study of the social organization of ideology and, more precisely, of the institutionalization of indoctrination and propaganda. The diversity of ways political systems organize and institutionalize their ideological functions seems to be a topic far from neglected by both scholarly work and journalism alike. Yet, at a closer look, the scholarly treatment of the ways of the ideological function gets organized and embedded in institutionalized structures reveals massive lacunae. As one becomes more familiar with the topic, it becomes clearer and clearer that, in this case, the issue is not just about the proverbial "gaps in the literature" that are to be filled. The reality is that, in order to put this research line on solid footing, one needs to start with very basic, foundational questions: How do we conceptualize and theorize about the social organization of ideology? How should we think methodically—in theoretically and empirically informed ways—about the institutionalization of indoctrination and propaganda? How should we conceptualize and theorize about the social and political instrumentation of ideology in regimes or systems that assume that historical missions of salvation or radical transformations are the stringent organizing and legitimization principles of their very existence? What are the best ways to document and study the specific domains of institutionalization of indoctrination, like, for instance, the way it gets inserted and implemented in education systems? This book is an attempt to outline several converging and complementary venues approaching the responses to these and similar questions. The exploratory investigations reflected in it, thus, have to be read as a propaedeutic for better analytic engagement with the problem of indoctrination and its institutionalization.

It is commonplace within political science textbooks to note that modern political systems have embedded into their structures distinctive organizational arrangements, whose function is to propagate, monitor, enforce, and manage a set of ideological positions, which have a central role in both defining and supporting the institutional architecture of those systems.

In most cases, these organizations or organizational units operate in the shadow of routine, without much salience. In fact, that is precisely a mark of democratic-liberal regimes: the toning down (or even absence of in large areas of social and organizational life) of these formal ideological vectors.

Yet, while in some political systems these entities and the functions they express remain mostly veiled, latent, and not very outstanding elements, in others they come to occupy a pivotal, manifest position. They are intrinsically intertwined with the very fundaments and operations of those systems. When that happens, one of the main features of these institutional arrangements is that they are rarely standalone. They operate by penetrating and planting their units within other existing organizations. And thus, almost all other institutions and organizations, each having its distinctive social role and position in the system, come to be monitored, censored, and managed on their ideological dimension from the inside by these political-ideological units and agents. At the same time, these units are operating, coordinated through an overarching (national and sometimes even international) systemic structure.

Thus, the entire institutional configuration of the political and social system is pervaded and altered. Distinctive patterns start to emerge. At that point, we already know that we are dealing with a peculiar form of a political system or regime. In it, a set of supreme ideas and values, taking a particular ideological form, comes to occupy a position such that they are considered the ultimate and exclusive drivers and regulators of social life. Those in charge with interpreting and guarding those values and ideas—and with the correctness of their application in practice—gain a dominant social position. Obviously, all of that has major institutional and governance implications.

Probably the easiest to grasp and the best-known illustration of this type of political phenomenon is the institution of the so-called "political commissar," operating under various names and forms in Communist regimes.[1] The standard definitions describe it as an official of the Communist Party, especially in the Soviet Union or China, responsible for political education, indoctrination, and reinforcing the loyalty of the military to the government. The standard function of the Army in any political system or regime is to defend the country and to develop and deploy human and material capabilities in this respect. The function of the commissar was to make sure the Army in a country that turned Communism was internalizing the Communist worldview, mindset, and interpretation of world events and that it was loyal in thought and action to the Communist Party's aims. It was the deepest, most profoundly reaching (in socio-psychological and indoctrination terms) conduit between each army unit and the Communist Party, a Party that was the political, ideological, and organizational center of the system and the ultimate standard in the interpretation of the Communist vision and ideology. That role required engaging in a continuous monitoring, indoctrination, and guidance process, always following the lines given "from the Center."

The "political commissar" is an excellent illustration not only of the nature of this type of political-ideological practice but also a reminder of the fact that its model could be extended (and indeed was extended in the Soviet Union, China, and Eastern Europe) to the other social institutions beyond the army. From factories to schools and hospitals, almost all organizations in Communism had, at one point or another, a special ideological office or agent, by now defined as "ideological worker"—different from those of the Communist Party, the political police, or the informers of the political police. This office was responsible for both directing and supervising the ideological training and indoctrination as well as monitoring and enforcing the official worldview and interpretation of the current events in all those institutions. The result in all Soviet or Soviet-inspired regimes was that it became "generally impossible to delimit precisely the field of propaganda. It is only one aspect of a total program of action that ranges from primary education to industrial and agricultural production, and which encompasses all literature, art and leisure. The entire life of the citizen becomes the object of propaganda." We come, thus, to find an office (or at least an agent, the ideological worker) exercising this function in most domains of organized activity in Communist regimes. Among them—as one may expect—the institutions of education and especially higher education were the object of a special attention.

These elementary observations about the "political commissar" or "ideological worker" and its functions in Communist regimes give a clear indication of the nature and importance of the phenomenon examined in this book, irrespective of the name or label under which it is known in real life or the scholarly literature. Indeed, such an accentuated institutionalization of the ideological element and its associated structures and mechanisms is a feature of a large class of regimes and political systems and a recurring phenomenon in history. And yet, the historical evidence shows that although that function may be present in any political system, there are some systems in which it grows and spreads to become the defining feature of the system. And when it comes to that, their strongest and most extreme form has manifested in modern times, so far, in Communist regimes. That means that in our attempt to understand the circumstances and implications surrounding the accentuated institutionalization of the ideological element (which takes place in a large class of regimes and political systems) one of the most fruitful ways to start is to explore it first in its Communist ("real life Socialism") avatar.

This book is a contribution to the study of this institutional phenomenon and its operations. Let's call it, for now, the institution of the "political ideological commissar" or "ideological worker," though as one could easily see, the function and its institutional and organizational embodiments have materialized and continue to materialize in recent history under different shapes and names. The objective of the book is to contribute to a better understanding of these apparently simple and familiar, yet, in fact, complex and poorly understood institutional arrangements and their associated indoctrination and social control practices. This is an exploratory study. Its main goal is propaedeutic and heuristic. It is an attempt to determine what a tentative review of the relevant literature and of a pertinent case study could teach us about the ways to intellectually engage such phenomena: How should we approach and think about this type of phenomena?

The fact that an exploratory study like ours gives a special attention to the education system, and especially higher education, should not come as a surprise. In "real life Socialism," indoctrination in higher education was a centerpiece of the national political strategies of social transformation. Universities were among the first targets of any Communist, collectivist regime. By keeping them as a constant reference point in our approaches, one anchors the investigation at the very core of the phenomenon of interest. At the same time, the phenomenon and its social and organizational forms could not be understood independently of the larger political and social systems they are a part of. The fact that we always keep in mind the social and institutional embeddedness of the ideological institutions opens up a two-way analytical and interpretive traffic. By exploring the avatar of this totalitarian function in its Communist materialization, we not only get a better grounded understanding of the nature and operations of the institutions of indoctrination and ideological control, but we also get a better understanding of the broader social and political system itself. The place and role of these institutions reveal important aspects of the organizational and administrative logic of the Communist and totalitarian regimes.

In brief, this book is meant to be an exploratory contribution to a larger research program focusing on the analysis of the nature, structure, and functioning of these indoctrination and propaganda institutional forms as well as on their relationship with the broader governance systems they are a part of. On the one hand, the book will explore the existing relevant literature and will discuss some elements of conceptualization and theoretical framing that are able to orient—both in substantive terms and as models of possible approaches—our general efforts to describe, analyze, and understand the phenomena in case. New potential venues of theoretical elaboration will also be identified, and in several cases, these venues will be tentatively engaged. On the other hand, the book will balance the exploratory theoretical approach with an exploratory empirical investigation.

This book will take the organization of indoctrination in Socialist Eastern Europe between 1945 and 1990 as a historical and empirical reference point, and, within that population of cases, it will focus on one country and one specific problem: the organization and evolution of the indoctrination function in Communist Romania. It will place a special focus on (higher) education with a view to get a better grasp on the intricacies of the phenomenon in real life settings. Concentrating on Communist Romania, the book will chart and analyze various elements and facets of both the organization of indoctrination and the functions and institutionalization of the "political-ideological commissars" in the education system while tracking their evolution over the forty-five years of Communism in that country. Our hope is that the two dimensions of the book—on the one hand, the historical and descriptive overview of the Romanian case, and on the other hand, the approach through the theoretical lenses based in modern institutional analysis, political economy, and organizational theory—will manage to offer, in conjunction, a constructive contribution to the advancement of this line of research.

Before moving ahead, it is necessary to clarify a couple of "method and approach" points. As mentioned, this is an interdisciplinary project, in which the interface between social sciences and history is preeminent. Given the social sciences facet of the project, we need to address, from the very beginning, two basic questions about case selection and analytical focus: Why Romania? Why education? In other words, this: What kind of more general significance could we associate with their study in depth, in addition to the intrinsic historical value of the exercise?

Obviously, in our approach, our first concern was to give our study a solid empirical grounding. Hence, as already suggested, out of the population of historical and empirical cases, we have identified a real case study that is clearly circumscribed in historical and institutional terms. It is only via the in-depth familiarity with such case that we could truly understand and appreciate how the organization of indoctrination and ideological social engineering operates in real life in its political, social, and administrative settings. As already noted, the strongest, most extreme, and longest-lasting forms of indoctrination institutions documented so far in modern history were associated with the Communist regimes. Their success in eliminating or marginalizing both religious and secular challengers, and their thoroughness in operation, was unparalleled. So, it is natural that, in trying to identify the most analytically fruitful possible cases, we have selected ours from the category of "real life Socialism" countries and their historical experiences.

Before looking more precisely at our particular case chosen from that category (i.e., Romania), let us first illuminate why, out of multiple domains—social, economic, cultural, and so forth—we have given more attention to education and why we think that, especially at this exploratory stage of the research agenda, one needs to prioritize it. An obvious reason is that because education—due to its very nature—was first and foremost the natural target for the indoctrination and propaganda practices. The most permanent, systematic, and accentuated forms of the ideological phenomena of interest to us, took place in this domain. But, in addition to that, there is a second, less evident reason. Even in Communist regimes, education continued to withhold one of its main general features as a social function by continuing to be a factor in social stratification.[2] Writing at the heights of the Stalinist era, Elisabeth Koutaissoff remarked that, even under Stalin, from the point of view of power, income, and prestige, there were three major forms of inequality in the USSR: first, "the power, prestige and often, though not necessarily, the higher income, enjoyed by Party members"; second, "the highly differential scale of wages"; and third, "the different levels of education leading to differentially paid posts as well as to diverse degrees of responsibility and social prestige."[3] The educational aspect of stratification is thus, next to the political and economic ones, part and parcel of the configuration of the system's architecture and hierarchy. Education, and especially higher education, had a crucial position in the system. Controlling education was a form of deep, structural, and long-term control over the entire system and its dynamics in both its structure and the mindsets of the citizens.

We have given a rationale of the approach advanced by this book by answering these questions: Why have a special interest in education? Why have a special interest in real life Eastern European Communist systems? Now, because the empirical anchor of this study will be an investigation of one country—Romania and more precisely, the organization and evolution of the ideological and indoctrination function in Romania during the Communist period (1948–1989)—we need to also address the following question: Why should one consider Romania as a salient and significant case in respect to our phenomenon of interest?

One way to answer is to simply point to the typical and illustrative nature of the case, standing *grosso modo* for any Eastern European country behind the Iron Curtain and its experience in this respect. But there is a second, more technical, answer pointing to what the 2009 Noble Prize in Economic Sciences laureate, Elinor Ostrom, called the "extreme case" approach to the use of case studies. Ostrom invites us to learn from biologists' approach when they are facing situations of studying complex processes that are poorly understood. The strategy is to identify cases "in which the process occurs in clarified even exaggerated forms." The case "is not chosen because it is representative for all forms." Rather, the case is chosen "because particular processes can be studied more effectively using it than using another."[4] That is to say, the extreme case method selects a case because of its extreme value on the variable of interest. "An extreme value is understood here as an observation that lies outside the mean of a given distribution."[5] In this respect, it is transparent why—following the extreme case logic—our case is selected, as already noted, from the population of political systems with accentuated, salient features of indoctrination and ideology (even more precisely, from the subpopulation of Communist cases identified by us as the most salient modern exemplars of such nature). One may also add that even within that set, the case of Romania stands out. As the following chapters will remind us, Romania's evolution from the brutal period of Stalinism to the eccentric dictatorship of Nicolae Ceaușescu, with its peculiar personality cult, is indeed outstanding.

As a further elaboration of the "typical" versus the "extreme" case theme, we should also note that, as Seawright and Gerring explain,[6] the extreme case method always "refers back to a larger sample of cases lying in the background of the analysis." Once we are aware of that, we realize that shifting the reference background cases—that is to say, the population of systems one is taking as a reference—leads to a shift of accent. In our situation, we could see our Romanian case in either the background of the entire population of cases of political systems, with its full range of variation, or, alternatively, in the background of a subset of it (i.e., the Communist systems). The same unit of observation and analysis may thus be interpreted, in function of the background of reference, and angle of interpretation, either as a representative or as an extreme case. Obviously, it all depends on the reference point and the objectives of the analysis

That is to say, when it comes to the variable of interest, using the class of Communist systems as a background, the Romanian system and the indoctrination institutional arrangements could be seen as representative. It may be a typical representative of the class in the measure in which, based on what we currently know, we have no reason to suspect that the Romanian regime during the period covered by our investigation was, at its core, anything else than a standard adaptation of the Soviet/Communist system, including in respect to the institutionalization of indoctrination in educational systems. Conversely, seen in the background of a larger set of political systems, including liberal democracies, and focusing on some of its facets, some of its features may be naturally emerging as salient or extreme.[7] In brief, the Romanian case gives the reader some degrees of freedom in adopting this interpretive strategy while going through the details of the case.

To sum up, the investigation is exploratory, multilayered, and open-ended. Our hope is that, at a minimum, by simply charting the literature and bringing to the table a set of relevant concepts and theoretical frameworks as well as by identifying some possible venues of advancing the research agenda, the book will make a contribution to our efforts to better conceptualize and understand the phenomenon and what is at stake. Also, by bringing to the table and exploring in-depth a case that is unambiguously circumscribed in historical and institutional terms, we hope to contribute to a more empirically grounded approach to the topic. The study may be seen (in function of the background cases taken as a reference) as either a typical, representative case study or as an extreme case study. Irrespective of how one approaches the case, our investigation is framed to advance our understanding of the social organization of ideology and the institutionalization of indoctrination.

Now that the general contours of the project have been tentatively outlined, let us briefly go over the structure of the book. As we have noted, our objective is to try as much as possible to go beyond the journalistic and common sense interpretations by engaging a minimal set of theoretical lenses able to help us to put some order and render intelligible the complex facets of the phenomena in point. The ideological and indoctrination processes and their associated institutions and practices are, in fact, a nexus of social, political, economic, and cultural factors. As such, they could be charted and examined under different—sometimes converging, sometimes parallel—approaches pertaining to different literatures and fields. The eclectic and interdisciplinary approach is thus unavoidable. The first part of the book looks at the relevant literature and identifies several salient ways in which the existent literature has responded to these challenges. At the same time, the book tries to further elaborate and calibrate some of concepts and theoretical lenses pertaining to this literature. Although far from comprehensive in covering the pertinent literature and the variety of frames and narratives used to deal with the phenomenon of interest, the section gives a rather robust sense of the main way the academic discourse has been shaped in this respect in the last 45 years or so. The result is an introduction to the problem of social organization of ideology as a major political factor and an illustration of the models of how one could think theoretically in the efforts to decipher and explain the features or patterns associated with indoctrination.

The second part of the book is dedicated, as noted, to an overview of the Romanian case. At this point, the book moves to explore the potential of an approach in which the historical case study becomes the main vehicle. In this type of approach, the emphasis is not on the conceptual and theoretical apparatus, but rather on the effort to identify the rich texture of the institutions, social actors, patterns, and events that are associated with the institutionalization of indoctrination in this Eastern European country during the Communist period. In exploring the Romanian case, we will start with the discussion of the central national institutional instrument for implementing the indoctrination function, as defined under the leadership of the Communist Party: The Agitation and Propaganda Department (later to be renamed "Section"). Then, we focus on the agent (the propagandist, the ideological worker) and its role and operational principles. Once that is done, we will be in the position to take a closer look at the strenuous dynamics set into motion by both agent and institutional arrangements as they operated in the evolving circumstances of the Communist regime during the second part of the twentieth century. We will find out that the emerging image is one of a dynamic processes of ongoing institutional change and adjustment, never fully successful, even by the indulgent and self-congratulatory propagandistic standards of the Communist Party. The resulting picture is far from the official narrative or image of a "triumphant march." We will reveal an ongoing muddling-through: a never ending patching and tinkering while, at each juncture, the Communist authorities were trying to contain a process that seemed to recurringly escape their full control.

Read in conjunction, the first two parts of the book will offer the reader complementing perspectives, each approaching the topic from different angles. The first part approaches from a broad angle—both in terms of the generality of the empirical material covered and of the scope of the conceptual and theoretical lenses and frameworks used. The second part approaches from the angle of a series of factual observations based on historical data and archival records, bringing to the table a sense of the complexities and dynamics of the real-life Communist system. The Romanian case will reveal, first and foremost, important insights about both the efficacy and the limits of indoctrination systems and ideocratic regimes. The most important insight we will gain is how difficult it is to implement and maintain a politically and ideologically correct line operating on totalitarian principles, even when one controls the entire state apparatus and has access to a massive set of institutional instruments designed precisely for this reason. Thus, the initial insights brought forth by the case will take us to another level of questions and investigative venues, inviting a more methodical attempt to understand the nature and dynamics of the phenomena.

The third part of the book will make several tentative steps in the direction of those venues. Using the clues offered by key observations coming from the case study, it will identify, in the already existing organizational sociology literature, a fresh way of framing an additional explanatory level of the institutional processes associated with propaganda and indoctrination. Its successful application to the interpretation of the Romanian case will demonstrate the feasibility and the potential of this type of research strategy, one that identifies conceptual instruments already forged in well-established fields like sociology, institutional theory, or political science and then applies them to specific problems and cases of interest. Based on that, several possible research agendas could be outlined, some of them along comparative lines—exploring the external validity of the insights advanced by our investigation—and some along analytical lines that consider the internal validity of the explanatory frameworks employed in our discussion of the case study. Therefore, the book will end up—appropriately so for an exploratory study—with a set of open questions and some possible modes of addressing them. Dealing with them and with the other questions and research venues that have emerged as salient in our inquiry will be the task of the next steps in the development of a research agenda, out of which the current study is just a preliminary, tentative, exploratory investigation.

NOTES

1. A variety of terms have been used over time to identify this function: *propagandist, ideologist, agitator, ideological worker, political commissar, lecturer, activist,* or *cadre.* Although each of these terms has its specific meaning—depending on the time in the history of Communism, context, and the duties assigned to each category—with few exceptions, the preferred generic term in the Communist vocabulary for the person conducting propaganda is *propagandist.* All point out to a specific institutional function in the Communist system. In our study, we will use, in most cases, these terms interchangeably as a default. However, each time when the specific meaning is important in context, we are going to be explicit about it.

2. E. Koutaissoff, "Soviet Education and the New Man" in *Soviet Studies,* 5, no. 2 (1953): 103–37.

3. E. Koutaissoff, op.cit. 103–37.

4. Elinor Ostrom, *Governing the Commons: The Evolution of Institutions for Collective Action* (Cambridge University Press, 1990).

5. Jason Seawright and John Gerring, "Case selection techniques in case study research: A menu of qualitative and quantitative options" in *Political research quarterly* 61, no. 2 (2008), 294–308.

6. Jason Seawright and John Gerring, op.cit., 301–2.

7. Two more comments of a methodological nature are in place. Following Seawright and Gerring (op.cit., 301–2), let us note that for each generalization and conclusion reached in the process—as long as one does not forget that there are some background cases that give meaning to the case in point—the analysis "is not likely to be subject to problems of sample bias." This observation puts us in the position to draw attention to the intrinsically open-ended nature of our research project. The very type of case study approach that we are using implies and requires it. The extreme case approach, write Seawright and Gerring, is a purely exploratory method, "an open-ended approach." This type of method "may morph into a different kind of approach as a study evolves" and indeed, in many cases it "serves as an entrée into a subject, a subject which is subsequently interrogated with a more determinate (less open ended) method" (Seawright and Gerring, op.cit., 302).

PART I

The Institutionalization of Propaganda and Indoctrination: The Phenomenon through Conceptual and Theoretical Lenses

The first part of the book introduces the phenomena of interest for the study, while it simultaneously presents and discusses the most salient conceptual and theoretical lenses created and used by the diverse interdisciplinary literature dealing with them. Some of these conceptual tools are the result of empirical observations and historical investigations, while others are the result of deductive theory construction and analytical reasoning applied to observational and historical data. All of them contribute in significant ways to our interpretations and explanations of the complex set of phenomena associated with the institutionalization of propaganda and indoctrination.

At the same time, the following chapters advance the theoretical agenda by suggesting novel ways of elaborating, combining, and applying the existing conceptual and theoretical resources. They do that in ways that offer significant insights, both regarding the practices and institutionalization of propaganda and indoctrination and regarding the theoretical apparatus used to explore them. The contribution in this respect takes mainly two forms. Either existent but underdeveloped underlying lines of arguments or conceptual models are further specified and articulated, or links between so far unconnected themes, concepts and approaches are identified and advanced as possible bases for analytical and interpretive frameworks of the phenomenon of interest. The exploratory, propaedeutic nature of these efforts should be always kept in mind. Their goal is to equip us with the epistemic and methodological resources needed for an intellectual journey into a territory that is perhaps evoked much more than it is truly analyzed and understood in the public discourse and, sometimes, even within academic settings.

Chapter 1

Ideocracy, Totalitarianism, and the "New Man"

Ideology, indoctrination, and propaganda have to be seen as part of complex social phenomenon, with multiple political, economic, anthropological, institutional, and historical facets. This chapter takes a closer look at a possible way of conceptualizing essential aspects of such ideology-related social facts in their institutional and political context. Starting from the assumption that combining alternative theoretical lenses in order to frame, describe, and analyze these types of phenomena is unavoidable in our efforts to study such phenomena, the chapter concentrates on three related conceptual schemes. The first is centered on the relatively new conceptualization based on the notion of ideocracy. The second is centered on the related, but much more familiar concept of totalitarianism. These are both united at a third level by the problem of the role of the "models of man" in the theories and practice of governance systems. This preliminary approach to the problem of the institutionalization of indoctrination along the lines of these converging three perspectives will help us establish, with a higher theoretical acumen, the contours, magnitudes, and significance of the phenomenon.

In the analysis of any governance and political system, three dimensions are always present, more or less explicitly: First, the incentive structures and the incentive-driven processes given by the condition of conflict, cooperation, and competition as well as by the environmental factors that the specific system has to deal with; second, the institutional arrangements and structures of legitimacy and authority that shape and respond to those incentives through systems of rules and social roles; and third, the beliefs, ideologies, and doctrines that define, legitimize, and frame the institutional structure. The ideological dimension is, thus, always essential for describing and analyzing any political system or governance regime. This is a general statement that could be further operationalized and calibrated.

The interest in disentangling the particular function and weight that ideas, ideologies, and their institutionalization have in governance systems leads—via comparative analysis—to the identification of a particular type of political system in which they play a very preeminent role with profound implications for the institutional and incentive structures. As we have seen, it is the class of these systems that offer the proximate set of "background cases" for our investigation. Let us now take a closer look at this type of system through a set of conceptual lenses that allow us to penetrate beyond the surface and identify underlying principles, patterns, and structures.

IDEOCRACY, TOTALITARIANISM, AND INSTITUTIONAL LOGIC

In his path-breaking book, *Totalitarianism, Terrorism and Supreme Values*, Peter Bernholz uses the term *ideocracies*[1] to describe the class of systems in which the ideological factor is institutionalized as a supreme principle of government. Ideocracies, he argues, have sufficient, distinctive features that establish them as a class in themselves, different in nature (not just in degree) from other types of political systems.

One of the most important features of Bernholz's contributions is an original theoretical framework linking ideocracies to totalitarianism. The two, he contends, are intrinsically related. In fact, they are phases of the same process. Crucial to his argument is the notion of "supreme values,"[2] a combination of ideas, images, and doctrines claiming absolute truth and historical validity. The installment of "supreme values," believed to be absolute and nonnegotiable, is the essential element setting this process into motion. Once a political system has made "absolute values" the centerpiece of its institutional and governance structure, a series of intrinsically interrelated developments are set into motion. In Bernholz's words, "the invention and introduction of an ideology with supreme values is a necessary condition for the development of a totalitarian regime."[3] Yet, it is not a sufficient condition. Full blown totalitarianism is made possible only when the power of the state is mobilized in support of the ideology in question.

Building on these observations, Bernholz introduces an analytically illuminating distinction: regimes based on ideologies that have reached their aims do not employ coercion and terrorism because their respective populations have already accepted the behavior and beliefs implied in the supreme ideology. He calls these regimes "mature ideocracies." In contrast, "totalitarian" regimes are systems that still have not managed to impose the beliefs and behaviors demanded in the logic of the supreme ideology. The relationship between "ideocracy" and "totalitarianism" is summarized in the following way: "A totalitarian regime is an ideocracy which has not yet reached the aims implied by its supreme values and which tries to pursue them with the spiritual and secular power available after it has gained domination of a state."[4]

Thus, Bernholz is able to construct not only a taxonomy but also the beginnings of a theory explaining the dynamics and transformation of such systems. He creates a framework within which one could theoretically situate the conditions and factors that may lead—in specific circumstances—to totalitarian regimes, as well as those leading to their transformation and breakdown. Using that framework, Bernholz further constructs a series of models capturing the logic, formal features, and properties of the systems operating on the totalitarianism–ideocracy continuum. He bolsters his interpretation with a survey of the empirical evidence. In his inventory of the historical cases closest to the ideal type implied by these models, he identifies and lists regimes such as those of Saudi Arabia and Iran (or in the past, the Jesuit State in Paraguay or Massachusetts Puritans) as mature ideocracies. The list of totalitarian systems comprises the cases of the Soviet Union, China, Nazi Germany, Cambodia, North Korea, Eastern Europe, Cuba, and the Islamic State.[5]

Bernholz's work thus introduces a fresh perspective that links his theory to the traditional literature on totalitarianism but also departs from that literature in substantive and challenging ways. Bernholz notes that the fact that the "supreme values" may be different in content from one system to another in very substantive ways does not mean that this heterogeneity of content precludes the construction of a general concept of "ideocracy." What matters is that, irrespective the content of beliefs, they have a certain form and function and certain general properties that have significant social consequences. Among those properties, two are axiomatically preeminent. Ideocracies have an underlying logic derived precisely from their ideas-centered feature. First, all "supreme values" are, at least according to the underlying creed, lexicographically preferred to do all other aims. Second, they are all considered to be absolutely true.[6] With that, the door toward any pluralism, in a real and significant degree, gets closed, ceasing to be an option in systems embracing such values as foundational governance principles. That, obviously, not only restricts the range of the set of political institutions that could be adopted, but also induces certain features in the regular social institutions.

In addition to the belief in the absolute truth of supreme values around which the social world should be organized (a belief implying the attitude of sacrificing everything for the sake of those values), another vital element has to be noted. The ideologies of this type are usually associated with a message promising a better life in the future. In this respect, the future is strongly contrasted to a past or present state of affairs, which is considered unjust, dysfunctional, and repressive. It is not so much a precise plan or a logical argument. It is more a set of mental images of a possible future and a series of expectations that the "things to come" will be better if the ideological line is followed. Thus, images of the future, which in many cases take utopian overtones, and their associated mindsets become an important factor in legitimating and motivating attitudes and actions. Reasserting and reinforcing them is part and parcel of the system's operations. All of the above have important consequences that reach to the level of institutors and governance processes.

Implicit in the logic of ideocracies is the objective to convert all people to the "true creed." Or, more precisely, the objective is converting all those who are convertible and deserve to be converted because some people may be open to conversion while others may not be. The imperative of conversion—full alignment to the ideology—emerges naturally from the logic of supreme values, unfolding politically and institutionally on the entire range from persuasion to coercion. The idea that force may be needed in order to achieve these goals, and that the secular power of the state—as a legitimate monopoly of coercion—has to be used in this respect, comes naturally. If there is one and only one appropriate worldview, mindset, or value system, then all the rest are deemed as dysfunctional and perhaps dangerous deviations. Hence, there is a need to weed out the bearers of inimical views and values known as "deviationists."

Consequently, there are two distinct attitudes (and two institutional strategies) toward the two major groups. First, there is the group of already converted or convertible. This group needs to be dealt with by creating for them a specific set of institutions and organizations out of which the implementation of indoctrination and propaganda are vital. Second, there is the group of people who are not convertible, according to the supreme ideology. These people have to be suppressed or—if they are considered to be a danger—driven out and eliminated. In all cases, these goals require a different set of institutional arrangements. Within range of this variety of alternatives, the organization and implementation of public shaming, ostracism, and exclusion and, at the extreme, forced labor camps, prisons, and execution camps are essential.

And thus, the logic of supreme values and ideological behavior is generating in its social and political embodiment an entire set of institutional and organizational forms and developments. Each is calibrated to different social groups, identified as such in the function of their position toward the central tenets of the reigning ideology. And it is important to add that all of the above have to operate under the assumption or corollary that force may be needed in order to achieve these goals, and the secular power of the state—as a legitimate monopoly of coercion—has to be used in this respect. In brief, an entire institutional architecture is therefore entailed, flowing naturally from the logic that is defining the totalitarianism–ideocracy continuum.

FRAMEWORKS OF COMPARATIVE ANALYSIS, THE "MODEL OF MAN," AND THE "NEW MAN" IN COMMUNIST SYSTEMS

The previous section has shown how the concept of ideocracy could serve us to develop a series of insights regarding the role and place ideological institutions have in a totalitarian–ideocratic system; it was an example of how conceptual and theoretical framing helps us to get a clearer grasp of the phenomena of interest. Let us now introduce an additional conceptual framework that, once brought to the table, helps illuminate an important aspect of these phenomena and illustrates at an even more profound level what is at stake in an investigation like the one advanced in this book.

The starting point is the observation that our investigation, although anchored empirically through a case study, takes place within the conceptual set-up of a comparative analysis perspective. Making explicit the otherwise implicit conceptual framework helps us to identify and illuminate a crucial but usually neglected element that is decisive for our phenomena of interest. This neglected element is the "model of man" used in thinking, designing, and assessing comparative economic and political systems. Let us elaborate this crucial point for our understanding of the logic of totalitarian and ideocratic systems and movements, especially for their institutional arrangements.

Any argument regarding alternative economic and governance systems presumes (in many cases only implicitly) at least two models, and has built in it the unavoidable logic of comparison between ideal and real, status quo and desirable etc. The Koopmans–Montias[7] framework, traditionally used in the discipline of Comparative Economic Systems, captures in the most concise way the underlying components and logic of all such approaches. In this framework, an outcome of a economy (in the Koopmans–Montias case, an economy, but one could extend it to political or governance arrangements) is a function of three variables: the environment (e), the economic system (s), and government policies conducted within the system (p_s). At the same time, there are evaluative criteria (the norm n in their terminology) applied to quantitative and qualitative outcomes (o). Koopmans and Montias define outcomes as consequences of the economy in its operations—that is to say, in the policies, decisions, or actions of all participants. Norms are preferences held by some actors that are pertinent to the comparison, and they are defined as evaluative functions of outcomes. Summing up, an economy (ε) is specified by the three components (e, s, p_s); the relevant characteristics of ε are given by different outcomes o, and these are measured or compared by norms n. In other words, we conceptualize an economy/polity as the structure:

1. $\varepsilon = (e, s, p_s, o)$, where
2. $o = f(e, s, p_s)$ and
3. $n(o) = n[f(e, s, p_s)]$

This framework is a generic instrument for the orderly identification of each category of factors and the analysis of their relationship. For instance, when analyzing Socialism, we need to disentangle the systemic features (s) from the impact of the environment in which the system is operating (e). In a similar way, we need to know in what measure an outcome is the result of a policy (p) taken in the system, or of a system (s) itself. The application of this analytical framework to our problem is straightforward. For instance, at the most basic level, when we analyze our indoctrination institutions, we need to unpack (s) to see its structure and the place such institutions occupy in it. Are they systemic features or just a policy? Or are they just an accidental feature, determined by environmental circumstances?

For the purposes of our discussion, the point is that once engaged in analysis, more often than not, this argument highlights and brings to the light a crucial yet unstated variable in most discussions of economic or governance systems: the underlying presence of a certain "model of man" of human behavior, motivation, and social action. It is usually encapsulated in an ideal type of the "social actor model." Whether or not one wants it and whether or not one makes it explicit, both analysis and predictions about the system are based on certain assumptions or expectations about human attitudes and behavior.

These attitudinal and behavioral assumptions are based on certain broad beliefs about human nature. What would the expectations regarding motivation be? Are—as a rule—altruism or opportunism expected? Are the social or institutional rules designed to foster social cooperation or social competition? In what forms and with what intensity? How are social actors supposed to react to the rules in that case? Why should one suppose that citizens, consumers, or producers will react that way and not otherwise? How generalizable is the rule or system design, and why? In other words, one realizes that in almost all governance or institutional issues, a lot is being predicated on and hinges on the type of "model of a man" employed. Therefore, it is fully justified to add (m), the model of man, to the comparative analysis framework, giving us this:

1. $\varepsilon = (m, e, s, p_s, o)$, where
2. $o = f(m, e, s, p_s)$ and
3. $n(o) = n[f(m, e, s, p_s)]$

This is a move of profound analytical implications. Its immediate outcome is that it focuses our attention to the "human factor," helping us explain what otherwise may seem to be a puzzle: why so many *institutional* experiments in alternative governance, political, or economic systems turn so fast into *anthropological* experiments—experiments trying to induce changes of human nature. If we become aware of the "model of man" assumption in comparative systems analysis, we see in a new light why all discussions about alternative economic/governance systems (even the most deterministic social engineering ones) sooner or later have to gravitate to the problem of the mindsets, values, and intrinsic motivation of social actors and, ultimately, the problem of human nature. It becomes more evident why, in the end, all plans for radical social change (i.e., Communist, Socialist, totalitarian) move very fast from ideas about social order and institutions (institutional design) to concentrate almost instinctively and obsessively on the problem of indoctrination, mindsets, and the creation of a "New Man."

Another way of making the point is to note that, given all of the above, advancing ideas and designs about governance and political systems could be predicated on two alternative approaches. The first approach assumes that the social actors will continue to display human nature "as is" and "as we know it." The second assumes that the social actors would/should change their attitudes, preferences, mindsets, and behavior to approximate "x" ideal type of social actor, or "model of man." Each approach has its own promises and challenges. Obviously, our investigation is mostly interested in the second one.

In this respect, let us note the paradox and circularity revealed by all schemes of radical social system change and their associated institutional designs: the feasibility of the system is predicated on a change in human nature. But the feasibility of the change in human nature is predicated on the feasibility and effectiveness of institutional interventions aiming at a change in human nature. Consequently, institutional interventions, the institutions, and organizations aiming at the adjustment of human beliefs, values, mindsets, and attitudes emerge as the decisive piece of the institutional system. If that is the case, the focus on indoctrination and propaganda does not anymore seem to be something secondary and accidental to certain types of systems. Indoctrination emerges as pivotal to the social engineering of the process of social change and the logic of the governance of the system.

The contrast between the two approaches could not be clearer, and the distinction is far from alien to the political science literature. On the one hand, there is the tradition in which institutional structures have to accommodate a given, "imperfect" human nature. In this tradition, analysis and design are predicated on a model of man that captures that imperfection in a simplified way for institutional design purposes. An extreme form of the argument in this tradition is Hume's much quoted "knave" argument, which is paradigmatic in this respect:

> Political writers have established it as a maxim, that, in contriving any system of government, and fixing the several checks and controls of the constitution, every man ought to be supposed a knave, and to have no other end, in all his actions, than private interest. By this interest we must govern him, and, by means of it, make him, notwithstanding his insatiable avarice and ambition, co-operate to public good. Without this, say they, we shall in vain boast of the advantages of any constitution, and shall find, in the end, that we have no security for our liberties or possessions, except the good-will of our rulers; that is, we shall have no security at all.[8]

On the other hand, there is the second approach in which human nature has to change in order to accommodate a given or desired institutional structure. Its gist is concisely expressed by Che Guevara[9] in the radical change, or revolutionary change tradition: "To build communism," he wrote, "it is necessary, simultaneous with the new material foundations, to build the new man."[10]

The emphasis on the problem of the "model of man" reveals why it is so significant for the ideocracy model of Bernholtz and, by implication, why it offers such an excellent key to our approach to the nature of the Communist experiment. The position defined by Che Guevara is a natural, logical outgrowth of the ideocratic and totalitarian nature of Marxism. The very moment one gets closer to implementing the institutional, political, and economic implications of the ideocratic programs, the totalitarian facet emerges to salience. As Paul Hollander put it, "Creating the totally politicized, obedient, self-sacrificing New Man was the shared dream of totalitarian rulers."[11] All features of ideocracy are thus present in the classic Marxism–Leninism, a fact that makes it an excellent case study for the type of phenomena we are studying (see Tismaneanu[12]). First, for the totalitarian, all-encompassing forms of an ideocratic ideology are there, ready to be fully developed. Second, within that mix, the problem of human nature, as a key variable to be manipulated in order to fit the systemic, totalitarian vision, becomes salient.

The evidence in this respect is overwhelming. In *Three Sources and Three Essentials of Marxism*, Lenin proclaimed, "The teachings of Marx are almighty since they are true. They are complete and harmonious in themselves. His doctrine provides man with a unified worldview, which is not consistent with any superstition, any reaction, any defense of bourgeoisie suppression."[13] Engels was convinced that, "Like Darwin who discovered the law of the evolution of organic nature, so Marx found the law of evolution of human society."[14] With those credentials, the conclusion is—with all its soteriological and messianic practical implications—foregone: "Only the philosophical materialism of Marx has shown to the proletariat the way out of the spiritual slavery under which our oppressed classes have suffered until now."[15]

Armed with such certitudes, it is not a surprise that any hesitation regarding the social and human costs implied by the social change and the economic and political schemes involved is dismissed. The conduit in the implementation of these "supreme values" and ideocratic ideals—to use Bernholz's terms—is explicitly articulated and assumed by the foremost authorities of Communism. "We are reckless and we do not ask for your consideration," wrote Marx. "When it will be our turn, we will be reckless and will not palliate terrorism."[16] Terror, violence, and coercion are considered natural, desirable, and unavoidable: "A revolution is certainly the most authoritarian event which exist," wrote Marx. "Through it one part of the population forces its will on the other part, with the help of rifles, bayonets and guns, i.e., with the most authoritarian means; and the victorious party has to make his domination durable by the terror which is infused by its arms."[17]

However, as Lenin made clear—and the theme introduced by this point is crucial for our study—social control and coercion are not limited to the revolutionary phase. Social pressure and violence are an inherent part of implementing the new system: "Until the higher phase of communism has arrived, socialists ask for the most rigorous control through society and the state." The fact that, even after the success of the revolution, the ideological pressure and coercion have to continue is of utmost importance for the topic of our investigation. The absolute, ultimate, and unmitigated nature of the process is vividly synthetized by Lenin who wrote, "class struggle still goes on and it is our task to subordinate everything to this struggle." In a striking conclusion, Lenin takes to the ultimate implications of his unabashedly Machiavellian argument: "We also subordinate our communist morality to this task. We assert that is moral which serves to destroy of the old exploitive society and the gathering of all the workers around the proletariat."[18]

Let us focus now on the Leninist call for the "most rigorous control through society and the state." This strategic priority has a double function. The first is intuitively obvious: to defend the newly established regime and system and consolidate its reach and grasp. The second is, however, also aiming at a larger time horizon: to socially engineer and maintain in the citizens' mindsets, perceptions, and values those adjustments that are deemed necessary for the creation of the "new man"[19] and, by implication, the "new system." The idea of a "new socialist human being" is a constant in all Marxist-Leninist movements and states, and it is a prima facie key for understanding many of their institutions and policies. As remarked by Paul Hollander, "Why these systems adopted this goal, how it related to their other attributes, and why they failed to create this supposedly superior human being remain questions of great interest."[20] These questions remain even now after the first great wave of social experiments in the name of Socialism have receded into history.

Therefore, focusing on the problem of the model of man and the "New Man" in Communism (and, for that matter, in Socialism) means more than drawing attention to a colorful element of the social and ideological practices of Socialist systems. The problem seems to offer a real analytical and interpretive key to the system, leading us beyond surface to a deeper level of analysis. For instance, in his *Creating the "New Man": From Enlightenment Ideals to Socialist Realities*, Cheng defines the new Soviet person in a manner that circumvents the official image. Cheng describes it as follows: "ideological conformity, political loyalty, devotion to the Party, selflessness, and self-sacrifice"[21] perfectly suited to be the "cog" and the "screw"[22] of the new system. That is indeed a very different profile from the official one.

The point is that by focusing on the "models of man," multiple tensions are immediately revealed. There are tensions between the official image and the real-life citizen and activists. Or, even more sharply, tensions exist between the manifest image of the "multilaterally developed socialist man" and the professional Communist activist as the conformist, obedient, or amorally opportunistic real-life result of the system. Or add to the list tensions like those identified by Brooks[23] as tensions between "the official images of new citizens and activists on the one hand, and new political systems on the other." In brief, moving the issue of the "New Man" from the background to foreground in the analysis of ideocracy and totalitarianism opens up multiple avenues of analysis and insights at multiple levels.

To sum up, we have now a clearer understanding of the double institutional task of a system, like the Communist one, in which human nature is seen as a malleable target variable in a grand-scale institutional and governance design. The first task is creating the institutional structure of the new system. The second is creating an additional institutional structure, aimed at shaping, preparing, configuring the members of the population to approximate as close as possible the "model of man" deemed to function optimally within and for the new system—a "New Man" for a "new system." Note that this task is not just related to Socialism or Communism. Bernholz alerted us to a whole range of systems that have features of "ideocracy." The ideocratic logic requires, sooner or later, addressing human beings as malleable human variables. This is why one could never reemphasize enough that, on the one hand, "the failed efforts to create the New Man were among the distinctive qualities of communist one-party states," while at the same time, "the awareness of these efforts is an integral part of a better understanding of these systems."[24]

TOTALITARIANISM: THE NOTION REVISITED

We are now in the position to revisit some of the features of the phenomena of interest to our study as reflected and described in the totalitarianism literature (for an introduction and overview, see Gleason[25]). We will use the classical discussion of Friedrich and Brzezinski as a vehicle.[26]

In *Totalitarian Dictatorship and Autocracy*, Carl Friedrich and Zbigniew Brzezinski develop one of the most influential definitions and descriptions of totalitarianism. At the same time, they create the conditions for opening up the path for a comparative analysis of totalitarianism, including its manifestations in forms and circumstances far from the standard, well-known cases of National Socialism, Communism, and Fascism that are typically used as illustrations in the literature. Although they do not explicitly take that path of comparativism, their work is foundational in this respect. We will postpone the discussion regarding these comparative approaches extending the analysis beyond the standard cases until the last part of the book. At this juncture, we will just overview some of the key observations made by Friedrich and Brzezinski. These observations help us to further articulate the larger conceptual map of the phenomena of interest and also signal some underlying links connecting the various approaches and theoretical frameworks that explore the phenomena.

Friedrich and Brzezinski start their description in familiar territory. The essence of totalitarianism is to be seen in the aim of "total control of the every day life of its citizens, of its control more particularly of their thoughts and attitudes as well as their activities."[27] The pattern of traits in a totalitarian dictatorship consists of "an ideology, a single Party typically led by one man, a terroristic police, a communication monopoly, a weapons monopoly, and the centrally directed economy."[28] Of these, they note, the last two are also found in constitutional systems. If that is the case, a noteworthy question is whether the presence of any of these traits in a system suggests a trend toward totalitarianism. Indeed, this is a crucial question for comparative analysis, as it suggests the possibility that a social or political system may move in a totalitarian direction in a sequence of stages, starting from different sectors of the society in small and partial steps and extending to the level of taking over the entire system. This observation correlates to the remark that there are some intrinsic connections between these traits that reinforce each other. This makes for a fascinating set of conjectures that may define a research agenda: looking at totalitarianism not just in systemic, national-level (state-level) regime manifestations, but also in more localized and personalized organizational or sectorial forms. That being said, at this stage we will not engage that direction.

At this juncture, the main point is that Friedrich and Brzezinski draw our attention to the fact that the distinctive, specific difference of modern totalitarian regimes is really the organization and methods developed and employed with the aid of modern technical devices. These technical devices have either a standard technological progress nature (such as that of communication) or an institutional technology nature (such as those related to bureaucratization, rationalization, and span of authority management). Such developments facilitated and were instrumental to the objective of total control.

When they discuss the ideological facet of totalitarianism, one could recognize in Friedrich and Brzezinski the standard lines: the total control at which totalitarian movements and regimes aim is put to the service of an ideology "dedicated to the total destruction and reconstruction of a mass society." The key element of that reconstruction is "the effort to remold and transform the human beings under its control in the image of its ideology."[29] This effort, "while not achieving such control, has highly significant human effects."[30]

The most important contribution is brought to the table when discussing the techniques and technological facet of totalitarianism. Friedrich and Brzezinski stress the fact that totalitarian regimes are historical novelties, and the nature of that novelty is crucial. Totalitarianism, they wrote, "emerges as a system for realizing 'totalist' intentions in the circumstances of modern political and technical conditions." Those conditions are the source of the specific difference, and they should be the main object of our attention. And if we do that, they claim, we realize that no system like totalitarian dictatorship has ever existed before. There are obvious similitudes to autocracies of the past, but those similitudes are far from capturing the real dimensions of the modern totalitarian phenomena. That specific difference is organizational and technological in nature.

Friedrich and Brzezinski insist that totalitarianism has to be seen largely as a function of the increased technological and organizational capabilities of modern societies. Four of the six traits are technologically conditioned. Even in the case of the remaining two (ideology and party) that have no significant relationship to the state of technology, there are nonetheless some connections to be identified. The mass conversion continually attempted by totalitarian propaganda could not be carried out without massive mass communication instruments.[31] Technological advances in terms of capabilities of control, monitoring, and communication are critical in understanding the preconditions for generating a totalitarian potential in a society.[32]

In brief, totalitarian societies "appear to be nearly exaggerations but nonetheless logical exaggerations of the technological state of modern society." That being said, the ideological belief system dimension is not neglected or dismissed. Even the "secular religion" interpretation of totalitarianism is fully acknowledged. Friedrich and Brzezinski note that totalitarian ideology involves, both in its rhetoric and in the manifestations of its supporters, a high degree of conviction of certainty. The official doctrines fueling totalitarianism follow a millennial pattern, radically rejecting the existing society and embracing utopian elements. That gives the ideology a quasi-religious quality. In fact, they "often elicit in their less critical followers a depth of conviction and the favor of devotion usually found only among persons inspired by a transcendental faith."[33]

Last but not least, a very important remark that has a huge promise for comparative analysis refers to the belief-systems dimension. Friedrich and Brzezinski insist that ideology and party are conditioned by modern democracy. Totalitarianism is seen by its own leaders as a natural extension of democracy. It is presented as the true form of democracy, the fulfillment of democracy. That has important implications. The entire vocabulary of democracy is taken over and its semantics are twisted. Double speak and the falsification of beliefs—two phenomena strongly associated with totalitarianism—are thus further facilitated. That being said, even if the ideological belief system dimension and the associated problem of language and public discourse are recognized as important by Friedrich and Brzezinski, in the end, the crucial aspect is considered the technological one.

For our purposes, it is more important to add here a couple more features that the totalitarianism literature has noted regarding totalitarianism, irrespective of the definitional or theoretical nuances. Totalitarianism advances anti-pluralist worldviews. These worldviews are expressed through a rhetoric based on formulaic utterances and conceptual dichotomies that are invested with normative value and purposefully constructed to obstruct distinctions, complexity, and intellectual and normative nuances. That vocabulary is used in generating myths, catechisms, and social events taking the form of rituals, reinforcing the cleavage between the elect, who are on a historical or metaphysical mission, and the rest.

Citizens, or groups or social classes, considered relevant historical (or change) agents are constantly mobilized to combat or facilitate some global, historical trends or developments. Some of the mobilization is against backsliding, and some of it is in the direction of accelerating some trends. This mobilization takes, in most cases, the form of the active pursuit (with a view to ostracism and purging) of other classes and categories of people, defined collectively as "objective enemies" or "enemies of the cause." With that end in view, some ascribed features that place people in some categories, in function of an ideological taxonomy normatively laden, such as race or descent, generate various forms of totalitarian dynamics. The examples of a "class-based" totalitarianism or a "race-based" totalitarianism were, in fact, historical realities. Finally, and importantly, the use of pressure, public shaming, and organized and instrumented harassment to intimidate, stigmatize, isolate, and regiment specific targeted individuals and groups, defined on the lines described above, is essential to all these dynamics. The validation and sometimes institutionalization of terror is contemplated in many cases, and in some cases, it is enacted.

In brief, the totalitarianism literature, in addition to creating a typology on the lines surveyed above, opens up a venue for a broader comparative analysis. One last thing needs to be mentioned at this juncture: totalitarianism—with its ideocratic aspirations—is not just related to Socialism, National Socialism, and Communism, and it has specific features that emerge whenever they find a way to manifest themselves. Totalitarianism tendencies may manifest itself in regimes and systems of no ideocratic aspiration. The totalitarian trends and processes do not need to take over the entire state to become manifest. Specific sectors, institutions, or organizations may start to operate on totalitarian lines long before the state succumbs to the totalitarian dominance. This aspect of totalitarianism as a creeping social phenomenon—manifesting at microsocial and organizational levels—has very important implications for the ways in which we understand its nature and impact. As we will discuss in the concluding chapter of the book, it has significant implications for comparative analysis.

In conclusion, we now have a better sense of the fact that the social functions, roles, and organizations we are interested in for our study are far from being accidental, marginal, or a mere footnote to the imposing architecture of totalitarianisms and ideocracies. On the contrary, as our initial intuition suggested, they have a function, structure, and modus operandi that make them an intrinsic part of essential importance to these systems. The next chapter will explore all these venues. The chapter will take a closer look at the function of the ideological and indoctrination institutions, concentrating on the Marxist/Communist case. We have seen *prima facie* that such institutions have a rationale based in a metahistorical vision pivoting on the Communist supreme values, and a view of the desirable future created by the transformation of social order under those values. However, we have already noticed that the functions of indoctrination and ideological control are far from limited to that.

NOTES

1. Peter Bernholz, *Totalitarianism, Terrorism and Supreme Values* (Springer International Publishing, 2017).
2. Peter Bernholz, op.cit., 2.
3. Ibid., 2.
4. Ibid., 2.

5. Ibid., 3.
6. Ibid., 4–5.
7. Tjalling C. Koopmans and Jojn Michel Montias, "On the Description and Comparison of Economic Systems" in *Comparison of Economic Systems: Theoretical and Methodological Approaches,* edited by A. Eckstein (Berkeley: University of California Press, 1971), 27–78.
8. David Hume, "On the Independence of Parliament" (1742) in *Essays Moral, Political, and Literary*, ed. Eugene F. Miller (Indianapolis: Liberty Fund, 1985), 98. Madison's argument is, in many respects, an echo of the same position, restated through the means of an implicit thought experiment: "But what is government itself, but the greatest of all reflections on human nature? If men were angels, no government would be necessary. If angels were to govern men, neither external nor internal controls on government would be necessary" (James Madison, Federalist 51). That is to say, under one definition of (m), the operating model of man (i.e., men behaving like angels, nonopportunistic, and prescient), both the system (s) and policies (p_s) lose their significance, their reason of being in existence. Having a governance/political system becomes unnecessary. But we cannot hope that men would be ever turned into angels. Therefore, we need to assume the status quo regarding human nature. The model of man to be used would be, by default, the human one. At the same time, we have established that, indeed, the governance system itself—the way one is thinking, assessing, or designing it—is intrinsically connected to the ways we think about human nature.
9. Ernesto Che Guevara, *Oeuvres 1957–1967*, vol. 2 (Paris: François Maspero, 1971), 371–72.
10. Ernesto Che Guevara, op.cit., 371–72.
11. Paul Hollander, *Slavic Review* 70, no. 1 (2011), p. 206.
12. Mentioned among Vladimir Tismaneanu's volumes: *Stalinism for All Seasons* (Berkeley: University of California Press, 2003); *Fantasies of Salvation: Democracy, Nationalism and Myth in Post-Communist Europe* (Princeton, NJ: Princeton University Press, 1998); *The Devil in History: Communism, Fascism and Some Lessons of the Twentieth Century* (Berkeley: University of California Press, 2012); *Reinventing Politics* (New York: Free Press, 2000); *Promises of 1968: Crisis, Illusion and Utopia* (Vienna: Central European University Press, 2010).
13. Lenin, *Three Sources and Three Essentials of Marxism,* 1913.
14. Peter Bernholz, op.cit., 11.
15. Lenin, op.cit.
16. Peter Bernholz, op.cit., 11.
17. Ibid., 11.
18. Ibid., 11., and Lenin, *Selected Works*, vol. 9.
19. Yinghong Cheng, *Creating the "New Man": From Enlightenment Ideals to Socialist Realities* (Honolulu: University of Hawai'i Press, 2009).
20. Paul Hollander, op.cit., 205–6.
21. Yinghong Cheng, op.cit., 220.
22. Ibid., 134.
23. Jeffrey Brooks, *International Review of Social History*, 55, no. 3 (2010): 529–30.

24. Paul Hollander, op.cit., 206.

25. Abbott Gleason, *Totalitarianism: The Inner History of the Cold War* (Oxford: Oxford University Press, 1997).

26. Carl J. Friedrich and Zbigniew Brzezinski, *Totalitarian Dictatorship and Autocracy* (Cambridge, MA: Harvard University Press, 1965).

27. Carl J. Friedrich and Zbigniew Brzezinski, op.cit., 16.

28. Ibid., 21.

29. Ibid., 17.

30. Ibid., 17.

31. Ibid., 27.

32. The emphasis on technology and modernity raises, obviously, some issues and tensions with the Ideocracy framework. It may be the case that Bernholz's model does not adequately capture the nuances of the process of transition to full blown Ideocracy in premodern settings. Or, it may be the case that Friedrich and Brzezinski's emphasis on modernity and technology is constraining the extension of the concept too much. One way or another, the two approaches continue to be convergent and complementary, even if the details of their working together are still to be clarified and elaborated.

33. Carl J. Friedrich and Zbigniew Brzezinski, op.cit., 26.

Chapter 2

The Functions and Logic of the Indoctrination and Propaganda Institutions

Any discussion of the ideological and indoctrination institutions of the Communist regimes starts in the realm of the obvious. One does not need to be an expert to note that the *prima facie* functions of those institutional arrangements have to be derived from the substantive rationale based in the logic of the Marxist worldview and its implementation. The so-called "manifest" functions of these institutions are derived from the ultimate aims (or ends-rationality) as defined by the Communist–Socialist creed. In addition to that, any serious discussion has to at least explore the hypothesis of the existence of less salient functions or logics that are latent and based on instrumental rationalities not having much to do with the Communist credo. Two of those—one illuminated by the logic of public choice models of autocracies and the other based on the logic of insecurity—deserve a special attention as statecraft instruments. Both are examples of alternative ways of interpreting the function of the institutions of interest to our study. They both bring to the fore additional facets of the phenomenon in case.

The relevance of this line of investigation for our understanding of the nature of these institutions and of the system in general could hardly be exaggerated.[1] The functional approach is irreplaceable, whether or not the goal was genuine (to truly create a new type of human being, i.e., the "multilaterally developed socialist man," for the sake of a lofty new governance system), or, alternatively, "this new citizen was going to be totally politicized, highly committed, and reflexively loyal to the power holders" in a logic of domination and manipulation having nothing to do with lofty goals of Communism. As Paul Hollander put it, either way, "their success in this endeavor would have opened up limitless possibilities for controlling and manipulating society" because the New Man "would invariably put the interests of society (as defined by the rulers) ahead of his or her own personal interests."[2] This command and control facet is a constant in all approaches. However, once we go beyond this basic observation and start elaborating the different lines mentioned above, we will be able to bring to light otherwise hard to detect aspects and patterns that increase our understanding of the phenomenon in considerable ways.

THE MARXIST RATIONALE AND THE "NEW MAN" FOR THE "NEW SYSTEM"

The rationale based in metahistorical vision, as articulated in the Marxist canon, offers the standard interpretation of the nature and function of indoctrination institutions in Communist regimes. We have already used it as a default background in our discussion so far. In this section, we are only going to briefly restate it and marginally elaborate some ensuing points.

From this perspective, the indoctrination, propaganda, and ideological-control institutions have a straightforward and easy-to-understand function: they are an indispensable instrument in creating the "New Man" for the "new system." Paul Hollander was simply stating a basic principle in the analysis of Communism when he wrote that a defining characteristic of Communist systems was "the apparent determination to create a New Man (human being) that has paralleled their commitment to create a new society."[3] If the Communist experiment and their "new society, new man" vision is taken at face value, sooner or later, one has to recognize that the centrality of the education and indoctrination process cannot be emphasized enough. "Each of these systems pursued the ideal New Man through heavily politicized formal education, massive doses of propaganda disseminated by the mass media, and the attempted integration of education and manual labor."[4]

In this respect, Makarenko's official take is emblematic. Education in Communism has to be about disciplining, correcting, and shaping political conscience; instilling loyalty to the right social class and the Party; and developing aptitudes to obey and give orders:

> We wish to educate a cultured Soviet worker. Consequently, we must give him education, preferably secondary education, we must teach him a trade, we must discipline him, he must be politically conscious, a devoted member of the working class, a komsomol and a Bolshevik. We must educate in him a sense of duty . . . and he must be made aware of his obligations to his class. He must know how to obey a comrade as well as to give an order to a comrade. . . . He must be persevering and steeled, self-controlled and able to influence others; if the community punishes him, he must respect the community and the punishment

must be gay, cheerful, smart, capable of fighting and building, of living and loving life: he must be happy. And he must be such not in the future, but now, today, and every day.[5]

Communist education is, therefore, far from being limited to instruction or civics. Instead, it is part of a programmatic effort of restructuring human consciousness and character through social engineering of attitudes, sentiments, and beliefs. Irrespective of how one interprets the rationale of the efforts (and in the next sections, we look at the second level, less doctrinaire, and latent motivations), the proclaimed desire to change man's behavior patterns coupled with the belief in the plasticity of human nature are fundamental, functional, and structural rationale for the Communist project.[6]

It is very important to note that the approach is predicated on a very strong belief that human nature is infinitely malleable. This very consequential philosophical anthropology assumption is a corollary of the general Marxist philosophical worldview. In our study, we are less interested in exploring the philosophical and doctrinal Marxist foundations than we are in focusing on the applied-level, practical, organizational, and institutional policy implications. And, in this respect, our attention goes not to the "nature–nurture" thesis and debate implicit in the malleability assumption, but rather to the implication in the practical realm of these foundational beliefs when it comes to the organization of the social engineering of human beings through a political, institutional, and governance apparatus implementing the Communist vision.

As already noted, Lenin argued that the transition from the "incipient" or "lower" stage of Communism to the higher forms or stages (i.e., from Socialism to Communism) cannot take place by mere institutional change. The mindsets of the citizens, their motivations, attitudes, and human behaviors have to be radically transformed.[7] That transformation was to be achieved by "raising the level of consciousness." The population was to be molded into the New Man, an anthropological novelty, to be socially engineered by a systematic process of indoctrination and propaganda targeting consciousness.

The Soviet leaders were not at all shy about this; on the contrary, they were very open and straightforward. Speaking at the session of the Academy of Sciences of the USSR in honor of the thirtieth anniversary of the revolution, M. M. Rozental, quoted by Koutaissoff,[8] offered a typical example in this respect: "Socialism, which is being implemented as a result of the proletarian revolution, creates a new man." Socialism brings to the fore "a great revolutionary upheaval which must radically transform the consciousness and psychology of millions and tens of millions of people."[9]

The supremacy of Communist values must be instilled from the beginning, early in life. Therefore, it should be no surprise that the process started from early childhood as the indoctrination techniques were "brought to bear on the immature and receptive mind of children." To succeed, the Marxist creed always has to be on guard against competing beliefs, values, and worldviews. Thus, the entire life cycle of a citizen gets targeted as organizations and policies get institutionalized and operationalized at all governance levels of the Communist state. Very soon, "all the powers of a totalitarian state, both coercion and all the techniques of mass persuasion, are being used to mold the new type of man."[10] We are talking about a systematic, systemic, ongoing, and strategically calibrated effort.

The approach focused on the manifest and explicit function derived from the ideological creed and the institutional structure materializing that function, is not difficult to follow in its implications. For instance, if we follow the logic of the Marxist Communist perspective, we could immediately identify why particular Communist indoctrination and propaganda approaches and themes are unavoidable and why they necessarily take certain forms.

Let us focus, as an illustration, on the observation that the preeminent challenges to the Communist worldview, creed, and narrative came mainly from the West and the past. First, the standard of living and the lifestyle in the West were an ongoing challenge. The idea that capitalist technologies and management were more efficient than Socialist ones was another challenge. Second, the past may also be a source of beliefs echoing real, historically verifiable collective memories about alternatives to the current regime—thus, religion, ethnicity, nationality, and even family ties may be problematic.[11]

Therefore, the practice of creating a New Man requires not just indoctrination but also protection. The targets of the process and the process itself have to be insulated from the flows of information coming from the outside or coming from the bearers of the historical memory of the pre-Communist past. Obviously, the Iron Curtain was a first line of defense. Institutionalizing such a quarantine and a roadblock system was essential. It was not just a military and security priority but also an ideological one. In addition to that, the most powerful line of defense and preemptive initiatives had to take place in schools, universities, and all other organizations where the minds of the citizens could be scrutinized and molded according to "the Party line."

To sum up, one compelling interpretation of the rationale of the indoctrination institutions could be easily identified in the logic of the Marxist doctrine. If one takes the claims of the doctrine at face value, then the institutional apparatus, as well as some particular features of the approaches taken, including some general themes developed in all newly installed Communist regimes, follow naturally from the ideocratic logic of the doctrine. Institutions implement the doctrinal task, and their instrumental and manifest function is linearly derived from the main objective: the creation a new system via creation of a New Man.

But this is not the sole possible interpretation of these institutions and their function and practices. As we have already indicated, the goal of creating a "New Man" may not be taken always and in all aspects at its face value. Or at least, its functions may be considered as being more complicated than suggested by the linear interpretation, limited to the manifest functionalism. The role of the ideological institutions could, hence, be seen from a rather different angle. This alternative perspective continues to emphasize the role of ideas, but it does so in a rather different and, perhaps, unexpected way.

IDEOLOGICAL INSTITUTIONS AS INSECURITY-INDUCING DEVICES

An article published by C. W. Cassinelli at the peak of the Cold War drew attention to an alternative take on the function that the ideological factor may have in totalitarian systems.[12] The doctrine-based approach (i.e., the approach taking the ideological claims regarding the new system and the New Man more or less at face value) is contrasted with the "insecurity-creation-and-management"-based approach. Cassinelli's ingenious argument starts by claiming that the focus on doctrine is not fully satisfactory in explaining the way totalitarianism treats ideas and its uses of ideology. A doctrine is not at all the clear cut and unambiguous thing as it is assumed to be by many scholars of Communism. Texts may stay unchanged in their letter, while their interpretation may be in continuous flux. In fact, texts are just a pretext for specific interpretations. Those interpretations and, even more precisely, the authority making the interpretation, are what really matter in the end.

A telling example is Stalin's manipulation of a shifting Communist "orthodoxy" in order to control the Party and its leaders. By declaring what was the correct (orthodox) line and what was not, Stalin drew a wedge between those loyal to "the Party line," and those punishable for lack of loyalty. The purges of Soviet activists used "the correct Party Line," and the alleged deviations from it, as a pretext in most cases. The arbitrariness of the "line" put all players other than those defining the "line" in a defensive, uncertain, and insecure stance.[13]

Thus, it may be the case that the linear relationship between doctrine, on the one hand, and the social construction of Communism and of the "New Man," on the other hand, is not what it seems to be. Even if a given, constant doctrine is assumed, wrote Cassinelli, the contradictory and arbitrary "ideological" practices cannot be accounted for.[14] To explain these practices, we need an alternative. The hypothesis of ideology and its interpretation as a strategic "insecurity" creation and manipulation instrument provides a possible solution.

"Totalitarianism," explains Cassinelli, derives its meaning from "total control." Yet, that could be interpreted in two different ways. The first takes "total" to mean "complete disciplinary control over all aspects of life, including all beliefs and ideas." This interpretation implies "a thorough ordering and regimentation of society, and the doctrine is its keystone." The second, however, derives its meaning from the "total" destruction of the human personality—from the subversion of "fixed authority, orthodoxy, stable personal relationships, in general the 'atomization' of society." Under this second interpretation, the thorough, total undermining of the social order and the insertion of a structural uncertainty and insecurity in the system, under an overarching arbitrary power, is what makes a system totalitarian.[15] Interestingly enough, the creation of these types of circumstances of anomy, insecurity, and uncertainty is achieved via ideological control and manipulation as well, and it requires the same institutional infrastructure and apparatus as the first one.

This perspective radically changes our interpretation of the system. For instance, if we look beyond appearances and rhetoric, the effort of training leaders in "ideology," explains Cassinelli, serves not so much to make them masters of a doctrine but "to condition them always to be aware of an unstable, arbitrarily shifting gospel handed down by the Leader." The main objective is getting across to them "the vital necessity" of being "ideologically correct" and thus, "preventing the cadres from engaging in independent thought."[16] The test, he further explains, is given by the simple fact that no matter how completely one "masters Marxism," one gains no insight into the way in which the Party line may at any time change.[17]

If that is the case, then any intellectual enterprise having its own standards and autonomy is a challenge to a regime with a basis in anomy-creation that is governing by inducing ultimate insecurity and uncertainty under the appearance of a rigid social order. Any scientific, scholarly, and artistic activity is targeted. Studies in arts and sciences become an extension of the shifting ideological interpretations driven by the Party leadership and the power plays of their rivalries and stratagems.[18] The entire system operates in undermining any sources of initiative outside the range approved by the Communist leaders at multiple levels: from direct demobilization and democratization to structural uncertainty creation. As Cassinelli notes:

> The Leader makes nonsense of art, history, and science, assuring at the same time that their remaining content emphasizes his own power. He trains his cadres to expect from him the "orthodoxy" which they oppose at their peril, but which they cannot anticipate. He tells the masses of the increasingly bountiful life he has created for them, while he gives them low pay, poor services, and shoddy consumer-goods and attacks them with arbitrary programs of terror. To

the totalitarian, ideas are weapons; by constructing an iron curtain he insures the monopoly of his own.[19]

The two interpretations of the rationale of ideology and ideological institutions discussed so far (the creation of the "new man for the new system" and the insecurity-inducing "ideological weapon" as a statecraft institution) are not mutually incompatible. It is not sociologically impossible that, once in place, the ideological institutions we associate with the notion of "ideological commissar" function could operate both ways. Some insights regarding this possibility may be gained if we take a closer look at the specific operations of the ideological and propaganda apparatus.

Authors studying Communism noted very early in their studies that Communist regimes propagate three principal types of indoctrination themes. The first is, as one may expect, the theory of Marxism–Leninism, a central part of the training of leaders.[20] Indoctrination and mindset-molding activities work according to the doctrine. In this respect, the institutions and the practices have a quasi-educational role. They build a certain profile of an ideal "New Man" as described earlier. However, Cassinelli[21] explains, in the training of their real activists, Communists instill a rather different profile. The professional activist, or the ideological worker, has as ultimate features a subservience to obedience and ruthlessness. Therefore, there is an additional layer, a deeper lesson, or a second order training taking place through these institutions. The key factor is given by the fact that, in the end, doctrine is malleable because its interpretation is malleable. What is taught always has to be calibrated to shifting leaders' foreign and domestic policies. Hence, "no matter how thoroughly one learns it he still is unable to anticipate when and understand why changes are made in the orthodox doctrine." To be able to adjust and adapt to these shifting and uncertain operational environments, a certain alertness to these shifts becomes second nature. And thus, if a profile is emerging, it is one of a purely opportunistic being, devoid of a real doctrine. Ideological necessity and the training generate a de facto situation in which the substantive doctrinal issues become secondary. It is true that a certain familiarity with some doctrinal tenets is necessary and that the training programs provide that. Yet, at the same time, subservience to leadership is learned not as a doctrine-based or principle-based practice, but rather as an instinctive, second nature. With that second nature comes a cultivated opportunism and duplicity.

The second type of indoctrination and propaganda stresses the benefits and excellence of living under Communism. In this case, the key fact is that the contrast between reality and propaganda is stark. Administrating this gap and its potential implications for citizens' attitudes and behaviors becomes an ongoing task for the apparatus. The Soviet citizen is free, rational, and a master of his destiny due to the liberating activities of the Socialist system. The Communist state provides a life of comfort and the correct existential and historical significance and meaning to the Soviet citizen. Communism is the realization of humankind's most noble ideals.[22] The overall result of this stark contrast between real life in Communism and the never-ending official propagandistic description of that life is reinforcing a double-speech, double-standards institutionalized hypocrisy, and a preference falsification process for all citizens.[23]

The third type of indoctrination and propaganda is even more contextual, short-term, and dynamic. It consists of providing explanations and justifications of the Party policies and positions, past and present, on a rolling basis.[24] It is an ongoing circumstantial exercise of fitting ideological narrative, facts, and power plays. It is part and parcel of the day-to-day management of the system. Obviously, in the process, the same discrepancies between reality and the ideological Party line becomes salient. Again, the apparatus has to administer this cleavage. And again, as one may expect, this institutionalization of the preference-falsification process has a strong formative impact on citizens' perceptions, attitudes, values, and behaviors.

All of the above have given us a sense of the contrast existing between what is meant to take place as a result of indoctrination and ideological control (i.e., the ideal results expected by the Communist leadership and what may take place in reality). That, in itself, is a huge step forward in understanding the phenomenon of the institutionalization of indoctrination and propaganda. We are thus alerted to some latent functions of it but also to the unintended consequences and processes set into motion by it. By looking at the tensions between the various levels and logics at which these institutions operate, we also get some hints about possible answers to the question: Why a failure to create a New Man?

Obviously, one should not see the manifest and latent rationalities and their logics as mutually exclusive. Their operations take place in tandem, sometimes one taking the forefront, sometimes the other, sometimes some people are acting according to one, and sometimes other people acting according to another. For the purposes of our argument, let us note that an approach illuminating the logic of insecurity induction as a political control technology (stratagem) helped us gain a more nuanced insight. At the same time, it has also helped us make the transition from an ideas-/doctrines-centered approach to an interest and stratagems approach in understanding the rationale of ideological institutions.

RATIONALITIES BASED IN PUBLIC CHOICE STRUCTURES

What will be called in our argument the "public choice" perspective is an approach framed by political economy and institutional analysis that emphasizes the incentive structure and the strategic rationality of decision making regarding political and collective action. Applied to our topic, it takes us beyond the view that concentrates exclusively on repression, coercion, and anonymization of the citizens and their communities as main—or even exclusive—defining instruments of Communist and totalitarian governments. From this perspective, a totalitarian system is based on a larger portfolio of mechanisms, institutions, and practices, and one should study them as a set. Three elements are essential: coercion, incentives, and preference manipulation. The public choice approach links the motivation of the dictator (or the authoritarian oligarchy) to these strategies and their relevant institutions.[25]

In this respect, the ideological-indoctrination apparatus is one key element of this portfolio. It may be seen as a part of a special type of coercion, carried out not against actions and behavior but against thought and speech. Or, it may be seen as pertaining to a class, totally different from coercion, more or less on the lines of manipulation—that is to say, an instrument of preferences formation and preferences management. One way or another, trade-offs emerge between the "instruments" in the portfolio. A mix of tools implies alternative allocations of resources and strategic decisions. In brief, the public choice approach accepts the standard definition of totalitarian government in which the emphasis is on the use of the government's coercive power "to transform economic and social relations, beliefs, values and psychological predispositions."[26] Yet, it goes beyond this.

If repression and indoctrination are seen as part of a larger package of policies and strategies available to totalitarian regimes, then the factors determining the *contents* of the package and the *trade-offs* ensuing between them are central for our understanding of how these regimes operate. The immediate implication is that the logic of repression and indoctrination is always strategic and calibrated to the factors determining the balance of power in a system. As Ronald Wintrobe (who, together with Gordon Tullock, is one of the founders of this approach) noted this:

> Repression is an important tool in the hands of the dictator; but just as a monopolist in the economic marketplace may try to impede (block, repress) entry by alternative sources of supply for the purpose of raising profits from exchange, a political dictator does not repress for the sake of repression alone but in order to increase power. In political exchange, the dictator provides individuals or interest groups with public services or patronage in exchange for support.[27]

Building on these insights, Svolik[28] takes a step further. He draws attention to the fact that authoritarian politics are shaped by two fundamental conflicts. The first is the tension between rules and ruled (i.e., between the masses and the leaders). Slovik refers to the political problem of keeping under control the majority excluded from power as "the problem of authoritarian control." However, that is not the sole—and, in many cases, not the most important—problem. Any totalitarian or authoritarian system usually has to be run through an alliance: a coalition of elite Party members, traditional elites, regional and central leaders, or military officers. Therefore, a second domain of political conflict emerges. Those allies in power sharing may challenge the top leadership anytime. This is the problem of "authoritarian power sharing." The predominant political conflict in dictatorships, explains Slovic, "appears to be not between the ruling elite and the masses but rather one among regime insiders." Obviously, monitoring and control within the ruling class/group is essential.

The result is the emergence of two distinctive features of any system based on such command and control authoritarian structures of power. First, such systems "inherently lack an independent authority with the power to enforce agreements among key political actors, especially the dictator, his allies, and their repressive agents." Second, some form or another of violence and conflict is an unyielding ever-presence in those systems. These two intrinsic features uniquely shape the dynamics of such systems—irrespective of the labels we are using to define them (authoritarian, totalitarian, dictatorships). The model outlined above alerts us that the indoctrination and propaganda institutions that are at the center of our investigation may have a double role in this respect. On the one hand, they are all obviously related to the problem of authoritarian control. On the other hand, they also have a role related to the problem of power sharing.

It may be the case that although the mainstream literature has mostly concentrated on the first (authoritarian control in relationship to the masses), what we called the "political commissar" and "indoctrination institutions" may have a function in the second respect as well. They may be rather important in administering the balance of power among the leaders and elites contributing to the management of the problem of authoritarian power sharing.

We have seen so far how the logic of what we called the public choice approach illuminates how the ideological factor may be essential to the system and yet part of a set of trade-offs. As such, it is part of a set of options in the administration of the system, and it may play several roles.

A very good further articulation of this point is made by Guriev and Treisman.[29] They start with the observation that to survive as a ruler of a system, one has to be both competent, in charge, and effectively in control at the same time to signal that competence and control. Following Slovic, they note that members of the elite have to be co-opted and kept in a closed and monitored coalition. If they are alienated and become hostile, one of the easiest strategies is to pull the incompetence charge against the leader(ship). That operation has, at least in theory, the masses supporting it. However, being informed is decisive for effective and successful action, and there is a difference between elite members and masses in terms of how they get their information about the situation.

The informed elite watch and judge the rulers' performance closely and directly due to access to top decision chains. But normal citizens take their clues in this respect based on the information available from mass media and from their own living standards and quality of life (determined by the tax rate set by the authorities and overall economic performance). Hence, the signals of competence and being in control should come via those two venues. If that is the case, the channels of information, and anything that helps frame perceptions, become central.

Therefore, the indoctrination and propaganda lines discussed earlier as "excellence of living in Communism" and "justification of Party's politics" do not seem so egregiously absurd in their counterfactual reality dimensions. Their insistence on covering the communication channels, no matter their blatant double speak, manipulative intentions, and falsification of preferences, is grounded in the cold-blooded rationality of the system, mixing noise with the signal as part of the logic of survival and control of the leadership in the system.

The bottom line is that the autocratic strategy and the resilience and survival of the regime are dependent on the technology of censorship, propaganda, and repression, and that is a reality irrespective of the particular ideological bent (left or right, Socialist or national Socialist) of the regime.[30] The dictator or the leadership could invest resources in propaganda via state media or private media. They also could use "carrot" or "stick" strategies: control, bribes, fines, or violence, could increase censorship and also could invest in equipping the police with the tools of repression.[31] All these imply certain costs and a series of trade-offs between alternative uses of available resources, including trade-offs between productive uses, government spending on welfare, government spending on monitoring and coercion, and investment in indoctrination and propaganda instruments. "Propaganda" here should be understood broadly: from varieties on the theme that "the leader is competent" to justifications and excuses for poor economic performance. It can also include government advertising, distorted or fake news, planting of stories, creating fake independent media, or hiring agents of influence to operate undercover in the media.[32] Guriev and Treisman identify two stable equilibria: in one, the dictator co-opts the elite; in the other, the dictator controls and manipulates information via media. They also find that using force is, in many respects, a second best to be used against the general public "only as a last resort after co-optation, censorship, and propaganda have failed."

In general, one thinks in terms of trade-offs and substitution in this type of approach. Censorship and co-optation are substitutes. Repression against potential revolutionaries is a substitute for the information-based techniques for maintaining power. Obviously, under some parameter values, equilibria exist in which no repression against the public is needed at all.[33] The model suggests that such regimes may survive in many circumstances simply by manipulating information and public beliefs about the state of the world and the incumbent's situation. Yet, at the same time, the model also illuminates the fact that "under other parameter values for which there are no equilibria based on co-optation, censorship, or propaganda, an equilibrium based on repression of potential protests may exist."[34]

Thus, the model offers insight into a number of observations and puzzles about nondemocratic, totalitarian, and authoritarian systems. For instance, the multiple equilibria associated with different strategies in dealing with these trade-offs illuminate why, in some cases, censoring and propaganda are chosen, while in other cases elite co-optation is favored. Regimes that are authoritarian or even totalitarian may survive using relatively limited coercion and violence. Repression, explain Guriev and Treisman, "is not necessary if mass beliefs can be manipulated sufficiently by means of censorship, co-optation, and propaganda." Indeed, because major repression in the model "is only used if equilibria based on co-optation and censorship have disappeared," violence "signals to the general public that the regime is incompetent and therefore vulnerable."[35] The insights emerging from the model are open-ended. Yet, they inspire a certain discipline and analytical order on our interpretation of concrete examples and case studies of relevant phenomena.

To sum up, this tour of models and frameworks illuminating the alternative functions and rationalities that may operate behind indoctrination, propaganda, and their institutionalization has offered us a more nuanced understanding of the nature and functions of ideology and indoctrination organizations. A combination of social-engineering doctrines and the strategic utilization of doctrines and their institutionalization, as well as some unintended consequences of both, offers us a rather good set of conceptual tools for analyzing and understanding the phenomena of interest. One of the most important insights regards the motive of why the ideological institutions themselves—irrespective of their particular organizational form—have to be, in the end, adaptive and dynamic. They have to change not only the content and accent of operations but also, sometimes, shift from one function to another to have, at once, multiple (related but different) roles. We are thus provided with a set of conceptual lenses that could be very useful in our investigation of the structure and dynamics of real-life cases and situations.

THE BEFORE AND AFTER: TWO MODELS, TWO STAGES, TWO INSTITUTIONAL PRACTICES OF PROPAGANDA AND INDOCTRINATION

The next and last step in our effort to put together a theoretically informed general perspective on the phenomenon of indoctrination and propaganda institutionalization in Communist and totalitarian systems starts with the observation that to understand the ideological indoctrination and monitoring institutions at work, we need to go beyond the approach centered on the functions and the general institutional and operating features derived from the logic of those functions. This is a perspective we have explored so far, but we need to add to that the historical—the evolution-in-time perspective. Before moving ahead to the second part of our book, let us briefly focus on this second perspective; more precisely, let us on one of its conceptual aspects related to the problem of the stages in the evolution of such phenomena.

Looking at the evolution in time aspect, one could easily notice that totalitarianism (and ideocracy) comes in phases, each phase having its own parameters, constraints, objectives, and dynamics. The Communist strategy is calibrated to that reality. Broadly speaking, there are two ways Communism defines its stages and tactics: First, as a challenger to an existing social order and system—a logic and strategy of subversion, generating an organizational structure aligned with the objective of overthrowing a social order from the inside. Second, as a dominant force building and defending a particular form of social order and governance system. In this case a strategy and structure of domination and consolidation through the control of national centers of power is required.

In the next part of our book, we will be concentrating on the second stage as it materialized in our case study. But to understand it, we need to have some familiarity with the instrumentation of ideology and beliefs in the first stage. So, we have to delve into a couple of things about that stage as well. The differences and continuities between the two stages matter. Understanding the organizational arrangements related to them requires a familiarity with these points of continuity and change.

Regarding the organizational aspect, it is very important to note that Communism (in both its phases and modes) was a formidable organizational phenomenon. One cannot underscore enough that effective organization was one of the key strengths of Communist parties and movements in comparison to their competitors and adversaries. In a sense, the success of Marxism is intrinsically related to the fact that Communist leaders understood to place their political practice at the forefront of the organizational revolution taking place in the twentieth century.

This reality was increasingly noticed and exposed at the very beginning of the Cold War. Then, Western scholars finally started to take seriously that Communism and totalitarianism could be demythologized as real life and effective organizational phenomena. Scholars discovered, sometimes to their surprise, the extent to which the entire Communist movement was how deliberately organizationally constructed and organizationally effective.[36] They noted, for instance, that Lenin was adamant about the organizational factor. Lenin was fully aware of the significance of the rationalization and organization movement gaining ground first in America and then all over the world, and he was a pioneer in thinking about the implications for politics and governance.

There is no better argument in this respect than "the method of practical action" he advocated for when it came to propaganda and ideological work within the confines of the existing capitalist, bourgeois regimes. In one of the most penetrating and succinct analyses of the time, Jean-Marie Domenach[37] explained that Lenin realized early on that consciousness must be awakened, educated, and mobilized into the battle beyond the narrow workplace and employment relations. That is to say, the transformation of the workplace and employment relations was a necessary but not sufficient condition. An elite group of professional revolutionaries, "the conscious vanguard of the proletariat," was to be created as instruments for an institutional structure targeting the entire polity and society. The principle of specialization and division of labor was to be taken at this new level, and its organizational force was to be unleashed in the service of the Communist revolution.

Therefore, within the Party, a special corps of agitators is created with the function of indoctrinating and leading the masses. Once created, their activity "becomes the means of transmission, the essential link of expression, at once highly rigid and infinitely flexible, which continually enlightens the masses, prepares them, leads them gradually to join the vanguard in understanding and eventually in action."[38]

But things go further than that. The genius of organization is demonstrated by a closer look at their activities. Propaganda and indoctrination are not merely repetitious Pavlovian exercises using images and mantras. In fact, the entire procedure is ingeniously structured around two pillars. Technically speaking, Domenach reminds us,[39] propaganda of the Bolshevik type can be reduced to two fundamental forms: political revelation (or denunciation) and slogans or watchwords. Each has its own logic and implies specific mechanisms and practices.

Following Domenach's classical take, let us start with the so-called "political revelations." The origins of the technique were in Marx, who had already noted that "it is necessary to render genuine oppression even more severe by adding to it the consciousness of oppression, and to make shame even more shameful by throwing upon it the light of publicity." Lenin took that insight and systematized it into a method of "organized political revelations in every sphere." The "revelations" were strategic debunkings of the ruling classes, pointing methodically to their selfish interests. Embracing all spheres of social life, they were presented by Lenin as necessary and fundamental for the preparation of the masses for their revolutionary activity. The exercise was predicated on the assumption that there was a façade (a veil) of ideology and, obviously, a reality behind it. Revelations were operations executed by the Communist specialists, giving the masses the "true picture" of the reality behind the façade manufactured by the ruling classes.

One way to see them is as "demystifications." In every situation, and especially in those that have something to do with (and are of direct interest) to the masses, the propagandist must go behind surfaces to demonstrate to the masses what the true realities are and how to interpret them once they are demystified. The propagandist is able to do that because he is trained and equipped with the proper tools (Marxism). That means always presenting the case in terms of class struggle. Anything else deviating from this method and its predetermined conclusion was deemed as superficial and unhelpful to the cause. Domenach offers one of the best, most concise, and effective accounts of the procedure: "A war, a strike, or a political scandal furnish him opportunities; but more often the propagandist will work from more trivial and concrete facts in order to connect what appeared to be only an accident to a general political explanation, which is, of course, that of the Communist Party."[40]

To illustrate this point, as a purely hypothetical example, Domenach invites the reader to imagine the following situation: The beauty parlor business goes through a general lull. The reason may be merely supply and demand, fashion, or circumstantial factors that all may be able to explain the slump. But the Communist propaganda will not bother with such explanations. Instead, it will build a chain of arguments linking the parlor business situation to NATO, capitalism, and imperialism. People don't have money to go to the parlors because they are not paid enough as all the money go to the military budget imposed by NATO, which is an organization created to support the capitalist exploiters and against the workers. The devastating and unprecedented situation of the parlors is the direct result of the capitalist class and of capitalism at work. Thus, a direct linkage is created between any hypothetical or real-life problem and something called "the capitalist system." That link, once revealed, it is denounced. And thus, what otherwise might be a temporary or normal phenomenon is more or less directly linked to the standard targets of Communist propaganda.[41]

Let us focus now on the second pillar of propaganda and indoctrination, the one defined by the so-called "slogans." Understanding the nature of the propaganda and indoctrination institutions requires us to be aware that, again, the issue of "slogans" is not left to chance by the Communists. It is a domain well thought of as a matter of organization and practical effectiveness. As Domenach explains, the "slogan," or "watchword," is the combative and constructive aspect of propaganda. It is "the verbal translation of one phase of the revolutionary tactic." It is action and context oriented, "a driving concept, expressing as clearly, briefly, and euphonically as possible the most important objective of the moment."[42] Examples of "slogans" should always be seen in conjunction with their circumstantial objective. If the objective is to rally the masses and overthrow a regime or government, then appropriate slogans are "All Power to the Soviets," "Land and Peace," "Bread, Peace and Liberty," "For a Liberal, Democratic Government," and so forth. If, however, one wants to consolidate the grip on power, then appropriate slogans are "Stabilization," "Socialist Edification," "To Reach and Exceed the Plan in Four Years," and so on.[43] The domain of slogans is always dynamic and contextual. Hence, it requires continuous attention and alert management.

The management and calibration are always in function of what was called "the Political Line." The "Political Line" is a prerogative of the Communist Party that had the authority and monopoly in dictating it. Needless to say, its content and direction are given by the contextual interests of the Party. Those interests, as already noted, have no bounds in morality. Morality itself is subdued to the "Political Line." The "Political Line" is driven by an ongoing Machiavellian exercise of calibrating discourse and power politics to the evolving circumstances. "Every slogan," said Lenin, "must be deduced from the sum of the particularities of a given political situation."[44] Each slogan has to operate between/with two factors: the political situation and the level of mass consciousness. It has to connect and stir the masses, and, for that, it has to address their consciousness as well as their latent desires or fears as stirred by the related contextual evolutions. "We are accused of creating mass opinion," Trotsky comments on this success, explaining how much was accomplished by Bolsheviks with so limited means:

> The paucity of means available for Bolshevik agitation was striking. How is it, then, that with such a weak apparatus and with so few printings of Bolshevik literature that the ideas and slogans of bolshevism were able to impress themselves on the people? The answer to the enigma is very simple: the slogans which correspond to the acute need of a class and epoch themselves create thousands of channels for their own dissemination. The revolutionary milieu is marked by a high conductability of ideas.[45]

Now that we have a clearer view of the basic ingredients and building blocks out of which propaganda campaigns are built, let us take a look at the functional roles required by them. Because, again, as one may expect, Communists follow a certain method and organizational logic at this level as well. The task of propagating "revelations" and "slogans" requires, in each case, a particular approach with specific techniques and training. The result of this basic fact of further specialization and division of labor was the emergence of two subtypes of specialists: propagandists and agitators.

Plekhanov is considered to be the one who introduced the classical definition of each: On the one hand, the role of the propagandist is to inculcate many ideas to a single person or to a small number of people. On the other hand, the agitator only inculcates a single idea or a small number of ideas. By contrast, however, he inculcates them to a whole mass of people. As one may expect, that goes back to Lenin, who elaborated the modus operandi and the division of labor between the two agents of Communism. The agitator identifies a social problem and diagnoses it unfailingly as one of the egregious results of capitalism, rousing "discontent and indignation against the crying injustice, leaving to the propagandist the responsibility of giving a complete explanation for the contradiction." As a result "the propagandist[46] works principally through the written word and the agitator through the spoken word."[47]

The next level is of a pure organizational nature. The agitator and propagandist are not fully effective if their efforts are not followed up by the "organization" of the targeted group or community. Again, Lenin was at the origin of this approach: Communists were urged to engage with the people "to go into all classes of the population as propagandists, as agitators, and as organizers" and to mold the society in ways congruous with the Communist designs. The use of denunciations and political revelations prepares the way for "political organization," which basically means creating core groups responding to the Communist Party "Political Line" both in thought and action, if possible. To achieve this, explained Lenin, the entire fabric of the social system of the country needs to be penetrated: "it is necessary that we have 'our men,' . . . everywhere and always in all social strata, in every position which will enable them to see and understand the internal springs of the state mechanism."[48]

Thus, while acting as revolutionary forces against a government or regime, the agents of Communism are operating as a disciplined, methodical apparatus. As Domenach noted, every mistake and every problem in the society is "unmasked," "denounced," and "systematically woven into a central political theme." It is a vast ongoing operation, that covers all aspects of society, from the local to the national level. Each social circumstance provides ammunition for political "revelations" and "denunciations." The ensuing immense process, driven by the Communist propaganda, is fueled by Communist agents, ready to provide—and in some cases to fabricate—the raw material. By placing its agents in all strata of society and all social institutions, the

Communists have more than a network of informers. In fact, the information network is converted at will into an enduring propaganda and denunciation mechanism, ready to operate under the Party's coordination. Even when they get in power, notes Domenach, the Communist parties have retained Lenin's 'passion for political revelations' organized "before the entire people."[49]

Last but not least, it is important to mention at this point that Lenin's system of propagandists and agitators, which operated based on the proper "political line," also involved an element related to practical action, the so-called "propaganda of deeds." The idea is that in order to inspire trust, propaganda and indoctrination need to signal from time to time that they are anchored in reality. To be able to influence and motivate, they need to manufacture concrete acts as examples to support its claims. These "deeds" are persuasion tools, tricks of the propaganda trade, and activities having a purely political marketing role. They are political "happenings" calibrated for specific audiences.

If the Communists are acting in opposition to a regime they want to dethrone, these are meant to support social demands and have demonstration effects in fomenting civil unrest and revolutionary conditions. However, once in power, things change radically, and most of these "deeds" are meant to illuminate real achievements, which are supposed to be displayed as previews and samples of general actions and achievements to come in the future under Socialism and full Communism. The aforementioned "deeds" are meant to bolster the image of the future and keep the expectations regarding the Communist goals connected to "real life" examples and developments. Propaganda of deeds provides to the people concrete evidence that the Communists are not just "talking the talk" but also "walking the walk." This is achieved through the display of a sample of how the Communist society will look when Communist goals are achieved. In other words, it is supposed to be a reassuring signal regarding the feasibility of the project.

To conclude, following the principles outlined above, the Communists (operating as a revolutionary anti-regime force) were in the position to construct an unprecedented system of propaganda and agitation penetrating state institutions and targeting the proletariat, the peasantry, and the army. In the initial stage, the objective was to undermine social order and create confusion, strife, and demobilization. But when the revolution was won—or was imposed by Soviet tanks in Eastern Europe—this type of activity was not discontinued. On the contrary, it was recalibrated, amplified, and intensified. It entered into a new stage. It was not only that "political commissars" (now operating under the designation of "ideological workers") were attached to military units, but they were sent to attend and shape public events and insert themselves into public life in mass media; art, intellectual, and cultural milieus; factories; communities; villages; professional associations; and so forth. Communist propaganda and indoctrination cells became not an exception but a rule in all aspects of society and polity. The result was "a vast psycho-political system which, through press, radio, theatre, films, local and factory bulletins, conferences, meetings, and the like, was able to reach into corners of the country."[50]

And thus, once the Communist Party takes control of the political system, all agitation,[51] propaganda and indoctrination activities, and strategies are immediately redefined, reorganized, and recalibrated to the new circumstances. At the same time, they are institutionalized as a key component of the party–state apparatus. Obviously, the educational system has to be at the core of this enterprise. The intrinsic link between indoctrination and education makes the assault and takeover of the education system inevitable. As Zinoviev[52] put it, "Propaganda, agitation, and instruction are a unity which must be realized according to the Leninist conception of education." Hence, very quickly the education system becomes the pivot of the total propaganda scheme. From the bases anchored in higher education, the "political seminars," the "schools of ideology," and the "study groups" are staffed by "hundreds of thousands of "propagandists" or "agitators."[53] Thus, the education system becomes a cradle of propagandists and activists who start to operate in official capacities in cultural associations, factories, professional associations, sporting clubs, and so on, appearing to submerge the entire political, economic, and intellectual activities of the state and society.

To sum up, there is no surprise that, once a country comes to be controlled by the Communists, the educational system immediately becomes one of their main targets, on the lines discussed above. The institutionalization of indoctrination starts as a mass scale, state-run operation of the Communist regime in the educational system. We have noted that the Communist takeover operates in two phases. First, Communism operates as a challenger to an existing social order and system, organized with the objective of overthrowing a social order from the inside. Second, it operates as a dominant force, building and defending a particular form of social order and governance system, which requires a strategy and structure of domination and consolidation through the control of national centers of power. We are now in the position to approach our topic and take a closer look at the details of the Romanian case. Our in-depth discussion of the Romanian case will start from the moment the second phase kicks in: the phase defined by a strategy and structure of authoritarian and dictatorial domination.

NOTES

1. Paul Hollander, *Slavic Review 70*, no. 1 (2011): 205–6 and 10.5612/slavicreview.70.1.0205 by Yinghong Cheng, *Creating the "New Man": From Enlightenment Ideals to Socialist Realities* (Honolulu: University of Hawai'i Press, 2009).
2. Paul Hollander, op.cit., 206.
3. Ibid., 206.
4. Ibid., 206.
5. A. S. Makarenko, "Pedagogi Pozhimayut Plechami," written in 1927, in *Izbrannye Pedagogicheskiye Sochinenia*, 1949, vol. 4, quoted by E. Koutaissoff, "Soviet Education and the New Man" in *Soviet Studies*, 5, no. 2 (1953): 134.
6. E. Koutaissoff, op.cit., 129.
7. The substitution of the service motive for the profit motive is an essential feature of the psychological revolution.
8. E. Koutaissoff, op.cit., 128.
9. Ibid., 103–37.
10. Ibid., 135–36.
11. Ibid., 135; "Public criticism and self-criticism was another tool in the campaigns of politically inspired self-improvement."
12. C. W. Cassinelli, "Totalitarianism, Ideology, and Propaganda," *The Journal of Politics*, 22, no. 1 (1960): 68–95.
13. C. W. Cassinelli, op.cit., 90–91.
14. Ibid., 70–71.
15. Ibid., 90.
16. Ibid., 93.
17. Ibid., 93.
18. Ibid., 91.
19. Ibid., 94.
20. Ibid., 86.
21. Ibid., 87.
22. Ibid., 88.
23. Timur Kuran, *Private Truths, Public Lies: The Social Consequences of Preference Falsification* (Cambridge, MA: Harvard University Press, 1997).
24. C. W. Cassinelli, op.cit., 89.
25. Ronald Wintrobe, "The Tinpot and the Totalitarian: An Economic Theory of Dictatorship," *The American Political Science Review*, 84, no. 3 (Sep. 1990): 849–72.

> I use basic tools of economic theory to construct a simple model of the behavior of dictatorships. Two extreme cases are considered: a "tin-pot" dictatorship, in which the dictator wishes only to minimize the costs of remaining in power in order to collect the fruits of office (palaces, Mercedes-Benzes, Swiss bank accounts), and a "totalitarian" dictatorship, whose leader maximizes power over the population. I show that the two differ in their responses to economic change. For example, a decline in economic performance will lead a tin-pot regime to increase its repression of the population, whereas it will lead a totalitarian government to reduce repression.

26. Jeane J. Kirkpatrick, "Dictatorships and Double Standards," *Commentary Magazine*, November, 1979 and also Jeane J. Kirkpatrick, *Dictatorships and Double Standards: Rationalism and Reason in Politics* (New York: Simon and Schuster, 1982), 101.
27. Ronald Wintrobe, op.cit., 850–51.
28. Milan W. Svolik, *The Politics of Authoritarian Rule* (Cambridge: Cambridge University Press, 2012).
29. Sergei Guriev, Daniel Treisman, "How Modern Dictators Survive: An Informational Theory of the New Authoritarianism," *National Bureau of Economic Research*, no. w21136 (2015).
30. One could also add, at the extreme range, manufacturing conflict and the potential confrontation with foreign powers in diversionary strategies blaming external forces for internal failures.
31. Sergei Guriev, Daniel Treisman, op.cit., 4.
32. Ibid., 4.
33. Ibid., 5–6.
34. Ibid., 5.
35. Ibid., 5–6.
36. Philip Selznick, *The Organizational Weapon: A Study of Bolshevik Strategy and Tactics*, Vol. 18 (New Orleans: Quid Pro Books, 2014).
37. Jean-Marie Domenach, "Leninist Propaganda," *The Public Opinion Quarterly*, 15, no. 2 (1951).
38. Jean-Marie Domenach, op.cit., 265–73.
39. Ibid., 266.
40. Ibid., 266.
41. Ibid., 266–67.
42. Ibid., 267.
43. Ibid., 267.
44. "Slogans stake out gradated platforms with which the communists can force other political groups to take stands either for or against collaboration with them on specific objectives which are likely to be seductive to the masses."
45. Jean-Marie Domenach, op.cit., 260–68.
46. Lenin also suggested that there is a certain level of theoretical systematization—and hence a higher intellectual level—which distinguishes the propagandist from the agitator.
47. Jean-Marie Domenach, op.cit., 268.
48. As Domenach notes, "These men have a double role: first, to propagandize and agitate by every available means: but to do that "always being careful to adapt their arguments to the milieu in which they work"; see also Jean-Marie Domenach, op.cit., 269.
49. Ibid., 269.
50. Ibid., 271.
51. The direction of this polymorphic activity was vested in an agency called "Agitprop" (a combined abbreviation of "agitation" and "propaganda") that has its representatives on all echelons down to the Party cell, and which will always continue

to be an essential part of Communist activity. See also Jean-Marie Domenach, op. cit., 271.
   52. Ibid., 272.
   53. Ibid., 272.

PART II

The Romanian Case (1948–1989): Descriptive and Narrative Facets

The second part of the book will offer an overview of the main historical elements and patterns of the institutionalization of indoctrination in the Romanian context of the Communist regime. The following chapters will explore a set of key aspects, putting a special emphasis on the education system and, within it, on higher education. In this task, we need to keep in mind the framework outlined in the first part of the book. Every factual detail, narrative element, or observation has to be seen in a broader perspective, shaped by the theoretical and conceptual instruments discussed in the first two chapters.

For instance, we need to keep in mind that the manifest goal of the propaganda machinery was to attempt to transform young Romanians into "New Men and Women." In Romania, as in Soviet Union and in all other Eastern European countries, the strategy to create the New Man employed the range of methods we are already familiar with from the first part of the book. While the first chapters have identified and outlined them and the logic behind them, now, in the following chapters, we will see them at work in a more concrete historical setting. Similarly, we need to keep in mind the two rationalities introduced and discussed in the first part of the book as possible modes of explanatory structures. First, are the rationalities based on ideology that intrinsically and instrumentally motivate decisions and the policies and institutional structures. Second, are what we have called the rationalities based in "public choice." Many of the decisions, phenomena, and patterns documented and described in the following chapters have to be seen as part of strategic political moves mobilizing institutions as devices for access to power or redistribution of resources or as part and parcel of political power games taking place within the members of the Communist political elite.

In brief, the second part of the volume will overview the historical record, emphasizing and identifying within it those aspects and facets that help us get a better sense on the specifics of the phenomena of interest in our investigation. We identify the rich texture of the institutions, social actors, patterns, and events that are associated with the institutionalization of indoctrination in this Eastern European country. Within this framework, we put—as noted—a special emphasis on the education system, and, within the education system, we give, from time-to-time, specific attention to higher education. Obviously, the survey captured in the following chapters is just charting and moving on the surface of the phenomena of interest. Each of the aspects identified may be the object of a separated in-depth analysis, using specific theories or concepts that have been introduced in the first part of the book. However, the objective of this second part of the book is not the direct application of those specific theoretical frameworks or the testing of some of the hypotheses that may be built using those frameworks. Instead, the goal is to offer the reader, through a series of factual observations based on historical data and archival records, a sense of the complexities, depth, multiple dimensions, and facets of the realities of the institutions and the process of indoctrination in a real-life Socialist/Communist system. Thus, read in conjunction, the first two parts of the book will offer the reader complementing perspectives, each approaching the phenomena of interest from different angles.

In addition to the relevant Romanian historical and political science literature, this part of the book is based also on the investigation of archival records from the Central Committee of the RCP[1] Collection; the Propaganda and Agitation, Chancellery, Cadres, and Organizational sections, retrieved at the Central National Historical Archives in Bucharest. In addition, we consulted a number of verbatim reports of the meetings of the Politburo or the Central Committee Secretariat and a considerable number of files belonging to cadres and propagandists active in education, especially in higher education, available at the Archive of the University of Bucharest. Yet another type of source were children's and youth publications[2] and textbooks. Finally, another type of source, used less than we wanted to, was the memoirs of people who were active in the Party structures, in which they expressed opinions on certain details of the relationship between the propagandists' powers and their obligations, shedding light on certain social aspects. Romanian historians have obviously studied extensively the issue of propaganda and education, and in writing this part of the book, we have acknowledged with gratitude their contribution to the research done in this respect. There is a significant literature regarding the Romanian Communist propaganda that singles out, within the scope of each work, various details of the workings of the Romanian system of indoctrination. In this respect, we note authors such as Vladimir Tismăneanu, Lavinia Betea, Nicoleta Ionescu-Gură,[3] Oana Ilie,[4] Călin Hentea, Marin Radu Mocanu, Marin Nițescu, Florin Șperlea, Eugen Denize, Adrian Cioflâncă,[5] Cristian Vasile,[6] Cristina Preutu, Marian Petcu,[7] Ștefan Bosomitu, Flori Bălănescu, Eugen Negrici, Cristian Sandache, Tiberiu Troncotă,[8] and Manuela Marin,[9] whose works constitute particularly valuable contributions to the contemporary Romanian historiography on this topic.

NOTES

1. Romanian Communist Party.

2. Among the relevant publications are both those addressing all Romanian citizens—*Scânteia* (The Spark), *Carnetul agitatorului* (The Agitator's Notebook), *Veac Nou* (New Century), *Lupta de clasă* (Class Struggle)—and those addressing the children and the youth—*Licurici* (Glowworm), *Arici Pogonici* (Prickly Hedgehog), *Cravata Roșie* (The Red Tie), *Luminița* (Twinkle), *Cutezătorii* (The Brave), *Scânteia tineretului* (The Youth Spark), etc.

3. Nicoleta Ionescu-Gură, *Nomenclatura CC al PMR* (Bucharest: Editura Humanitas, 2006).

4. Oana Ilie, *Propagandă politică. Tipologii și arii de manifestare (1945–1958)* (Târgoviște: Editura Cetatea de Scaun, 2014).

5. "Pentru o genealogie culturală a modelului propagandistic comunist" (For a cultural genealogy of the Communist propaganda model), in *In media res. Studii de istorie culturală*, eds. Andi Mihalache, Adrian Cioflâncă (Iași: Editura Universității Alexandru Ioan Cuza, 2007), 159.

6. Cristian Vasile, *Politici culturale comuniste în timpul regimului lui Gheorghiu-Dej* (Bucharest: Editura Humanitas, 2011).

7. Marian Petcu, *Puterea și cenzura. O istorie a cenzurii* (Iași: Editura Polirom, 1999).

8. Tiberiu Troncotă, *România comunistă. Propagandă și cenzură* (Bucharest: Tritonic, 2006).

9. Manuela Marin, *Originea și evoluția cultului personalității lui Nicolae Ceaușescu* (Alba-Iulia: Editura Altip, 2008).

Chapter 3

Indoctrination and Propaganda in Communist Romania

An Overview of the General Patterns of Organization and Evolution over Time

The Communist project and the dominance of the party–state required more than just indoctrination efforts. Ultimately, the resilience and survival of Soviet-type regimes cannot be explained without factoring in the constant state of terror as a result of the repression institutions (in Romania's case, securitate, militia, etc.). And yet, once all this is said, the role of the actions of the Party apparatus on the propaganda and indoctrination front remains salient and decisive. It was with the help of the latter structures that the Communist Party created the ultimate conditions for exercising its monopoly over the society and converted that monopoly into a totalitarian regime.[1]

And thus, we see how in Romania, as elsewhere in Eastern Europe, the institutionalization of indoctrination played a key role in this complex transformation. In its drive to gain totalitarian control, Communist propaganda ingeniously and tenaciously manipulated old and well-tried symbols. We see how, in time, Romanian Communism[2] developed a political culture that borrowed from both nationalism and the internationalist Leninist tradition. To that, one may add the conspiracy mindset that prevailed in the Romanian Communist Party, as well as an ideology turned into a dogma that clashed with the most blatant Machiavellian and Byzantine spirit. All of the above merged into a "totalitarian blueprint" with its own distinctive features.[3] And as all this mix had to be held together somehow, indoctrination and propaganda entered into the picture at multiple levels and in multiple ways.

According to Socialist educator Makarenko's teachings[4] that were widely disseminated in Romania as elsewhere in the Eastern Bloc, collectivism was to be the ruling principle in the building of a Socialist society; consequently, there was no room for individualism in this new type of society, where collective interests prevailed over individual ones.[5] "Our involvement in the life of a collective in almost all the important and unimportant areas of our life: *that* is the foundation of our psychology. Ideology unifies the individual consciousness and unites millions of little 'I's' into one huge 'We.'"[6] As early as 1918, the Soviet leaders decided that the young generation was to become a "generation of communists"[7] and, therefore, urged, "We must transform our children into true communists. We must teach them to strongly influence their families.[8] We must take them under our control and, to put it bluntly, nationalize them. From their first days, they will be under the influence of the communist kindergartens and schools."[9]

The model of the New Man[10] was imprinted on all from the youngest age. School-age children were expected to identify with it and become familiar with the qualities associated with it. Citizens did not have a choice. One could not opt out. Once Communism took power and the nationwide Sovietization process was set in motion, the fate of Romanian citizens was decided. Whether in the primary school or later in life, the propaganda was a constant throughout the Communist period, part and parcel of everyday life from the early years of Communism until its downfall. As we shall see, the Romanian propaganda and indoctrination evolved into an extremely complex institutional mechanism with an ever-expanding structure, requiring the constant renewal of its techniques, resources, and operations.[11] A noteworthy feature of this apparatus was its constant effort to overcome its bureaucratic and dogmatic nature, adapt to the challenges coming from society, and constantly change in relation to the changes taking place in the Communist power. The bureaucratic apparatus of the propaganda underwent repeated resets and reforms, restructuring its sections, units, and operations. That meant that the role of the propagandist—or the ideological worker—required periodical reassessments, updating of the activity, and continuous training.

To sum up, we are confronted with a complex and dynamic system, fully equipped with its institutional arrangements, agents, dissemination channels, and specific practices.[12] As such, the Romanian case illustrates, in multiple ways, features that we associate with the notions of totalitarianism and ideocracy. The functions of the ideological commissar laying at the foundations of this system continued to define the nature and logic of the system throughout its entire life span from 1948[13] to 1989.

This chapter will take a closer look at the institutionalization of propaganda and the propagandist[14] in Romanian education with a focus on the broad patterns and dynamics in the context of the main national and international events occurring in that time span. We will start by tackling the institutional dimension of the propaganda via an analysis of the structure of its central institution, the Agitation and Propaganda Department—later the Agitation and Propaganda Section—and its territorial subunits. (The frequent reorganizations of the institution due to functional requirements have to be seen in the context of the regime's evolution, as they reflect the pivotal position that the regime gave to it.) Beyond this central institution, under the command of the Central Committee of the RCP and its territorial subunits, there were other organizations that shared the task of indoctrination and propaganda in education (e.g., educational institutions such as kindergartens, primary schools, secondary schools, universities; cultural centers; and libraries). In addition to indoctrination, the latter category also targeted how citizens socialized and spent their leisure time. It is only when we put these pieces together that we are able to start recreating and analyzing the tangible profile of the propaganda institution and identifying its functions, characteristics, and the connections between propaganda and the education system.

Once that is done, the stage will be prepared for the main character to take center stage: the ideological worker—under their various guises (agitators, propagandists, ideologists, or lecturers), depending on the stage of Romanian Communism—as operatives and vehicles for the Party leadership's message in educational institutions. That will be the task of the next chapter.

THE SET-UP OF THE SYSTEM

After the Communists' accession to power in Central and Eastern Europe, the Soviet leaders from satellite countries established a monopoly of power that followed the doctrines and the orientation that Stalin had given to Bolshevism. The notion of "dictatorship of the proletariat" served as the foundation of those systems, while the Stalinist design for the countries subordinated to the USSR relied on a unitary strategy to transform their national political cultures into copies of the Soviet model. In a short time, historically speaking, those countries implemented the strategy, successfully transplanting, under the aegis of proletarian internationalism, the characteristics of the Soviet type of totalitarian system. The Romanian Communist Party was no exception. From a marginal, illegal, sect-like group[15] with a little over one thousand members[16] in a country of almost 20 million people, it rapidly grew to become a massive party.

Once it took over in Romania, supported by Soviet army, the main objectives of the Romanian Communist Party—quickly rebranded as the Romanian Workers' Party (RWP) for tactical and propaganda reasons—were to strengthen and expand the Party's influence in all areas of social activity. Stalinization was a radical program: it aimed to annihilate civil society and to control the intellectual life and culture. Any contrary opinion that failed to toe the official dogma was banned, and its originator silenced. Every aspect of public life was strictly regulated. The result was the annihilation of any form of free, critical thinking or initiative.

While totally submitting to Moscow's interests, it claimed to offer to the Romanian people "the chance to build the socialist society together." And while this offer was wrapped in an illusion of generosity, in practice, the RWP used two main methods. The first was repression—the task of the securitate (political police) and the militia (standard police force), with the intervention of the military in extreme situations. The second was persuasion via indoctrination—the task of a massive propaganda apparatus, which maintained a constant sociopsychological pressure of the citizens.[17] The main actor in this society-wide process was, of course, the "propagandist"—the ideological workers institutionalized as ideological cadres,[18] or individuals indoctrinated to see themselves as belonging to the chosen caste called to fulfill a historical mission.

To get a sense of the dynamics of the institutionalization of the Communist propaganda apparatus in Romania, one needs to approach it not only in relationship to the Soviet model but also in light of the developments of the Romanian circumstances. We have seen that the Communists managed to prevent the return of democracy in Romania, taking control of the executive via the government headed by Petru Groza on March 6, 1945. From then until full submission to Moscow, the events and the actions of the political actors unfolded in a predictable way. The political offensive was pursued in stages, including taking over the legislature following the rigged elections of November 19, 1946, forcing King Michael I into exile, and finally proclaiming the Romanian People's Republic on December 30, 1947. At this time, the traditional established political parties were also forced out of the Romanian political scene.[19] The last one of them, the Social-Democrat Party, was incorporated by the Communists following the merger congress of February 21–23, 1948, which marked the birth of the Romanian Workers' Party. It was only in the summer of 1965 that the Party officially embraced its true identity as the Romanian Communist Party.[20]

From the very beginning of the process, whose chronology was outlined above, the RWP leaders—such as Chișinevschi,[21] Alexandru Moghioroș, Leonte Răutu,[22] and Miron Constantinescu[23]—enforced the Soviet orders and made sure that Romania imported mimetic institutions from Moscow. The regime closely followed the Soviet model: a society whose top tier consisted of the Party nomenklatura (i.e., a complex, hierarchical structure that included the members of the Politbiuro; the Orgburo; the Secretariat, the Chancellery, and the various sections of the Central Committee; the file and rank members of the Central Committee; the Party active in the regional and municipal committees; the members of the government and the diplomatic corps; the highest ranking officers of the army, securitate, and militia; the leaders of the main public institutions [including education]; and the local and central press). In addition to its vast repression apparatus, the Romanian Workers' Party created the indispensable propaganda machine.

The newly created Agitation and Propaganda Department emerged rapidly as a key institution in the Communist architecture of power and control over the Romanian society. The responsibilities of the Propaganda Department (later, Section) and its structure were from the very beginning fully integrated with the other institutions of the Communist state. The role of the main agents disseminating the Party's message (i.e., the ideological/propaganda workers, the lecturers, agitators, activists, or in one word: the cadres) has to be seen in this larger context of the evolving party–state apparatus.

Established in 1948, the Agitation and Propaganda Department[24] of the Central Committee of the Romanian Workers' Party was designed from the very beginning as one of the key institutions of the Communist architecture of power. The department (later renamed section) was formally defined as the prime agent in the social engineering strategy to create the New Man and implement the materialist-dialectical ideology. But in addition to that, as already explained in our theoretical discussion of these types of institutions, it had other related functions, such as controlling and policing the Romanian cultural scene, recruiting cadres, and deploying them under its direction to implement political ideological lines that reflected the tactical objectives of the party–state.

From the very beginning, the department was designed to have a formal presence and influence at the top level of the political-administrative apparatus, in every ministry, in the form of an ideological bureau.[25] It had an overarching coordinating role and would convene regular meetings with local secretaries and other persons responsible for propaganda. One of these tasks was to explain the decisions taken by the Party leaders and make sure the decisions taken at the central level were implemented. At the same time, the department would receive complaints from its territorial structures about attitudes hostile to the new ideology, with the central authorities having an obligation to analyze them and indicate the best action to be taken.[26] Both top-down and bottom-up flows were institutionalized.

It is important to try to outline the entire range of functions because that shows that, irrespective of how the job description of the ideological worker was articulated over time, the best way to understand is to try to focus on its de facto functions in the system in addition to the de jure functions. The problem of legitimacy was central. In this respect, usually legitimating a ruling party relies on tradition, elections, ideology or religion, and the popular support. Communism was, however, perceived by a large part of the population as Russian occupation, imposed by force and electoral fraud. So, elections, tradition, and religion were out of question. The legitimacy of the Communist regime largely relied on its ideology. They had to historically validate the notion of class struggle, persuade that human progress and evolution are dependent on Communism, and constantly emphasize that individuals had to become involved in the life of the community and embrace "socialist" models of conduct.

The legitimation and interpretation functions of the propaganda were explicitly reflected in the party courses, with the Propaganda and Agitation Section broadly designing the curricula for the universities of Marxism-Leninism every year.[27] To that, one may add popularizing the history of the Party[28] and of the Romanian state in the Party schools or other educational establishments. The main documents that served as guidelines for the curricula were the basic doctrines of Marxism-Leninism.

As we have already noted, the "propaganda of deeds" was crucial in the Communist strategy. Even a well-built propaganda discourse would have been inefficient were it not backed up by practical achievements. The educational leaflets used for the training of propaganda workers stipulated that propaganda was not an end in itself, nor was it a dogma. It was instead a field that underwent continuous improvement, in sync with the development of the society. Connecting public rhetoric to the concrete achievements of Socialism was an important element in the strategy of legitimizing the regime.

Last but not least, legitimization was also induced through the so-called "wooden language," perceived as a means and a model of communication that could shape an individual's way of thinking.[29] Although criticized on logical and stylistic grounds, the "wooden language" was in fact an effective "grammar of persuasion" comprising a number of elements: the "prestige" of official sources, the "affirmation free of proof" that did away with any debate, "repetition" that made acceptable as certain whatever it was asserted, and "mental contagion" that easily created strong beliefs.[30] In brief, the propaganda system had multiple ways of operating in contributing to the legitimacy space of the regime. Some of them were related to the New Man and some of them were not.

Let us note at this juncture that—notwithstanding their scientific materialism with its focus on economic forces, technology, and social classes—from the very beginning, Communists were aware that they were supposed to engineer a "cultural revolution." Implementing this "cultural revolution" required controlling mass communications, reshaping the language (on the lines of the so-called "wooden language"[31]), requiring people to put doctrine and ideology above their personal interests, and denouncing them for failing at that. Long before Gramsci's vogue or Mao's cultural revolution, an influential Romanian propagandist, Sorin Toma, wrote, "the training of the new intellectuals was integral to this country's large cultural revolution and to the struggle for a truly flourishing culture that would be national in its form and socialist in its content."[32] In brief, a Romanian national-Socialist cultural revolution in the 1950s!

The literature dealing with this period notes that the Communist regime did not refrain from using all means available. As long as they were likely to assist in gaining control over the entire society, no means were deemed reprehensible. As a result, misinforming, encouraging prejudices and stereotypes, calling on resentment, inciting conflicts, fostering resentment, blackmailing, fueling misperceptions to be used to divide and manipulate, presenting a threat as imminent, and bringing false accusation[33] were all part and parcel of the modus operandi of the regime.

For instance, typical for the Communist propaganda, was an abstract representation of an "enemy" and the idea of an imminent worldwide plot against Communism. Hence, the necessity of a state of constant vigilance. The universal existence of the "enemy" was a fact that could hide even under the most benevolent of guises; therefore, one had to be vigilant all the time. The "enemy" was real, determined, and prepared to give the final blow to Communism at any time.[34] Concepts such as enemy, traitor, and plot were correlated with the representation of the capitalist world—where the situation was, of course, dire, and people were starving to death—a world of imperialists who were guilty for the pauperism of the rest of the world.) But the ideological context was secondary when it came to the Machiavellian value added: ultimately, this method of identifying, pointing at, and personalizing *the* enemy offered endless possibilities for manipulation.[35]

By 1948, the Communist regime had already developed an apparatus that penetrated most institutional sectors and a pyramid-like propaganda structure that was already playing a key role in exercising control over the society. During a meeting of the Bureau of the Central Section for Political Education that year, the situation of political ideological workers was at the top of the agenda. It was decided that their numbers should be raised up to 100,000.[36] This particular meeting was revealing for how the Party was ready from the very beginning to oversee and have an impressive number of ideological workers and propagandists on the payroll. After the Congress of February 21–23, 1948, the newly formed party, the Romanian Workers' Party, created its own apparatus that included departments (e.g., the Organizational Department of the Central Committee, the Propaganda and Agitation Department, Cadres Department, Administrative Department), sections (e.g., the Economic Section, Public Education Section, External Affairs Section, Army Section), and committees (e.g., trade unions, agriculture, work among the youth and the women).[37] In a first step, when the members of the Politburo first divided the tasks among them (on May 14, 1948), the Propaganda and Agitation Department was assigned to Ana Pauker. But the actual leaders of the propaganda were Iosif Chișinevschi and his adjunct, Leonte Răutu.[38]

Following the decision of the January 23–24, 1950, Plenary Session, the Agitation and Propaganda Department was to be responsible for Party propaganda, ideological work, Party work in various areas of the cultural life, and mass political agitation. Additionally, it was to recruit and deploy cadres to the various areas it was to cover. According to the documents, those areas were propaganda, Party education, agitation, press, sciences, public education, literature and arts, cultural-educational work, publishing, and human resources.

The department was structured into two large divisions, propaganda and agitation, each one with its own nomenklatura. In the propaganda division, the following positions existed: the director of the "A. Zhdanov" School of High Social Sciences,[39] the academic director, the assistant directors, the directors of the central courses for propaganda workers, the director and academic directors of the evening universities of Marxism-Leninism, and the directors of evening schools of Marxism-Leninism. As for the agitation division, it included the editor-in-chief, the assistant editor-in-chief, and the copyeditor of *Carnetul Agitatorului* [*Agitator's Notebook*], a party publication for the use of the local and central propaganda apparatus, as well as the directors of the central courses for agitators.[40] The public education area included the advisors and directors working for the Ministry of Education; the rectors of the universities, polytechnics, and other higher education institutions; the deans of the faculties of philosophy and history; and the heads of the chairs of social sciences, Marxism-Leninism, and dialectical and historical materialism.[41]

During the meeting of May 12, 1950, the total number of positions within the Central Committee nomenklatura was set to 17,329, with Agitation and Propaganda totaling 833 positions. There were 124 activists responsible for "political work."[42] Post-1950, the Propaganda and Agitation Section was the second largest in the general classification of sections, after the section including the Party's, trade unions', and youth's leading bodies.[43]

This structure of the Party apparatus would remain essentially unchanged until the fall of the Communist regime in December 1989, except for some fine-tuning and real-time adapting to the fluctuating interests of the highest tier of the Party. Among the most prominent figures of these beginnings of the Romanian Communist propaganda and agitation institutionalization—in addition to its ultimate leaders Iosif Chișinevschi and Leonte Răutu—let us mention Mihail Roller, Paul Niculescu-Mizil, Manea Mănescu, Cornel Onescu, Pavel Țugui, Nicolae Goldberger, Ștefan Voicu, Traian Șelmaru, and Sorin Toma.[44]

On January 26, 1953, during a meeting of the Politburo, Gheorghiu-Dej suggested that each section should be headed by two secretaries of the Central Committee, namely Iosif Chișinevschi, who headed the ideology sections, and Alexandru Moghioroș, who was responsible for the administration, nomenklatura, and economy sections.[45] The adjuncts of the heads of sections were in charge of the activities of several sectors and regions. Depending on the needs, the sections were split into several sectors, each with its own head of sector and political activists and specialized cadres (referents). The activists working for the sectors were called instructors, and their job was to make visits in the country and make sure that the decisions of the Party leadership were carried out accordingly. The team that coordinated the Agitation and Propaganda Section from 1946 to 1953 (i.e., Iosif Chișinevschi, Leonte Răutu, Ofelia Manole, and Mihail Roller) constantly surveilled that the subdivisions complied with the Party's official stance.

In 1955, the section was renamed the Propaganda and Culture Department and was made up of three subdivisions: a Propaganda and Agitation Section, a Cultural and Scientific Section, and an Education Section.[46] This structure was maintained until the 1965 reform when the Propaganda and Agitation Section was dissolved and replaced with two distinct sections: the Agitation and Propaganda Section and the Press and Publishing Section. The new Agitation and Propaganda Section included the propaganda sector, the lecturer sector, the documentation sector, the mass political and cultural work sector, the group of territorial instructors, one instructor for the central ideological institutions, one human resources instructor, and the support staff.[47] As we will discuss in the next chapters, this constant restructuring[48] of the Agitation and Propaganda Section throughout the life of the regime was more the result of political circumstances as well as more or less circumstantial assessments of the techniques and methods of implementation, and it was based on ad-hoc administrative observations, rather than an action informed by serious institutional evaluations and genuine self-criticism.

One way or another, restructuring was a constant throughout the lifecycle of the institution and the changes in the names used for it and its components make the analyses of its evolution a real challenge. Things seemed to be undisputedly settled in terms of substance. (Leonte Răutu[49] defined propaganda as "one of the Party's sacred things,"[50] and it was, obviously, hard to argue with that.) Hence, if there was any improvement to be made, that was supposed to happen mostly in terms of organization.

In the context of the 1960s, the section underwent several organizational restructurings, one of the most significant of them being the introduction of lecturers beginning in 1965. During the section's November 1965 meeting, the following main objectives were decided: "to establish whether the collectives of agitators should be maintained with the basic organizations; who should be their members, and how should they be used; how should they train them; what kind of materials they should edit; and how to organize political work?"[51]

Having decided to do without the work of agitators[52]—as the Party believed that society had reached a certain level of understanding by then and could do without this kind of propaganda—the lecturers were to be the new elite propaganda workers. In compliance with the official views, the lecturer was an experienced propagandist. And thus, after removing the agitators from the propaganda apparatus, some propagandists were deemed experienced enough to move on to a new stage in their specialization: the lecturer stage. Weighing this specific move against the political decisions taken at that time, the logic behind it becomes rather transparent. By declaring during the Ninth Congress that Romanian society was entering a new stage in its development, Nicolae Ceaușescu was paving the way for the type of propaganda that would help him legitimize his power and his future political and economic decisions.[53] A purge and a revamping of the apparatus was necessary at this stage.

But restructuring continued unabated even after Ceausescu gained total control over the apparatus. In November 1976, the Propaganda and Press Section was split into the Propaganda Section and the Press and Radiobroadcast Section.[54] The new Propaganda Section totaled sixty-four positions and included a group of territorial instructors and four sectors: the Sector for Mass Political-Educational Work, the Propaganda Sector, the Sector for Cadre Training and Educational Work in Schools and Universities, and the Information Sector.[55]

The job descriptions of the propaganda agents—the lecturer or the propagandist responsible with disseminating ideological doctrines—as reflected in the official records, were by that time not exactly clear. They were becoming more and more diffuse. We find a few details about their specific skills and duties in the leaflets and other publications edited by the Propaganda Section.[56] Also, there is not much data available on their exact role or the officially endorsed methods they used. Their training and the methodology employed to train them claimed to be based on the social sciences, as the methods these sciences used were considered to penetrate the consciences more effectively.[57] But according to the official stance, the lecturer was an experienced propagandist, not a social scientist.

The emerging image is one of a system undergoing a continuous process of organization and calibration in its role in supporting the regime. As already mentioned, the dialectics of Communist internationalization and nationalism is a fascinating feature of this system and its evolution. After Stalin's death (in March 1953), and especially after "Khrushchev's Secret Speech" of February 1956 at the end of the Twentieth Party Congress of the Communist Party of the Soviet Union, Sovietization lost its momentum. This was the signal, everywhere in Eastern Europe, for an ambitious reform of the Communist regimes. In Romania, Dej tried to change his legitimizing discourse without, however, changing its deep Stalinist foundations.[58] In other words, the

Bucharest leadership merely simulated the ideological "thaw" without actually putting it into practice. Even more, it resumed its repressive practices, as well as the forced industrialization and collectivization programs. Very soon, the propaganda brought back to life the cliché of class struggle, and Marxism-Leninism was reaffirmed as a valid ideological doctrine.

A moment of high significance in the evolution of the relations between the Romanian Communist regime and the Soviet Union was 1958, when the Red Army troops left Romania. As a direct consequence of the withdrawal, the means of control of the Soviet power were lessened. Dej's regime continued its repressive policy nonetheless; the repression being mainly aimed, with few exceptions, at preventing potential uprisings. In fact, until the beginning of 1962, Dej continued to loyally support Moscow's hegemonic status within the Bloc and the international Communist movement.[59] Later however, there was a gradual shift toward emancipation from under the tutelage of the suzerain elite, the highest point of this process being his April 1964 Declaration that officially marked the breakaway of Romanian politics from Sovietization.

The following years, even after Dej's death, were characterized by a lessening of the ideological grip. The social mobilization policy was not abandoned, but the propaganda cleverly used the concepts of nationalism and modernization as manipulation instruments. The regime's commitment to national values became one of the Party's key strategies to win over both the population and the intellectuals. At the same time, the unofficial and difficult to attain goal of Dej's politics was to maintain nonconflictual relations with the new Soviet leaders without, however, following suit in their efforts to tear down Stalinism. At the same time, he tried to hide his own Stalinism[60] under a nationalist discourse that proved convincing for many Romanians who nurtured a genuine aversion toward Soviet hegemony.[61] Dej's nationalism consisted of a collection of principles and justifications that sought to legitimate the Party as an independent entity, determined to forge its own path and to use its own resources as it saw fit, while claiming that the relations of Moscow and Bucharest were no longer hierarchical but egalitarian. Indeed, for the remaining four decades of the Romanian Communist regime, the RWP (soon to become RCP), through its leaders' cunning foreign policy, would position itself both theoretically and discursively as the defender of the national interest.[62]

The obligations toward proletarian internationalism would move into the background. As already noted, it was around this time that key identity concepts, such as homeland, nation, and family started to be widely embraced, or at least used, with a strong impact on the culture and literature promoted by the institutions with authority in those fields. This brought with it a dramatic change in discourse, topics, and doctrines, as well as a shift in value systems.

We see the nature and definition of the propaganda and indoctrination shifting. At the same time, we see the education system and the way its role was defined and understood adjusting accordingly. One interesting development is that the entire process with all its intertwined components starts to be increasingly defined on "scientific socialism" parameters. Following up and assessing these changes, a report of the Propaganda and Agitation Section of the CC of the RCP on the state of Marxist-Leninist education revealed that the effectiveness of the propaganda—and the cadres working for it—was very far from the standards set by the Plenary Session of the CC of the RCP dedicated to education, which had taken place the previous year.[63] In the report drawn up at the end of the assessment, the CC officials wrote that at the Plenary Session "it was asked of the cadres in the social sciences to become the main ideological centers, using the highest scientific standards." Yet, they had failed to rise to the standards.[64]

The process continued unabated in 1970s. In an internal newsletter issued in 1970 by the Propaganda Section, *propaganda* is defined as "an institutionalized set of activities dedicated to systematically propagating specific opinions among the members of society, to shaping attitudes and behaviors in accordance with the objectives of the socialist society."[65] Defined as a key instrument of ideology, politics, and the development of the Socialist society, propaganda had to be built in a scientific way with "an understanding of the complexities of life and the economic, social and human particularities of the age in which it operates."[66]

Yet, notwithstanding the scientific rhetoric, under Nicolae Ceaușescu's regime, propaganda continued to embrace new topics that were part of the new leader's rhetoric, helping to build his cult of personality that culminated in the 1980s. Historian Tiberiu Troncotă[67] splits Ceaușescu's era[68] into two broad periods: from 1965 to 1971, there was a stage focused on building a national Communism, with the Party playing an important role in the process of defining power; and from 1971 to 1989, there was a stage focused on establishing a cult of the leader's personality, with the Party fading into the background of the political scene and losing much of its public visibility.

In the regime's view, however, the threshold year of 1971 stood for the passage to a multilaterally developed Socialist society, which also caused a change in the institutional framework for implementing the social and educational policies.[69] That was also the moment when the shift toward the cult of personality started to take shape. That meant a move toward grafting the cult of personality on the already solidly grounded national Communism. In 1974, during the Eleventh Congress of the RCP, a *Code of Principles and Rules Regulating the Work and Life of the Communists and the Social Ethics and Equality*[70] was adopted as a foundational document that recalibrated and summed up in a few paragraphs the ethical meaning of being a true Communist. In turn, propaganda reflected all these shifts away from the internationalist stage of Romanian Communism and toward nationalist forms of Communism.

And thus, we are in a position to note a remarkable evolution through which the apparatus had to increasingly combine traditionally Communist topics with new national elements, rephrasing older official propaganda language in new ways. National history gets rewritten again. By rewriting the past and appropriating it within the framework of Communist propaganda, the regime defined and calibrated a new system of values that the individual was expected to adopt. These values were further grouped into broad themes—internationalism, the New Man, and increasing salient nationalism. At the same time, the regime actively destroyed or eliminated other systems of values or discourses that might have constituted an alternative to those propagated by the Communist regime. Paraphrasing Lasswell's theory,[71] historian Cristina Preutu lists three types of symbols that the Communist political power used in this respect: "demands," symbols that determine a specific preference in the receiver (here we can include the idea of unity); "identifications," keywords working as symbols (our/ours, unity) that dissolve the line between the individual self and the political self; and "expectations," symbols that determine certain expectations from those in power.[72] The Romanian synthesis of Communism and nationalism stands as a remarkable achievement in this respect.

In the 1980s during a series of meetings of the Agitation and Propaganda Section of the CC of the RCP, the recurring theme was the lack of clear definitions of the concepts of Socialist patriotism,[73] state, nation, nationality, people, or Socialist humanism.[74] This requirement for clarity did not solely concern the civic education of the citizens. It was, in fact, part of the process of building the framework necessary to implement Ceaușescu's cult of personality and his nationalist policy. The 1980s coincided with the climax of the cult of the Communist leader as a national leader, which also presented a huge challenge for the propaganda, as this cult of personality caused a divorce between the Party and the Romanians, while the gap between reality and the political discourse grew ever larger. The efforts of the propaganda at that time were focused on building a rhetoric about a unified, totalizing world where the Communist power and the Romanians people were one.

This enterprise generated a massive spiral of silence. The 1989 developments leading to the collapse of the regime demonstrated how large the gap was between the official propaganda and reality. The revealed level of preference falsification of the Romanian public was astonishing. It looks like the institutionalization of propaganda and indoctrination had major unanticipated and unforeseen consequences.

To conclude, this constant reorganization of the Agitation and Propaganda Section throughout the regime's existence was one of the most important features and symptoms of the system. The forces determining these reorganizations were mainly driven by political factors and the strategies of the Communist leaders. Yet, as noted, when it came to the "big picture," the Party structures of power remained essentially unchanged until the fall of the Communist regime in December 1989, except for some fine-tuning and real-time adapting to the fluctuating interests of the highest tier of the Party. That being said, such fine-tuning and adjustments were sufficient to induce ongoing alterations and restructuring of the massive indoctrination and propaganda apparatus that operated at the core of the regime's architecture of power.

NOTES

1. While the 1948 RPR (The Popular Republic of Romania) Constitution set forth that the Party was "the leading political force of the working class," the 1952 Constitution gave it increased control and power as it became "the leading political force of both the working people's organizations and the state organs and institutions," culminating with the 1965 RSR (The Socialist Republic of Romania) Constitution designating the Party "the leading political force of the entire society."

2. For histories of Romanian Communism, see Victor Frunză, *Istoria stalinismului în România* (Bucharest: Editura Humanitas, 1990); Dennis Deletant, *România sub regimul comunist* (Bucharest: Editura Fundația Academia Civică, 1997); Vladimir Tismăneanu, *Stalinism pentru eternitate. O istorie politică a comunismului românesc* (Iași: Editura Polirom, 2005); Adrian Cioroianu, *Pe umerii lui Marx. O introducere în istoria comunismului românesc* (Bucharest: Curtea Veche Publishing, 2005).

3. For more details on the history of Romanian Communism, see Vladimir Tismăneanu, *Stalinism for All Seasons: A Political History of Romanian Communism* (Berkeley: University of California Press, 2003). The work is a study of the mechanisms behind a political culture based on fear, suspicion, questionable legitimacy, false internationalism, populist manipulation of national symbols, and self-centered personalization of power.

4. Anton Semyonovich Makarenko (1888–1939) was a Soviet educator and writer who subscribed to the theory that all education should be centered on the collective and the spirit of work. His theses were published in several volumes, *Flags on the Battlements* (1938) and *The Pedagogical Poem* (1925–1935)—the latter was also a source of inspiration for the Romanian Communist propaganda.

5. Antoaneta Tănăsescu, "Un Făt-Frumos de laborator, un Făt-Frumos de tip nou: 'omul nou'" (A Prince Charming obrained in the lab, a new type of Prince Charming: the New Man) in *Miturile comunismului românesc,* ed. Lucian Boia (Bucharest: Editura Universității din București, 1995), 18.

6. Alexander Zinoviev, *Homo sovieticus,* trans. Charles Janson (London: Gollancz, 1985), 107.

7. For details on the transformist program, see Michel Heller, *La machine et les rouages. La formation de l'homme sovietique* (Paris: Calmann-Lévy, 1985), 180.

8. Note the rather transparent reference to the story of young Pavel Morozov as an encouragement to turn in family members. Mostly known under the diminutive Pavlik, Pavel Morozov (1918–1932) was featured for a long time in the Soviet press and schoolbooks as a hero and a martyr. He was the protagonist of fiction works, plays, films, and biographies. According to the official account, he denounced his father who had been withholding part of the crop to feed his family instead of turning it all in for requisitioning. After his father was convicted to forced labor, his sentence being later commuted to death, his family allegedly killed Pavlik. Archival research conducted after the fall of Communism contradicts this account.

9. Michel Heller, op.cit., 180.

10. As already noted, a multifaceted concept rooted in integralist, millenarist religious beliefs, the New Man was honed over one hundred years. In its 1950s Romanian iteration, the concept of the New Man was imported from the Soviet Union. There is an impressive Romanian literature on the topic: M. Nițescu, Monica Lovinescu, Sanda Cordoş, Ana Selejan, Ion Ianoşi, Antoaneta Tănăsescu, and Anca Hațiegan. One reference work, perhaps the most comprehensive to date regarding Romania, investigating the origins of the New Man is Dorin-Liviu Bîtfoi's *Aşa s-a născut omul nou-În România anilor '50* (Thus Was the New Man Born in 1950s Romania) (Bucharest: Editura Compania, 2012). Bîtfoi's book provides a detailed account of the early 1950s political, social, and economic life. It starts with a complete account of the 1950s in Romania and a list of the implications of the Communists' accession to power. Subchapters such as "Revelația prin Stalin" (Revelation through Stalin), "Casele poporului" (The houses of the people), and "Reapare pâinea albă" (The white bread reappears) are but a few motifs that outline what the author deems the psychosis of the beginning of a "new Middle Ages," looking into the details of the political, economic, social, and ideological changes that made it possible.

11. They are part of a broader strategy that includes *reeducation* with a view to suppress individuality; *manipulation* with a view to induce the *illusion of freedom*, a form of control within a closely watched territory completely cut out from the outside world by closed borders; the *intrusion in the private life; large-scale literacy* aiming to make everybody amenable to the official ideology; and instilling the belief that once installed, the new political system would last forever. These methods aimed also to erode individuality and the reliance on family, religion, and rational language as identity markers.

12. Cristina Preutu writes that "despite continuous efforts to organize and hone the methods of training the different categories of propagandists, one cannot speak of a cohesive communist bureaucracy. . . . From defining the propagandist as ideological worker, cultural activist, Party activist, and so on, to practicing certain behaviors and attitudes supposed to embody examples of the New Man, everything leads to the conclusion that, more often than not, the profile of the propagandist or the New Man was always derived from a set of tasks or functions." See also Cristina Preutu,

Propaganda politică în România socialistă. Practici instituționale și tehnici de comunicare 1965–1974 (Iași: Editura Universității Alexandru Ioan Cuza, 2017), 265.

13. The 1948 RPR Constitution set that the Party was "the leading political force of working class."

14. As noted, under the umbrella term *propagandist*, other derivative terms are often included: *ideologist, agitator, lecturer, activist,* or *cadre*. Although each of these terms has its specific meaning—depending on the time in the history of Romanian Communism and the duties assigned to each category—with few exceptions, the preferred generic term in the Communist vocabulary for the person conducting propaganda is *propagandist*, including at the meetings of the CC of the RCP or in specialized works. All point out to a specific institutional function in the Communist system.

15. Historically, the Romanian Communist Left was rather marginal and underdeveloped—first, because the country was slow to modernize, and, following from that, the conditions for an urban industrial proletariat actively involved in politics appeared rather late. For more details, see Vladimir Tismăneanu, *Stalinism for All Seasons: A Political History of Romanian Communism*, Berkeley: University of California Press, 2003.

16. For this topic, see Adrian Cioroianu, *Camarazii utopiei. Destine individuale și de grup din ilegalitatea comunistă* (Bucharest: Editura Universității din București, 2017).

17. As far as the intellectual life was concerned, the Communist Party aimed to annihilate any form of freedom of expression; literature, history, art, and philosophy had to be ideologically subordinated to the political sphere. In this context one should explicitly name censorship. For details on censorship, see Marian Petcu, *Puterea și cultura. O istorie a cenzurii* (Iași: Editura Polirom, 1999), 7; Maria Radu Mocanu, *Cenzura comunistă (Documente)* (Bucharest: Editura Albatros, 2001), 11; and Călin Hentea, *Propagandă fără frontiere* (Bucharest: Editura Nemira, 2002), 259.

18. For details, see also Dennis Deletant, *Communist Terror in Romania: Gheorghiu-Dej and the Police State, 1948–65* (London: C. Hurst & Co. Publishers, 1999), 75.

19. Some were dissolved, others were forced out. The National Liberal Party ceased to exist in November 1947, with many of its leaders dying in the Communist prisons or being forced into exile. As for the National Peasant Party, the government decreed its dissolution on July 29, 1947, and then arrested its leaders, tried them, and sentenced them for "plotting against Romania's legally established Government."

20. Eugen Denize, *Propaganda comunistă în România (1948–1953)* (Târgoviște: Editura Cetatea de Scaun, 2011), 5–14.

21. Iosif Chișinevschi (1905–1963), born Jakob Roitman, was a Communist activist and high official. He became member of the CC of the RCP in 1945, and from 1944 to 1957 he worked as the Party's chief ideologist and propagandist.

22. Leonte Răutu (1910–1993), born Leo Oigenstein, was the main architect of the Party's ideology and the institutional machine used for indoctrination purposes. From 1956 to 1965, he was the head of the Propaganda and Culture Department of the CC of the RWP. As Chișiniveschi's adjunct, he worked in the team of editors at *Scânteia* newspaper. After 1965, he held the positions of member of the Secretariat

of the Central Committee, member of the Executive Committee, and vice prime minister on education. From 1974 to 1982 he was also rector of the Party's Ştefan Gheorghiu Academy. In the latter half of 1981, he lost his influence, and was forced to quit and to retire. For details on the role played by Leonte Răutu in the context of Romanian Communism, see Vladimir Tismăneanu and Cristian Vasile, *Perfectul acrobat. Leonte Răutu, măştile răului* (Bucharest: Editura Humanitas, 2008), as well as Dan C. Mihăilescu's article, "Acrobatul cu plasa roşie" (The Acrobat with the Red Net), *Evenimentul zilei*, January 23, 2009, accessed August 27, 2014, https://evz.ro/dan-c-mihailescu-acrobatul-cu-plasa-rosie-836777.html.

23. For more details, see Gheorghe Buzatu, *Românii în arhivele Kremlinului* (Bucharest: Editura Univers Enciclopedic, 1996), 154.

24. This was one of the outcomes of the February 21–23, 1948, Congress. Later, with the restructuring of the RWP in January 1952 came a change in name from Department to Section. Its responsibilities over time ranged from checking whether and how PWR decisions were carried out by the Ministry of Public Education, the Ministry of Arts and Information, the RPR Academy, the Committee for Cable Radio and Radio Broadcasting, the Committee for the Cinema, the Committee for Cultural Establishments, the Committee for Physical Culture and Sports, the General Department for the Printing Industry, DGPT, AGERPRES, ARLUS, the creators' unions, and the Society for Popularizing Science and Culture. For details, see Nicoleta Ionescu-Gură, "Reorganizarea PMR-ului după modelul PC al URSS şi crearea nomenclaturii CC al PMR în Republica Populară Romănă (1949–1954)" in *Totalitarism şi rezistenţă, teroare şi represiune în România comunistă*, ed. Gh. Onişoru (Bucharest: CNSAS, 2001), 224. Under its new name, Section, it would oversee the editing of *Carnetul agitatorului* (The Aggitator's Notebook) and *Lupta de clasă* (Class Struggle) magazines.

25. ANIC, CC of the RCP Collection—Propaganda and Agitation Section, file no. 49/1948, 1.

26. Cristian Vasile, *Literatura şi artele în România comunistă (1948–1953)* (Bucharest: Humanitas, 2010), 55.

27. *Învăţământul politico-ideologic de partid 1975–1979. Probleme orientative şi bibliografii pentru cursuri şi seminarii* (Bucharest: Editura Politică, 1975), 9.

28. The mass demonstrations on May Day (International Workers' Day) or August 23 (Liberation from Fascist Occupation Day)—which will be dealt with later in the book—were, in addition to occasions to remember important events in the Party's history, also a means to present and promote the history of the Party. These rallies were also designed to instill allegiance to the regime. Related to this type of phenomenon with roots in Revolutionary France, a parallel was drawn between these types of manifestations and large religious celebrations. Raymond Aron claimed that "The French revolutionary cults shared something of the ambiguity of Rousseau's civil religion. Their basis was patriotism, 'a love of the ideal society, based on justice, much more than love of the national soil.' . . . The latter (the State) divorced itself from the old Church but tried to keep a religious character, to impose itself 'on the masses under the aspect of a Church with its feasts and its obligatory rites.'" See also

Raymond Aron, *The Opium of the Intellectuals*, transl. Terence Kilmartin (New York: W. W. Norton & Company. Inc, 1962), 281.

29. This wooden language is also present in the individual cadre dossiers, which mandatorily included an autobiography of the propagandist. This personal touch simultaneously meant an introspective process and a reconstruction of the self as close to the terms desirable for the political power as possible.

30. Gustave Le Bon, *Psihologie politică*, trans. Simona Pelin (Prahova: Antet Press, 2002), 98.

31. The Party documents and national conference speeches, and so forth, point to the activities of Party organizations that "take firmer action to make Party organizational and political work meet today's standards and requirements." Organizational work was supposed to develop skills and efficiency by "the qualitative strengthening of the Party ranks, of the connections with the working class masses, the consistent fostering of criticism and self-criticism, of the activist, revolutionary spirit, of the principle of collective labor and ruling, of the fight against self-sufficient tendencies, and of increasing responsibility of cadres in relation to the tasks assigned to them" (Flori Bălănescu, unpublished manuscript).

32. Sorin Toma, "Noua intelectualitate din țările de democrație populară" (The New Intellectuals in Popular Democracies), *Scânteia,* June 3, 1951, 3.

33. Henri-Pierre Cathala, *Epoca dezinformării*, trans. Nicolae Bărbulescu (Bucharest: Editura Militară, 1991), 19–20; Bogdan Ficeac, *Tehnici de manipulare* (Bucharest: Editura Nemira, 1996) and *Cenzura comunistă și formarea omului nou* (Bucharest: Editura Nemira, 1999); Vladimir Volokoff, *Tratat de dezinformare: de la Calul Troian la internet* (Bucharest: Editura Antet, 1999); Marian Voicu, *Matrioșka mincinoșilor, fake news, manipulare, populism* (Bucharest: Editura Humanitas, 2018).

34. Noteworthy here is a text in a volume by Mircea Sântimbreanu, one of the most popular authors of the regime, whose books were included in school reading lists. The text is called "Portocalii sălbatici" (The Wild Orange Trees), published in his volume *Să stăm de vorbă fără catalog* (Let Us Talk Without the Class Roster) (Bucharest: Editura Politică, 1976), 186. In the text he contrasts the order and benefits of Communism with the decadent, miserable capitalist world. The author looks at the hardships that children from the West have to face because they lack a collective ideal to unite them, and instead they fall prey to drug abuse and have to eat from dumpsters. They are the children of capitalism deprived of their childhood, victims of a disorderly, unjust, corrupt, and abusive system.

35. E. Denize, op.cit., 3–22.

36. Idem, 4–33, as well as *Procesul verbal al Ședinței Biroului Secției Centrale de Educație Politică din 2 februarie 1948* (Minutes of the meeting of the Bureau of the Central Section for Political Education of February 2, 1948), in AMR, microfilm records, roll no. AS1–1516, frame no. 1.

37. The sections made a major contribution to the implementation of the Party's political line in all of the state's areas of activity. It was via the sections that the Central Committee implemented the Party's decisions and directives and exercised control over their thorough implementation. Locally, the Party organizations—region,

raion or town—created an apparatus replicating that of the Central Committee, invested with duties and authority over a specific territorial unit.

38. For more details, see Lavinia Betea, *Psihologia politică. Individ, lider, mulțime în regimul comunist* (Iași: Editura Polirom, 2001), 139.

39. For more details, see E. Denize, op.cit., 43.

40. Ibid., 44.

41. Ibid., 45.

42. *Ședința Biroului Organizatoric din 12 mai 1950* (Meeting of the Orgburo of May 12, 1950), in AMR, microfilm records, roll no. AS1–405, frame no. 44–85. During the same meeting, it was decided that each county committee should include its own propaganda and agitation section, led by one head and one adjunct. These local sections were to include the following sectors: the Party propaganda sector (three activists); the mass political agitation sector (three activists); the dissemination of Party press and publications sector (one to two activists); and the scientific and public education sector (one to two activists). The lowest level equipped with its own agitation and propaganda section was the village *raion*, and the section was led by one head and included one propaganda and public education sector (two activists); one mass political agitation sector (one to two activists); and one culture, sports, and dissemination sector (one to two activists).

43. For details, see Eugen Denize's "Propaganda," in *România comunistă. Statul și propaganda*, Eugen Denize and Cezar Mâță (Târgoviște: Editura Cetatea de Scaun, 2005), 14–113.

44. Lavinia Betea, op.cit., 139.

45. *Procesul verbal și stenograma ședinței Biroului Politic din data de 26 ianuarie 1953* (Minutes and Verbatim Report of the Meeting of the Politburo of January 26, 1953), in AMR, microfilm records, roll no. AS1–407, frame no. 30.

46. N. Ionescu-Gură, *Nomenclatura CC al PMR* (Bucharest: Editura Humanitas, 2006), 13–25.

47. For details, see *Schema secției de propagandă și agitație* (The organization chart of the propaganda and agitation section), in ANIC, the CC of the RCP Collection, Propaganda and Agitation Section, file no. 46/1965, 8.

48. Historian Cristina Preutu notes that, out of the nine rounds of restructuring undertaken by the Central Committee of the RWP, five of them included the area of propaganda (see Cristina Preutu, op.cit., 45).

49. With Leonte Răutu at its head, the propaganda apparatus used the doctrines developed by the 1961 Plenary Session of the Central Committee to rewrite the history of the RCP around the merits of Gheorghiu-Dej's close circle in the fight to unmask the enemies of the working class. Răutu's adjunct and collaborator was Paul Niculescu-Mizil, the head of Propaganda Section after 1965 and Răutu's successor as the Party's chief ideologist.

50. *Expunere făcută de tovarășul Leonte Răutu despre sarcinile muncii de propagandă și agitație* (Comrade Răutu's memorandum on the responsibilities of propaganda and agitation work), in ANIC, the CC of the RCP Collection, Propaganda and Agitation Section, file no. 10/ 1960, 65.

51. *Notă-probleme ce urmează a fi rezolvate în munca politică de masă* (Note—issues related to mass political work to be solved), in ANIC, the CC of the RCP Collection, Propaganda and Agitation Section, file no. 3/1965, 109.

52. Along with the group of agitators at central level also discontinued was the *Carnetul agitatorului* (The agitator's notebook) magazine. *Scânteia* newspaper took over part of the supporting function for agitation work.

53. Cristina Preutu, op.cit, 49.

54. *Protocol nr. 11 al şedinţei Secretariatului CC al PCR din ziua de 29 noiembrie 1976* (Protocol no. 11 of the meeting of the CC of the RCP Secretariat of November 29, 1976), in ANIC, the CC of the RCP Collection, the Chancellery Section, file no. 110/1976, 2.

55. *Schema Secţiei de propagandă* (Organizational chart of the Propaganda Section), in ANIC, the CC of the RCP Collection, the Chancellery Section, file no. 110/1976, 87–185.

56. For more details, we recommend the publication *În ajutorul propagandiştilor* (Support for the propagandists).

57. Cristina Preutu, op.cit., 61.

58. For what came next, namely de-Sovietization without de-Stalinization that practically covered the entire duration of the Romanian Communist regime, political scientist Vladimir Tismăneanu suggests the term "national Stalinism," see Vladimir Tismăneanu, "The Ambiguity of Romanian National Communism," *Telos,* no. 60 (1984): 65–79 and "What Was National Stalinism," in *Oxford Handbook of Postwar European History*, ed. Dan Stone (Oxford: Oxford University Press, 2012), 462–80. Tismăneanu also discusses the concept in his *Stalinism for All Seasons: A Political History of Romanian Communism* (Berkeley: University of California Press, 2003).

59. The Third Congress of the RWP (June 20–28, 1960) marked the continuity with the pro-Soviet attitude of the Romanian People's Republic.

60. Of the various studies sometimes advancing opposed interpretations—that focus on the Romanian Communist leader Gheorghe Gheorghiu-Dej and his instinctive Stalinism, as well as the existence of a personal myth about Gheorghiu-Dej, see: Vladimir Tismăneanu, *Fantoma lui Gheorghiu-Dej* (Bucharest: Editura Univers, 1995) and the expanded 2nd ed. (Bucharest: Editura Humanitas, 2008); Lavinia Betea, *Maurer şi lumea de ieri. Mărturii despre stalinizarea României* (Arad: Editura Fundaţiei Ioan Slavici, 1995); Silviu Brucan, *Generaţia irosită* (Bucharest: Editura Univers—Calistrat Hogaş, 1992); Lucian Boia, "Un mit Gheorghiu-Dej?" (A Gheorghiu-Dej Myth?), in *Miturile comunismului românesc*, vol. 2 (Bucharest: Editura Universităţii Bucureşti, 1995), 173–82; Stelian Tănase, *Elite şi societate. Guvernarea Gheorghiu-Dej, 1948–1965* (Bucharest: Editura Humanitas, 2006).

61. The Russophobia quietly encouraged by the Romanian head of state—Russian language courses were no longer compulsory, the production of Soviet publications was limited, and so forth—never openly challenged the Stalinist political system as such and merely brought about a circumstantial liberalization. After 1960, in the same context of this de-Russification, Dej proposed that all statues of Stalin should be removed, and Braşov, until then *Oraşul Stalin* (City of Stalin), regained its old name.

62. Stelian. Tănase, op.cit., 256.

63. *Plenara CC al PCR din 22–25 aprilie 1968* (The Plenary Session of the CC of the RCP of April 22–25, 1968) (Bucharest: Editura Politică, 1968).

64. ANIC, the CC of the RCP Collection, Propaganda and Agitation Section, file no. 14/1969. 39.

65. For details, see Cristina Preutu, op.cit., 15.

66. *Expunere făcută de tovarășul Leonte Răutu despre sarcinile muncii de propagandă și agitație* (Comrade Leonte Răutu's memorandum on the duties of the propaganda and agitation work), in ANIC, the CC of the RCP Collection, Propaganda and Agitation Section, ibid., 39.

67. For more details, see the work of Tiberiu Troncotă, op.cit., "Introducere."

68. Historian Cosmin Popa splits Ceaușescu's regime into three stages: 1965 to 1969, marked by a restricted and circumstantial liberalization; 1969 to 1974, marked by transition and the dissolution of any liberalization tendencies; and 1974 to 1989, strongly marked by a Romanian brand of neo-Stalinism, a stage that began with the formal establishment of the personal dictatorship. For more details, see Cosmin Popa, *Intelectualii lui Ceaușescu și Academia de Științe Sociale și Politice (1970–1989)* (Bucharest: Editura Litera, 2018), 29–30.

69. 1974 was another landmark year for the political power. All the important changes in the foreign and domestic policies happened that year as Nicolae Ceaușescu became the president of the Romanian Socialist Republic. This led to the restructuring of cadres and increased control of each nomenklatura member to avoid the emergence of any internal opposition. Also, that very year, the decisions of the Ninth Congress of the RCP were preceded by the Press Law of April, under which the journalist became officially a propaganda worker, meaning the full control of informational means by the Communist leadership.

70. *Codul principiilor și normelor muncii și vieții comuniștilor, ale eticii și echității socialiste* included thirty-three moral and social principles that every citizen of the Romanian Communist society was expected to unequivocally accept and practice.

71. Harold D. Lasswell and Nathan Leites, *Language of Politics. Studies in Quantitative Semantics* (Cambridge, MA: M.I.T. Press, 1965), 13.

72. Cristina Preutu, op.cit, 215.

73. *Socialist patriotism* was defined as "an attitude, a means to understand and foster the interests of the homeland," more often in the form of "an attitude towards socialist work and education." For more details, see *Protocolul nr.18 al ședinței Comitetului Executiv din ziua de 6 iulie 1971* (Protocol no. 18 of the Executive Committee meeting of July 6, 1971), in ANIC, the CC of the RCP Collection, the Chancellery Section, file no. 76/1971, 52.

74. *Socialist humanism* referred to "the fight against the backward bourgeois conceptions and working to develop socialist unity." For more details, see *Protocolul nr.18 al ședinței Comitetului Executiv din ziua de 6 iulie 1971* (Protocol no. 18 of the Executive Committee meeting of July 6, 1971), in ANIC, the CC of the RCP Collection, the Chancellery Section, file no. 76/1971, 52.

Chapter 4

The Ideological Worker

An Overview of Its Profiles and Functions in the Context of the Romanian System

Sociologically speaking, the new Romanian Communist society had at its core a social hierarchy that replicated a formula created in the Soviet state, pivoting on a structure known as the nomenklatura.[1] Official documents presented it as a simple pyramidal structure, but in practice, it was more of a network of networks or a complex multilayered informal polycentric system.[2] Institutionally speaking, not long after the Communists took over, the state apparatus was invaded and replicated by Party clones, creating directorates for each ministry (after 1950, these became sections of Committee of Romanian Communist Party) that worked to set out the "political line" and then supervise and control, with great vigilance, how this line was put into practice. This is the socioinstitutional context in which we have to place and see the "ideological commissars" turned "propagandists" and "ideological workers."

The core of propaganda workers stood not only as a component of Communist bureaucracy but also as a professional category of their own, since many of them received payment in exchange exclusively for their propaganda work while exclusively associated to the propaganda machine and identified strictly by their function in it. This means that once involved with ideological work, one also had access to certain personal career benefits and income (albeit one that, as documents show, was not motivating them, a fact that over time resulted in some of them discarding their propaganda duties and returning to teach classes). With its own identity and distinctive social and professional status, it can therefore be described as a professional category; however, its relationship to nomenklatura was contingent, not intrinsic.

In brief, the tendency to conflating the activists and propagandist with the nomenklatura and see them as a privileged group is not fully accurate.

That being said, the role of the propagandist in the system was a special one. At the most basic level, they were supposed to handle the most direct form of political socialization at a face-to-face individual level—at once a mediator and a voice of power—with a task of informing, mobilizing, and "raising awareness" in order to advance the Party leaders' agenda. At the top level, the propagandists' own instruction level was higher, and their message aimed at the trainees was also much more subtle, meant to develop *"competences for analysis, orientation, discernment."*[3] Extrapolating from mass communication to propaganda, historian Cristina Preutu identifies six specific functions of the latter: legitimization, persuasion, interpretation, memorization, identification, and mobilization.[4] Legitimization—primarily in use during the early stages of the regime—is the method that propaganda uses to convince the population that its proclaimers are legitimate. The persuasive function refers to a power of convincing the populace. The interpretative function means the conferring of meaning to the class struggle and of maintaining conflict—permanent tension—with the notion that "the class enemy never rests." The memorial function has to do with the regime's commemorations and festive actions, with propaganda contributing to creating, organizing, and preserving a collective memory in tune with the ideology it transmitted. The identity function has to do with the *New Man* and—as historian Cristina Preutu asserts—with the attempts at changing man's self-references and inducing a behavior in support of the regime.[5] The mobilization function is a resultant of all the other functions.[6]

Propaganda was obviously essential in the training and instruction of the individual into the scope of Communist values. In practical terms, the propagandist's duty was to execute the orders received from the political center through the ideological-political chain of the Party.[7] Banking on the social function, the Communist power used the propagandist as an instrument who transmits the message, persuades, and changes attitudes while monitoring how well the message is received by individuals and groups targeted. Last but not least, the physical presence of the propagandist was thought of as the symbolic presence of power.[8] In addition to the functions related to conveying political messages and indoctrinating individuals with Communist ideology, the propagandist had another responsibility, that is to gather information from the field, which he would then pass on to the political leadership. This was in effect an informational double flow—from top to bottom and bottom to top. This flow was, on the one hand, inherent to the systemic effort of the regime to achieve total control, and on the other hand, for the adept to adapt and improve its functioning and stability, based on endogenous feedback. Hence the propagandist's function was rather complex, the latent functions being in many cases more important than the manifest functions.

TRAINING IDEOLOGICAL WORKERS: "PARTY EDUCATION"

In order to have propagandists and agitators readily available, a dedicated training system was needed, parallel to state education. It was called Party Education. The establishment of the Party Education system was not originally a Romanian idea, but it was implemented in other parts of the Communist bloc as well. The action of shadowing the state institutions with the Party's own institutions was a standard Communist practice. This is why the 1948 educational reform was deemed insufficient, even though, as a result of it, the Party took control of the national education system (see next chapter for a discussion of the educational reform). Hence, the Communists went even further: the Party created its own parallel education system. Once established, it would be pivotal to the Communist apparatus of command, propaganda, and control. Gheorghiu-Dej, speaking at the Romanian Workers' Party Congress of February 21–23, 1948, underscored the importance of this social meaning and education track: "we should grant the appropriate attention to Party education, in order to elevate cadres who are at once honest and vetted, with a solid ideological training."[9]

That same year, at a session of the Propaganda and Agitation Bureau that took place on May 15, the three levels of Party instruction, namely permanent Party schools, night schools, and individual study, were introduced.[10] Romania's Party schools[11] were established after a Soviet blueprint and fully operational by the late 1940s. The schools active alongside the RWP Central Committee were known as Higher Party schools, whereas those created alongside regional party committees were known as regular Party schools and offered three-month, six-month, or one-year courses.[12]

In 1948, there were three large Party schools, namely Ştefan Gheorghiu, which had been open on March 21, 1945; the Central Party School for Hungarian speakers, open since 1946; and the A. A. Zhdanov School, established in 1948. Their main tasks were preparing cadres for work in the central Party institutions, directing Party Education, instructing lecturers and public speakers for the social sciences departments within higher public education, and training propaganda-section leaders for central periodicals as well as the editors of ideological magazines.

The Andrei Zhdanov School of Social Science,[13] founded in 1948 and subordinated to the Agitation and Propaganda Section of the Central Committee, was meant to educate a new generation of Communists who had not been underground Party activists or part of the antifascist fight. In other words, it was an ideological incubator for new cadre who would further enforce the Communist apparatus. In 1949, it had two sections, press and propaganda, and in 1954, the Institute of Social Sciences was added. The school gained an important role in 1949, when it stepped up from a lecturer's school (six-month cycles of studies to completion) and became a superior school of social sciences (two-year cycles of studies to completion). The recruitment of the students was also adjusted to only accept Party activists who had already undertaken ideological and cultural training, preferably Party school graduates. The school had 100 students per year,[14] permanent and associate professors, and was run by the Agitation and Propaganda Directorate. In 1951, the permanent staff was made up of Leonte Răutu as director, Grigore Cotovschi as dean, and Solomon Știrbu as professor of philosophy and dialectical materialism.

In 1958, the Andrei Zhdanov Superior School was taken over by the Ștefan Gheorghiu Superior School[15] and was subsequently called the Ștefan Gheorghiu Social-Political Sciences Academy.[16] Beside regular teaching, the institution would also have classes for cadres with a state university degree—they could enroll in daily classes for a year or part-time classes for two years. The cadres would be members of the Party, of the state administration, or of one of the many mass organizations (in which case, the classes would take place several days a year).

Party cadres could also take doctoral classes (with a leave of absence). Ștefan Gheorghiu Party School[17]—which later became a university offering three-year courses—is the most well-known and longest serving institution of its kind. Admission was granted based on exams on Romanian language, geography, the constitution of the Popular Republic of Romania, and the fundamentals of Marxism-Leninism.[18] Upon graduation, there was a state examination in CPSU[19] history, political economy, dialectical materialism, and historical materialism. Each year, there were approximately 150 students enrolled in the daily classes and about 100 more in part-time classes.[20]

In 1949–1950, there were a total of 249,125 Party members enrolled in the university, compared to 1948–1949 when the total number was 100,046. The intention was to increase the number of Party members participating in this type of education by 40–50 percent in the following years to 360,000–390,000: 6,500 in middle and higher schools, 4,000 in Marxist-Leninist universities and night schools, and 20,000 in classes designed for Party activists in rural areas.[21]

It was important that county and *raion* committees were "very vigilant" in recruiting students so that no "foreign hostile elements" would penetrate the Party schools. Instead, there was a demand for "elements which carry prestige in the eyes of the masses, with Party work experience, a well documented background, with growing prospects."[22] The propagandists had to be carefully picked from those having a "healthy social background." The Party school students were not the only ones subjected to such political scrutiny. There was no exception made for teaching staff (e.g., headmaster, professors, lecturers, and assistants). Likewise, Party school curricula were permanently reviewed and revised, with the Propaganda and Agitation Section publishing abridged theses on each subject included into the curricula of such Party schools. Ștefan Gheorghiu University had 127 students in 1948 and 145 in 1950, whereas A. A. Zhdanov School had 129 students in 1948 and 143 in 1950.[23] The first Party cabinet had been set up in early February 1949 in Bucharest at 25 Batiștei Street.[24]

Ștefan Gheorghiu Academy, as a successor to the RCP Workers' University[25] and Andrei Zhdanov School of Social Sciences, was set up through Decree 121 of March 17, 1970, as a "forum for organizing, overseeing and coordinating the totality of research in social sciences."[26] In 1971, the Ștefan Gheorghiu Academy of Social Education[27] was reorganized and a new Central Institute for Training Leadership Cadres in State Economy and Administration was added. Its function was to train cadres[28] who would in turn train others in scientific Socialism.[29] The activity of this university was more than training students. In their status, the professors who taught at the Academy participated in international conferences representing—with authority the official voice—the position of the Party in various internal or external affairs.

The teaching material used was produced by the Propaganda Section of the Central Committee. The Political Publishing House compiled lessons on topics such as "Current problems of the RCP politics," "State-building in the RSR,"[30] etc., and every class had to begin with a statement announcing the latest political line from the Party. Likewise, Nicolae Ceaușescu's speeches, delivered on different occasions, had become indispensable in Party education.

In addition to the higher education level units strictly tied to the Central Committee, there were Party schools alongside the Party's County Committees. Additionally, Party schools operated on two levels, namely the higher education level, which functioned under the RCP Central Committee, and the secondary level, which was organized under the local Party. Party schools were the main form of education and instruction when it came to Communist cadres (ideologists, propagandists). They also had the function of imposing a model of thinking and behaving. As the Party literature noted, "party propaganda, political and cultural-educational work, the whole structure of forms and means of ideological activity have a primordial part to play in forming and molding the behavior of communists."[31] Lectures at such schools took place after office hours, with attendees selected from among the Party secretaries, members of baseline organizations, factory and plant workers, and some intellectuals.³² Rectors of Ştefan Gheorghiu Academy included Leonte Răutu (1972–1981) and Dumitru Popescu (1981–December 22, 1989). While the institution's name went through numerous changes, the name of Ştefan Gheorghiu, added in 1946 to honor an early twentieth-century Socialist militant, was a constant throughout all changes until 1989.

Leonte Răutu—as the longest serving rector of Ştefan Gheorghiu Academy—outlined in 1975 what a successful graduate needed to know:

> Any leadership cadre, no matter what specialized domains he may be active in, is primarily a revolutionary militant, a political man tirelessly engaged in the execution of RCP internal and international policy, and will prove himself to be boundlessly devoted to the Party, to our socialist nation, as well as applying in his life the principles of socialist ethics and socialist fairness, of socialist humanism.

Trainees of this school who matured during the ascendancy of a new Communist class were to steadily replace the elites of a previous generation, who would be gradually purged from the Party leadership in bitter struggles for power. These struggles and the constant "reorganization" they induced created a paradoxical sense of change in a system that was at its core basically stagnant.

The changes taking place in 1965, for instance, were a consequence of Nicolae Ceauşescu's coming to power, while the change in 1968 was caused by the change in the territorial-administrative structure of the country. It was only in 1973, and later in 1976, that changes were motivated by problems strictly regarding the propaganda system. In February 1972, Nicolae Ceauşescu had a meeting with the central and territorial leadership of the Propaganda Section. The event is relevant in observing how the system truly functioned. First, was a review of the fundamental issues facing the propaganda system, especially out in the field: its messages had a hard time reaching its target within society. This shortcoming, it was concluded, was not a mere failure in communicating the message by the propagandist but it was caused by insufficient technique, by the absence of infrastructure and technology necessary for distributing the messages.

The more effective diffusion of the propaganda required a continuous increase in the number of propagandists. Unlike other political regimes—which only required a rather small number of political messengers, with emphasis added instead on diversity in the propaganda means employed—the Communist regime was a system reliant on a large number of individuals who were specially trained for this task. As reported by historian Adam Burakowsky, 1963–1964, brought the largest numerical growth of the Party.³³ The cadre social structure was as follows: 44.16 percent workers, 32.98

percent peasants, and 22.86 percent intellectuals. Compared to the situation in 1962, there was a doubling of the number of peasants as Party members and candidates. Such a development made it possible to establish Party organizations in many localities where none had previously existed. Among the newly minted activists, over 900 graduated from either the central or county-level schools or from the night schools of the Marxism-Leninism universities.[34]

It was only natural that the number of propagandists would match this growth, as their training was much more carefully scrutinized by the leaders of the Party. Starting in 1972, control intensified along with propaganda, with the goal of coaxing as many citizens as possible into active engagement within the system.[35] With all this demand for propaganda work, those involved expressed dissatisfaction with pay, arguing that benefits received was not adequate compensation for their efforts and participation. The stenogram of a propagandists' session in the spring of 1968[36] suggests that a sizable number of those active within the county bureaus of the Party felt tempted to renounce and return to their careers in teaching, with most objections being raised about the small salaries they received—sometimes smaller than those of the teaching staff—and the heavy responsibilities they were assigned.

THE IDEOLOGICAL WORKER: THEME AND VARIATIONS

Propaganda (and the role of the propagandist implicitly) under the Communist regime cannot only be associated with the diffusion of the Party's message, though—as we have seen—this was, in its own terms, an extremely important component. The phenomenon is much more complex, even more so in the context of the education system. We have seen that the propagandist—the ideological worker—operated not only as part of a system of indoctrination but also as one of control, communication, and socializing. Throughout the Communist period, the propaganda apparatus acted differently and in varying proportions, following the Party's directions and responding society's reaction. Consequently, important functions of propaganda (e.g., normative, legitimizing, mobilizing, controlling, persuasive, and identitarian) were all present in the portfolio of the propagandist.

Nothing of significance in what was aimed at in ideological training, celebrations, mass gatherings—be they militant, historical, or sporting—festivals, competitions, student symposiums, and so forth, would have been possible without the involvement and the direct coordination by the ideologue-educator. The information that propaganda apparatus would write down in their field report notes for the various educational institutions came to be used as instruments, whereby those in power could check the system's pulse and the situation of schoolchildren, university students, and teaching staff handling the others' ideological training. Quite often, dissatisfaction was recorded among propagandists concerning their financial rewards for that office, with resulting resignations, dismissals, and reorganizations of the propaganda apparatus.

We have already discussed in chapter 3 how, once the Communists were in full control, the Propaganda Section began speeding up decisions for a more aggressive introduction of ideology into the education system. For instance, a report dated August 8, 1952 noted that:

> With a mandate received from the Central Committee of the Romanian Workers Party Propaganda and Agitation Section, two groups of comrades have been dispatched to Cluj and Iași respectively, in order to assess: 1. The ideological orientation among educational staff and the manner whereby they are becoming familiar with Soviet science 2. The communist education among the students, their combativity against nationalism and chauvinism 3. The cadre policy as relates to students and educational staff.[37]

During the first decades that followed the educational reform of 1948, a rigorous process granted ideological workers, especially faculty ideologues, their statuses and roles within the Communist machine. Discussing the phenomenon, historian Cristian Vasile has published archival documents[38] that refer to the Planned Program of the Central Committee of the Romanian Workers' Party Propaganda and Agitation Section from July 1 to October 10, 1952, relative to its Literature and Arts Section. They run as follows:

> 1. A seminary will be held at the CC Propaganda and Agitation Section attended by the leaders of the art and literature sectors and the secretaries of the core organizations in the main art and literature institutions (September); 2. The work of the Party organizations in the fields of art and literature in the Cluj (July 25) and Valea Jiului (September 15) regions will be analyzed; 3. A report will be submitted on the improvement of the material situation and working conditions of the art and literature people (July 10); 4. The reorganization of the history of world and Romanian literature departments at the C.I. Parhon University in Bucharest will be take place. A written memo on teaching history of Romanian literature will be submitted (September 1); 5. The RPR Architects' Union will be organized; 6. Middle school text-books for the history of Romanian literature will be approved (August 10). The program included other types of tasks: preparing debates on several novels, insuring the recruitment of students for the Mihai Eminescu School of Literature and Literary Critics, preparing a debate at the Writer's Union concerning the process of creating dramatic works, writing articles for *Class Struggle* magazine.[39]

During this period, specialized institutions started to print and distribute publications to support the ideological work. More focus was put on the skills needed to accomplish the propaganda and indoctrination tasks. The idea was that the propagandist in education needed to master psychological knowledge and practical skills to engage both the intellectual and the affective-emotional. At the same time, given the division into specializations (e.g., agitators, lecturers, propagandists, cadres, and activists), each had the obligation to respect the professional code of the field (each with its own method, techniques, and means) in which they had to carry out their ideological activity.

Paraphrasing George Chakotin,[40] historian Ștefan Bosomitu[41] notes—in his analysis of propaganda campaigns—that such campaigns were following a rather well-defined structure. That included (a) defining every group targeted by the propaganda (for instance, preschoolers, high school, and university students); (b) substantiating the psychological approach for each group (this required knowledge and methodology in child youth psychology); (c) creating tools for each group (e.g., written materials, meetings, public manifestations, and mobilizations); and (d) constant supervision of the campaign (e.g., evaluations, discussions, reports, check-ups). Bosomitu notes that these campaigns were based on the idea that people can be categorized into to well-defined groups: (a) active minority—comprised of circa 10 percent of the population and (b) passive majority—comprised of the remaining 90 percent of the population. The active minority was represented by the conscious vanguard of the proletariat, the Party cadres, and the propagandists, while the passive majority was represented by the masses that need to form a class consciousnesses. The propaganda aimed at the minority group was sophisticated, while the one targeting the majority was simple and direct, meant to influence emotions and not the intellect.[42] The audience addressed by the propagandists was differentiated. The minority would receive a variety of ideas, while the majority would receive one idea repeatedly.[43]

There was another distinction that we already introduced in the first part of the book, that between (a) the propagandist who had to present a wide range of ideas and address a limited group and (b) the agitator who had the mission to focus his efforts on presenting a single idea and to mobilize the masses.[44] This distinction explains why the activity of a propagandist in education was supposed to be so mindful of the group it was addressing (e.g., schoolchildren, university students) and to calibrate the approach.

The institutional control of the ideological worker—whether working in education or active in other areas—was directly performed by the Propaganda and Agitation Section. The Section was monitoring how the Party resolutions and directives were to be understood and applied, also informing the regional-, city-, or *raion*-level Party Committee on these issues.[45] "The Regional Party Committee is tasked with supporting the proper functioning of public education, which is why it must control the measures taken by the local state organs, to ensure that schools receive cadres that are honest and devoted to the working masses."[46] To improve functionality of its activity, the Section periodically sent activists out in the field, their role being to inform the subordinate structures of the Propaganda and Agitation Section on the activity of other Party organizations. An activist also had the task of providing information and clarification on the functioning of the Section, its sectors, Party schools, and courses and also sharing the notes and observations to the *raion-* or city-level Party committees. Upon return, he would report on his findings as a delegate, since "only this way might an activist have a real perspective on his own work."[47] Another control method—and also an obligation for local-level propaganda—was a periodic calling upon the propaganda secretaries from the City or *Raion* Party Committees so that they could report on the field situation or get instructions. These were required to report on issues such as the school year's opening or political work among primary- and secondary-school teachers.

Each propagandist was assigned their own file, one that needed periodic updating and evaluations based on periodic reports, promotions, warnings, or vetting received from the structure to which they belonged. Below is the standardized chart of a cadre model (from the 1970s and 1980s), which, it should be noted, were typified and did not change from one year to the next, with the exception of particular cases such as marrying foreign citizens (which required more in-depth vetting and more referrals attached to a file):[48]

RCP CENTRAL COMMITTEE

CADRE SECTION

Name: . . .

Party member since: . . .

Born on: . . .

Social origin: [those who could write themselves in as peasants with a middle-or small-sized farm had an advantage because they were seen more favorably]

Marriage status: [married people had an advantage]

Studies: . . .[obviously, attending Ștefan Gheorghiu Academy courses was a plus]

Profession and title: . . .

Foreign language: [in the 1950s, Russian was a plus, but in the 1970s and 1980s, speaking French or English was a plus]

This was followed by a detailed biography of the person up for review, in many cases writing in a formulaic style that included:

> "the ministry leadership endorses the work he did in directing and supporting the activity"; "in his leadership positions he showed competence, multilateral preparedness, responsibility, principle-mindedness and firmness"; "he contributed to the proper solving of issues pertaining to certain cadres being sent abroad"; "during the annual evaluation session, it was suggested to him that he display more promptness in his work and be more available to institutions of higher learning and research"; "in his teaching activity, he authored and taught a course in . . . , and as a Party activist and lecturer of the CC of the RCP he prepared and hosted numerous lectures and conferences and collaborated on compiling the analytical programs for Party schooling"; "He was assigned numerous tasks by the Party organization, namely: group organizer, basic organizational bureau member, member of the ministry-level Party committee."

Notes on family: parents have worked [on a collective farm, if from a rural area], parents had a Party membership.

Siblings: Party members/activists

Wife: Party member, currently employed as . . .

Children: [a similar note was made, if they were themselves Party members]

Cadre Section of the CC of the RCP views him as fit for the current office.

INSTRUCTOR: . . .

SECTIONAL LEADER: . . .

DATE: . . .

The activity of vetting Party members (as well as propagandists, agitators, and lecturers) was central to a cadre file. Each file had at least three referrals, or a maximum of six in more difficult cases, in addition to an autobiography. Evaluations (referrals) were highly important for determining how the upper echelons could decide to support and promote certain people. Usually, favorable ones sounded like this: so-and-so should be promoted "for a decent activity and for the way in which they were able to mobilize the students' collective," or "for distributing material for the celebration of August 23," "for cultural activity and for increasing the library collection," or "for work in directing and distributing the press."

In analyzing these cadre files, what emerges at a glance, other than details reflecting professional life (interesting to note that the pages contain no details as to their private lives or presumable hobbies), is the striking reliance on the so-called "wooden language." Without exception, propagandists' autobiographies are written in a formulaic manner, using stereotypes and cadences behind which phrases and the author become impersonal. The situation is identical in the case of evaluation and vetting, where—excluding some minor exceptions—formulaic phrases are repeated with no modification whatsoever from one year to the next.

The task of taking in recommendations fell on cadre sector instructors, their most often employed method being field visits and interviews with the people who were most likely to provide the most detailed references for the candidate in question. Files include "notes on relationships," "observations," "assessments," and an "autobiography" (which all required constant updating). Some files contain information not only on the person being proposed but also on their families (father, mother, brothers, and sisters). Only in this way could the sound social origin be proven, making one potentially eligible for ascent into the political elite of Communism.[49]

These are some generic examples that went into these references: "this comrade has a political and ideological level that befits his employment"; "he was up to the tasks for his ideological and organizational work, and showed awareness of the issues he was supposed to handle"; "he showed up well prepared for Party sessions and came up with various proposals on how to improve the work"; "high political and ideological level"; "a sense of responsibility in fulfilling the tasks"; "an active participant in discussions, also noted for always bringing up issues of great importance"; "mindful of his own political-ideological preparation."

The views expressed by an article in *Scânteia* (the official newspaper of the Communists dating to 1951),[50] regarding the ideological workers and, more precisely, their role within the propaganda apparatus, mode of selection, and training, is worth quoting:

> Our Party leads great battles on the field of socialist construction . . . it mobilizes large masses of people, its success in this political endeavor dependent on the communists' political and ideological preparedness. . . . A strong connection exists between the cadres' level of preparedness and the pace of work in socialist construction, with most tasks being successfully fulfilled once Party activists acquire a high degree of political and ideological preparedness. . . . a propagandist will have the honored task of acting as the ideological guide and political educator for the communists under his supervision.[51]

For this very reason, one of the most important tasks facing Party organizations was precisely to "ensure, in the best conditions possible, the selection of propagandists and the means of which to organizing their training courses." Similarly, propaganda work was only for the selected few, those with obvious skills: "only those comrades who proved themselves suitable for the tasks and requirements that are imposed on a propagandist." Hence, "the induction of new propagandists contingents should lead to an increase in the overall level of theoretical, political, ideological, and cultural training of existing propagandist cadres." The activists displaying a remarkable ideological level that "should constitute a backbone for the propaganda apparatus in Party schools and Party training."[52] In addition, there was a drive to attract the secondary school teachers, primary school teachers (especially those active in rural areas), homeroom teachers, and teaching guides from various educational units into the propaganda apparatus.

Whereas during the Dej years in government, most propagandists were recruited from among intellectuals and sent to Party schools for ideological training, later, especially after 1965 and in the context of the formal education system, propagandists were recruited from among teachers, librarians, and auxiliary personnel in that field. This led to a change of perspective.[53] In time, ideological workers became specialized and were asked to perform in specific areas, which required specific training befitting the age group expected to be targeted. Often, this resulted in the ousting of propagandists who did not meet the criteria.[54]

Selecting propagandists was done on the basis of personal interviews with discussions that were expected to highlight the propagandist's ideological knowledge and capabilities. Afterward, decision makers would submit proposals for confirmation by the regional bureaus. What followed was a thorough vetting of the candidate, along with a set of credentials and the candidate's own affidavit attesting his loyalty toward the Communist regime. Then the file was submitted for analysis. Such a detailed procedure reconfirms that the propagandist was no mere Party functionary, but rather was seen as a key element of the system. After the file was accepted, instruction followed. Next, there was a presentation of the tasks and responsibilities assigned as well as of the institutions and people to whom he was supposed to submit the reports and who oversaw the activity. Propagandists in the field of education were to be recruited from among Party and state activists, cultural sections inspectors, and the best professors and schoolteachers who were also Party members.[55] The Party documents specified that "members of *raion* and city committees have a duty to engage these personally in order to assess their knowledge level, if they have a calling for the job, and to define in direct terms the circle that he will be leading for the future school-year, with the relevant type of training he is to receive."[56]

Once the selection was complete, full attention was given to their training. This was achieved through special courses held by ideologically trained Party activists, and these qualification lessons and seminars—if they did not take place at the center—were constantly controlled by the Party district committees. Upon graduation, these committees had an obligation to place these propagandists (in manufacturing plants, factories, editorial offices, or educational units) while simultaneously ensuring their integration into the propaganda apparatus as a whole. In pursuing their goals, propagandists familiarized themselves with Marxism, the history of the Soviet Bolshevik Party, and the Romanian Communists' own "history of struggles." They needed to master Romania's history, geography, and the core notions of political economy and Socialism and, needless to say, to be sufficiently well read, as to allow them to present their lessons in the most attractive and convincing form. Gr. Cotovschi[57] in *Lupta de clasă* wrote:

> The communist education of Party members is a core task among Party organizations. . . . the propagandist will teach Party members to understand the importance of theory in the Party's practical activity, will support them in learning Marxist-Leninist science, will seek to bring out in them the moral profile of a revolutionary fighter, a Communist man.[58]

Those who had not graduated from Ştefan Gheorghiu Academy were instructed with lectures held by the local Party organization bureaus for a ten-to-twelve-day period, generally in late summer.[59] During the latter half of the 1960s, their specific training formula was based on seminars,[60] later extended to symposiums, conferences, consultations, and referral-based debates.[61] Individual study was also part of propagandists' training, namely "the study of Party documents and other bibliographic materials pertaining to the topic; information on the state of affairs, the facts of life, relating to students as a unit, so as to best illustrate the main ideas of the topic and to align studying with ideological necessities of the Party organization; procuring illustrative material that would support the topic: graphs, charts, sketches, slides etc."[62] A *Propagandist's Notebook*[63] was held by the Party committee, wherein propagandists had a duty of writing down, after each activity, the month, day, student attendance, and any observations regarding the attendees' participation in debates.[64] Alongside bibliographies sent in from the Party headquarters, the propagandists' activity was supported by a magazine called *În ajutorul propagandiştilor*, which included bibliographic reviews, field reports, and articles regarding a propaganda methodology and the profession of ideological workers.[65] The topics covered in this magazine included the following:

> Explaining Party policy; the role and place of the propagandist in the Party's ideological activity; educating attendees the communist way—a propagandist's main mission; a propagandist's method in individual study; a propagandist's personal training for expositions or debates; the permanent effort to improve one's own level of ideological, political, cultural, specialty skills, a defining feature of the propagandist.[66]

Among propagandists entering Party education, those who stood out during the classes could well be hired as teaching staff within the institutions that formed them. Party instructors had an obligation to monitor and verify the courses and the attendees. Historian Cristina Preutu has reviewed the transcripts that raise doubts about whether such classes had a consistent attendance. Reports indicate that attendance of these classes was not constant, with most of them, only averaging 50 percent attendance.[67]

The requirement was that each lecture be clear and concise, shedding light on the core ideas of a text and giving a systematic exposition to Marxism-Leninism as a science of societal development, a science of the oppressed and exploited masses, a science of the coming victory of Socialism in all countries, as well as a science of constructing Communist society.[68] One was never to ignore, in Communist education, the development of a critical and self-critical spirit among Party members, or even among school-age attendees.[69] Being a good personal example was also a matter relevant for the propagandist-teachers.

THE IDEOLOGICAL WORKER VARIATIONS: THE AGITATOR

As we have already noted, the function of the agitator was related and sometimes indistinguishable from the function of the propagandist in the system of the propaganda apparatus. Whereas the propagandist had a more complex range, distributing more than one idea to a targeted circle of individuals, an agitator had, in turn, the mission to promote just one idea to the many.[70] An agitator was perceived as a "guide and advisor to the masses, in permanent contact with them."[71] As envisioned by the Party, agitation had to be continuous, consistent, and present always and everywhere, but preferably in crowded domains: schools, universities, sporting grounds, youth reunions, etc. It mobilized "the base"[72] and even though its status was reduced after 1965, it was a constant presence at events such as demonstrations, public gatherings, or mass events involving youth.

Over time, however, the Party placed more and more emphasis on the propagandist's role and status. Meanwhile, the work of instructing agitators—with advisory sessions, seminars, and lessons—fell on the field instructors, who would hold their own yearly meetings at a regional level. The agitator never carried the same importance as the propagandist. The specific role was increasingly seen as insufficient for carrying through with the Party's agenda.

Unlike propagandists, agitators were not required to be Party members and, as such, did not receive continuous training of a certain level, but only got to attend a number of hours of instructional lectures each month. Nonetheless, agitators were viewed as a key link between the Party and the masses, and it was held that "the task of agitators is one of honor and of great responsibility, and communist agitation an art form."[73] It was considered that, unlike a propagandist, whose success depended strictly on ideological training and on the identification of effective pedagogical methods to apply on those whom they targeted, the agitator's success was more reliant on how they organized their act.[74]

The main features of political agitation were "exceptional principle-mindedness, class features, truth, combativeness, concreteness, clarity."[75] The agitator needed to be "devoted mind and soul to the Party cause,"[76] well acquainted with his or her line of work, an example for all others, and at the same time aware of all news involving the Party. An agitator needed to know how to address people "lively and persuasively, possessing the art of approaching a man's soul, displaying tactfulness and solicitude"[77]—or in other words, to attempt persuasion using examples, including one's own example, and making appeals to human emotions. As means of agitation, one would use both spoken agitation—which implied discussions and expositions—as well the written kind: wall newspapers, slides, documentary films, agitation displays, or exhibits.

Agitation—as described in the official training manuals[78]—had three main forms of manifestation: spoken, written, and visual. All three means of expression were also used in an educational context, where the same propaganda formula, more or less, was being employed, though, one should note, the messages it spread were modified in line with the targets' perception and level of comprehension—those of schoolchildren or university students, for instance. In fact, we have already noted that, broadly speaking, the activity in the area of education follows the same coordinates as in any other field, though one should be aware that the messages and the mechanisms employed for their spread required a certain specificity.

One of the main areas of operations for agitation was in the context of major ceremonies (school-year opening and closure, national festivities,[79] award ceremonies) that—irrespective of the form they took—would always include quoting from the work of Marxist-Leninist classics or from Communist Party documents. At the other extreme—small groups, rather than large gatherings—the agitator had an obligation to be alert, intervene, and enter pupil-group conversations, clarifying certain points of the ideological program and discussing news articles or Party brochures with them.

Written agitation comprised all things related to mass communication. The student press and the brochures or books that the Party put out for the students' ideological training, which agitators had an obligation to popularize, were at the core of it. Slogans, as already discussed in part 1, were crucial. A slogan was to feature one single idea as an exhortation that was quickly readable and meant to have an impact.⁸⁰ Here are some examples of messages on classroom walls or on the corridors of educational units, primarily schools: "Fight for the cause of Lenin and Stalin!" "Keep up the pace! For the glory of the Party and the prosperity of Socialist Romania!" "I honor my red tie and its tricolor fringe!" "The Party, Ceaușescu, Romania!" "Communists are our teachers in courage!"

Visual agitation comprised posters, graphs, boards, or banners.⁸¹ The importance of visual agitation within the scope of means and methods employed by the propaganda and agitation apparatus was covered in a session of the Organizing Office of March 22, 1952, which came up with a resolution detailing the quasi-mystical care that Communist leaders displayed when it came to their own public image. The idea was to instill a robust, proletarian-like optimism.⁸² The Party's leadership highly favored visual agitation, since it could prove more persuasive and could have greater impact when compared to spoken or written agitation.⁸³ Much attention was given to the details in this case. The instructions pointed out, for instance, that dark shades had a depressing, discouraging, and negative effect, while too lively shades of color would cause fatigue.⁸⁴ Evidently—when it came to the primary school pupils—propaganda was much more piercing and more visually striking. At the same time, the March 1952 session made an explicit point of asking that the portraits of Leninist classics and Romanian Workers' Party leaders be printed only by the RWP Publishing House, monitored and controlled by the Central Committee Propaganda and Agitation Section. Using portraits printed by any other printing office, institution, or organization was entirely forbidden.⁸⁵

Agitation, it was claimed, helped the Party to lead the masses by "lifting them up its own level of consciousness." But only if it were done in the right way. As one editorial in *Scânteia* argued, the strength of political agitation had to be based on the far-sighted ideology of the proletariat.⁸⁶ Likewise, according to the authors of that text, it had to be *reliant on truth*. It did not have to contradict facts. At the same time, it needed to be *clear*, using transparent and universally accessible language, and *concrete*, easily tied to the problems of regular folk. It also had to be on *the offensive*, unmasking international imperialism and class enemies within the country, and *operative*, by reacting in real time and promptly. But above all, it had to be *effective*, leading to concrete results.⁸⁷

Last but not least, one of the most noteworthy aspects of the activity of "agitation" was that an agitator was under the obligation of unmasking class enemies, identifying negative examples, and pointing them out.⁸⁸ In addition to these were responsibilities such as accompanying organized groups on tours of museums, exhibits, or memorial homes or the participation, alongside youth, in mass rallies or in certain festive occasions. That created ample room for "unmasking" real or imagined "deviations" from the "Party line" or "enemies of the working classes." As already discussed, over time, the role of the agitator diminished, but in the education system, agitation work, especially of the visual kind, maintained its importance, even more so as Socialist competitions were held between schools. If the problems encountered surpassed the agitator's skill level, they could always seek assistance from the propagandist or lecturer.

The status of the agitator became increasingly muddled after 1969. It was considered to be discarded altogether for being both redundant and antiquated, though Nicolae Ceaușescu later brought up the need for using agitators to keep people connected to the Party's policy. A proposal was even advanced to change the name of agitator to cultural instructor, political educator, or even propagandist. Yet, over time, the category of agitators could no longer fit into the propaganda system structure and was assimilated with the category of activists and propagandists.[89]

THE IDEOLOGICAL WORKER VARIATIONS: THE LECTURERS

Alongside agitators and propagandists, a new category of "lecturers" was created in 1965. Lecturers were broadly defined, in the typical Communist rhetoric of ambiguity, as those "members of the Party organs and respective committees, responsible cadres employed by the state apparatus . . . in research institutes, in cultural institutions, or as teaching staff."[90] A propaganda secretary of the county or city committee was directly responsible for the lecturers' activities, and the bureaus of such committees had an annual duty to revise the membership of any group of lecturers.[91] In turn, lecturers were divided into categories that were meant to streamline their propaganda work. They were organized by domains: philosophy, scientific Socialism, and Party construction. Meanwhile, in university centers—Bucharest, Iași, Cluj, Timișoara, and Târgu Mureș—groups of lecturers were formed out of regular students.[92]

In this respect, it is important to keep in mind that the major difference between a lecturer and a propagandist was that, whereas the latter supposedly had a general awareness of all the issues facing the Party and was trained to master a vast general knowledge, the lecturer specialized in a certain field and, as such, trained for a certain area. In an interesting twist, Party documents reveal that, very soon, the power of lecturers within the propaganda institution grew as they gained the upper hand over propagandists when they came to verify the propagandists in their work. Their creation in 1965 led to a revamping of the system. Adding a new element located between the source (the Party leaders) and the voice of propagandists made a difference.[93] The Communist hierarchy consolidated its grip on the system, and the Central Committee lecturers instructed and gave speeches to those active within local organizations, monitoring them and at the same time controlling the work at a grassroots level.

In 1976, the CC of RCP Secretariat ruled that the Central Committee group of lecturers[94] would comprise the following: "members of the CC of the RCP, of the Central Review Commission, of the Central Party College, selective members of the Great National Assembly and other responsible cadres of the Party's central apparatus, of ministries, of core state institutions . . . , teaching staff in higher education, scientific researchers."[95] Lecturers were instructed in accordance with their specialization. For instance, those who were involved in teaching history were dealing with topics such as "the role of personalities and of masses in the history of the Motherland and that of the Communist Party," while those who had roles in atheistic-scientific propaganda dealt with "the tasks of Party organizations in the field of educating people" as well as with "the essence of the materialist dialectical worldview."[96]

Given that this category of lecturers was introduced in 1965, it was only natural that their activity be linked to the ninth RCP Congress, taking place that year, as well as with the documents and the political line endorsed by Nicolae Ceaușescu. It was in relation to this Congress that the activities of this very category were set into motion, with lecturers clarifying, elaborating, providing consultations, and interpreting the Congressional resolutions. Between November 8 and 12, 1965, a group attached to the Propaganda and Agitation Section went on a control mission through some of the regions in order to monitor and assess how Congressional documentation was being studied and debated within Party schools, among teaching staff, and within the Union of Communist Youth political training courses.[97] At a later stage in 1972, lectures from the Central Committee of the Romanian Communist Party delivered over 750 field presentations and field debates for teaching staff and students.[98] It is hard not to speculate about the link between, on the one hand, this restructuring of the system and, on the other hand, the intense activity and impact of Nicolae Ceausescu's maneuvers and strategies, who at that time was in process of taking over the Romanian Communist Party and gaining control of the entire Romanian political system.

THE CHALLENGES OF PRACTICE

While things seemed to be straightforward in theory and on paper, implementation and practice did not always yield the desired results. The commitment of the ideological workers was often in doubt, especially during the latter stages of the Communist regime. A decline in enthusiasm for the mission and for "the construction of a multilaterally developed socialist society" seemed to be prevalent. What's more, the propaganda structure in its entirety had always had a set of contradictions at its core. The biggest of them was between official rhetoric and reality. The conclusion was simple and obvious: despite its claims, it could not base itself on truth since that would have ran against the very core of the ideological myths and wishful thinking around which the Communist regime had been built. Clarity in propaganda messaging was blurred more and more often, more and more saliently. In conjunction with the dilettantism displayed by certain cadres, it created a situation wherein the propaganda mechanism sometimes functioned in ways contrary to its own design and against the wishes of higher-up Party officials.

The transcript of a 1950 meeting, which looked into the successes and failures of propaganda work, stands out as illustrative.[99] A comrade active in the Party's middle echelons put out an activity report that featured the main issues up for discussion and went through those tasks that his sector had satisfactorily handled during that specific period: intensifying agitation for world peace as well as agitation in respect to countering Anglo-American propaganda. In addition, he noted that the agitation sector "has sought to fulfill its permanent duties, namely liquidating disdain for agitation work by some Party organs and mass organizations, the upscaling of agitators recruitment and their instruction and control by the leadership organs of base organizations, the popularization of agitation methods and approaches." As accomplishments, he went on to outline the following: "a three-day advisory session and subsequent seminar were held by the Central Committee with the relevant cadres of all county-level agitation commissions, which included instruction as to organizing agitation work in preparation for Stalin's birthday" as well as "in respect to some of the speeches given by Gheorghiu-Dej." In addition, "instructions were given as to organizing and running agitation courses, the instruction of agitators, the use of various agitation methods, of agitation materials."[100]

In one session of March 1968,[101] where the issue of propagandists was brought up for discussion, it emerged that some of these, mostly those attached to county-level Party offices, gave up their positions—due to payment grievances—and returned to their jobs as teachers. It was then recommended that their salaries be increased, though this measure never seems to have been enforced.

Yet, another reason for discontent among propagandists operating on the front line, alongside their low salaries, was the overinflated responsibilities that fell on them: in addition to active work in the ideological field, they had to carry out periodic controls of educational institutions, submit monthly reports regarding various events, and be vigilant about how press and propaganda materials were being distributed. Central figures of the Party often accused them of inefficiency and failing to grasp the messages, dropping hints that the work of propagandists was never up to the standards of their historical responsibility in educating the younger generations.

Party documents, therefore, suggest that the system was confronted from within, on one hand, with the dissatisfaction with pay and, on the other hand, with a crisis of confidence. An issue that arose within the Propaganda and Agitation Section in 1972[102] was linked to the frequent episodes of confusion and hesitation regarding the task of overseeing a propagandist's work. The transcripts of the session also reveal that agitators were uncertain about whether their involvement was as an individual, a group, or a brigade-level action, and they were unfamiliar with where their responsibilities would end.[103]

Moreover—given the personal implication in propaganda work, and even the cultivation of a personal style—the central leadership noted a lack of uniformity in the propaganda messages and approaches of these ideological workers (propagandists, lecturers, and agitators). Here is an excerpt from Nicolae Ceaușescu's contribution to that session,[104] pleading above all for a toning down of the rigidity in the propagandist's discourse and for drawing attention to the uselessness (and above all, the inadequacy) of various rules imposed on them: "True enough, we ought to have a number of guidelines, but overall we need to work with the people, since new rules and guidelines may pop up each month. Of course, some things will endure in the long run, but we'll be wrong to seek out new solutions by having instructions for all problems."[105]

This session resulted in another reorganization of the Propaganda and Agitation Section, with the propagandist taking on more relevant responsibilities within the horizontal mechanism and collaborating with other educational institutions in the field, namely primary and secondary schools, kindergartens, libraries, and community centers. Within the vertical mechanism, propagandists were required to participate in sessions alongside county secretaries, sectional leaders, and chief editors of various publications. A working method was established whereby regional sections would receive from the central leadership only a series of general working principles of the sections, so as to render their operations more flexible.[106]

Recruiting of top-level propagandists in the field of ideological education was a particularly sensitive task, given that these were meant to provide cadres for the future party nomenklatura. In this respect, the recruiting ground was from among inspectors of the education and culture sections and professors. Priority was given to those who had obtained their credentials and taught social sciences.[107] An internally circulated publication of 1971 recommended that all committees—county, municipal, town, or communal—give enhanced attention to the selection of propagandists and lecturers for political and ideological training: "Party workers, accountable cadres of the state of mass organizations, who should fulfill the task of lecturer or propagandist, provide expositions and chair debates within the various forms of political-ideological training."[108]

During the early 1960s, while speaking at a Party session with the secretaries and section leaders of regional Party committees, Paul Niculescu-Mizil reemphasized that propagandists had an extremely important role to play in matters of Party instruction. The task of promoting and rendering popular the Party's policies was crucial. Every speech and every lecture had to be prefaced by the most recent resolutions of the Party leaders.[109] A propagandist was not the "casual reciter, and therefore should not base himself on just material sent to him by the central offices."[110]

One would have a hard time estimating the number of propagandists active in the 1960s and 1970s, let alone how many among those were performing their ideological duties in the field of education. An analysis of archival documents gives us a sense of the magnitudes: Argeș Region reports produced in 1964 reveal the registration of some 856 Party and state activists as well as 1,106 educational staff and other intellectuals.[111] Brașov Region had 715 activists and 778 educational staff, whereas Bucharest had 4,138 propagandists, of whom 1,432 were Party activists.[112]

We have seen how during the 1960s and 1970s greater emphasis was put on training propagandists on their quality rather than on their head count. The reality was that, while the number of cadres grew in proportion to the extension and development of that institution, their perceived performance fell below expectations. Wherever the Party leaders viewed particular propagandists as unfit, they were purged out of the system.

During the second part of the 1960s, as a means to improve the quality of propaganda work, a series of surveys designed as working tools were carried out, allowing the Propaganda Section leadership to decide on how certain topics needed to be tweaked.[113] Monitoring and evaluating continued to highlight problems—be they, on the one hand, those that were generated by the absence of propagandists from sessions and debates that were compulsory for people of that status, or, on the other hand, those that reflected that some of them had poor skills and had only been superficially vetted when first proposed for the respective positions.[114] Consequently, one would note afterwards a modification of structures within the Agitation and Propaganda Section. Alongside the growth in numbers of cadres who were active in educational institutions, there was an increase of the personalization and calibration of messages. The messages, while reflecting demands issued by the upper echelons of the Party, tended to be personalized and calibrated to the capabilities, specificity, and training available to the actor in question. This meant a nuancing of the approach and the message.[115]

As the Section was reorganized, the message became more personalized, and the number of areas that required more specialized expertise grew. There was a noticeable growth in the number of propagandists with a higher education background, as the system now required people with a better training. Again, the revolving door to the education system was activated. In the field of professional education, teaching staff were sometimes asked to give up their positions for the precise reason of dedicating themselves exclusively to propaganda work.[116]

CONCLUSIONS

Our investigation has led us to the conclusion that the establishment and maintenance of an institutionalized system of propaganda and indoctrination was, in reality, less like a mechanical authoritative structure, but more like an ongoing process. It presumed a periodic reevaluation, an ongoing reconfiguration and reassertion, and a continuous training and (re)education dimension. Despite its intensity and magnitude, Communist propaganda met its objectives to a small degree. There were many Romanians who, in various ways, bought into propaganda to a certain degree. And there were many Romanians whose mindsets were affected by indoctrination, sometimes in ways they were not even fully aware of. However, we have reason to believe that the vast majority of the people went increasingly unpersuaded by Communist slogans, and they dismissed propaganda claims altogether.

The erosion of its ability to persuade—reaching its final stage in December 1989—had begun, in fact, much earlier, along with the pauperization, shortages, and economic distress that Romania had come to face. Propaganda and indoctrination could not offer any solutions to the grim economic realities of the daily life. In the end, despite all its reinventions, reform, revamping, and avatars, the Romanian system of indoctrination and propaganda failed to achieve any of its functions: neither the ideological function of shaping the "new men and women" that the regime intended to create, nor the pragmatic, or strategic function of regime survival through institutionally induced loyalty and obedience.

NOTES

1. For details on the nomenklatura, see Eugen Denize, *Propaganda comunistă în România (1948–1953)* (Târgoviște: Editura Cetatea de Scaun, 2011), 33–34; Nicoleta Ionescu-Gură, "Modernizarea PMR-ului după modelul PC al URSS și crearea nomenclaturii CC al PMR în Republica Populară Română (1949–1950)," chapter of

Totalitarism și rezistență, teroare și represiune în România comunistă (ed. Gheorghe Onișoru) (Bucharest: Editura CNSAS, 2001), 216–50; Florin Constantiniu, "Geneza nomenclaturii comuniste," in *Dosarele istoriei*, no. 4 (1996): 2.

2. At its most basic level and above and beyond the sociological interpretations, the nomenklatura was in reality a list of accountable offices, subject to election or party appointment and vetted by the Party's central leadership organs (the Central Committee) or by local ones (regional, *raion*, or city-wide committees). For that matter, even the nomenklatura's designation varied with affiliations: to the CC, to the region, or to the *raion*. People entering the nomenklatura were, in practical terms, the Party, their selection (in accordance to specialties and branches of activity) being centered on mainly political criteria: what mattered was their devotion to the Party, their Party membership status, their social origin, political past, family connections, workplace relations, and attendance of Party schools. *De facto*, this nomenklatura was not subject to approval by the Party leadership organs, but rather by its executive ones, namely the Secretariat and Politburo. Nomenklaturists were carefully selected and were promoted when this was called for. They followed along a certain path with a strict record of their careers and clearly defined responsibilities, but also with a set of privileges that distinguished them from other Party members. (Additional details regarding Romania in Stelian Tănase's work, *Elite și societate. Guvernarea Gheorghiu-Dej, 1948–1965* [Bucharest: Editura Humanitas, 1998], 52.) Even so, many authors argue that nomenklaturists did not represent an elite (in the sense of a "*social power structure known to exercise major influence or to be in direct control of how political, economic, social decisions are adopted within a certain community*," for details see Sergiu Tămaș, *Dicționar politic. Instituțiile democrației și cultura civică* [Bucharest: Editura Academiei Române, 1993], 216) were not a power to their own, and not a decision-making body, but rather the enablers of Party resolutions, the executors, and a cog in the mechanism that transmitted ideas set by the Party leadership.

3. Cristina Preutu, *Propaganda politică în România socialistă. Practici instituționale și tehnici de comunicare 1965–1974* (Iași: Editura Universității Alexandru Ioan Cuza, 2017), 137.

4. Cristina Preutu, op.cit., 157.

5. Ibid., 157.

6. For details on this, see Marc Angenot's volume, *La propagande socialiste: six essais d'analyse du discours*, Montréal, Editions Balzac, 1997, as well as Lavinia Betea's *Psihologia politică. Individ, lider, mulțime în regimul comunist* (Iași: Editura Polirom, 2001).

7. *Propuneri de măsuri pentru îmbunătățirea propagandei de partid*, in ANIC, CC of the RCP Collection, Propaganda and Agitation Section, file no. 1/1961, 157.

8. These aspects are emerging in the evaluation of successes and failures of propaganda activities presented to the Propaganda and Agitation Section. The agents' suggestions were analyzed by the political leadership and then forwarded in the form of instructions for future actions.

9. Congresul PMR, București, 21–23 Februarie 1948 (Bucharest: Editura PMR, 1948), 95.

10. *Procesul verbal al ședinței Biroului Direcției de Propagandă și Agitație al CC al PMR din 15 mai 1948*, in AMR, microfilm fund, r. AS1–1516, c.1.

11. In Romanian historiography, a significant contribution in this field is the volume coordinated by Sorin Radu—*Învățământul de partid și școlile de cadre în România comunistă. Context național și regional* (Iași: Editura Universității Alexandru Ioan Cuza, 2014).

12. For details, see also Nicoleta Ionescu-Gură, *Nomenclatura CC al PMR* (Bucharest: Editura Humanitas, 2006), 103–4.

13. Named after a renowned Soviet ideologue who died in the summer of 1948.

14. For details, see the editorial *"Biroului Politic al PMR a decis transformarea școlii de lectori A.A. Jdanov într-o școală superioară de științe sociale cu durata de 2 ani"* in Scânteia, July 22, 1949, 1.

15. A note should be made that Party education had an existence before the establishment of Ștefan Gheorghiu Academy of Social-Political Sciences. On Ana Pauker's initiative, March 21, 1945, saw the inauguration of the Romanian Communist Party Workers' University, whose first rector (1945–1948) was the ethnically Jewish literary historian Barbu Lăzăreanu, a constant contributor to the main Communist-oriented periodicals, namely *România muncitoare* and *Socialismul*, afterwards in the underground RCP (Romanian Communist Party) press. It remains a paradox that, during the time of Jewish deportations, his name had been taken out of the blacklist following an intervention by Queen-Mother Helena. In 1948, Barbu Lăzăreanu was one of the new waves of inductees into the Romanian Academy. Professors assigned to teach at the RCP Workers' University also included Mihail Roller, Ion Popescu-Puțuri, Ion Călugăru, and so forth.

16. A symbolic name referencing one of the founders of the Romanian Social-Democratic Party and a defender of the 1907 peasants' uprising.

17. In the early 1970s, the rector was Miron Constantinescu, succeeded by Leonte Răutu, who was discharged in 1981. The last rector of Ștefan Gheorghiu Party school was Dumitru Popescu, one of the main doctrinaires of Ceaușescu's Socialism.

18. More important in school admissions was the selection of the candidates, who were recommended by the CC Sections and by the Party Regional Committees. The recommendations were submitted for approval by a commission of the Central Committee.

19. Communist Party of the Soviet Union

20. Part-time classes had a duration of four years.

21. For more details on the analysis of Party education: *Procesul verbal și stenograma ședinței Biroului organizatoric din ziua de 29 iunie 1950*, in AMR, microfilm fund, r.AS1–405, c.16–42.

22. Idem, c.16.

23. Eugen Denize, op.cit., 77.

24. "Deschiderea primului Cabinet de Partid de consultanță marxist-leninistă," in *Scânteia*, February 15, 1949, 1.

25. A "leading school for the workers' education," Ștefan Gheorghiu Party School was minutely copied after the Soviet blueprint of propaganda schools, aiming to become the source of dialectical materialism for the "sons and daughters of our

people." In *Scânteia* of March 13, 1945, mention was made of how the University inauguration had been a "moving ceremony, for both the professors and the imposing number of students, recruited from among manual workers and intellectuals." During inauguration, the festive moment came with a rendition of The Internationale—as sung by the university student's choir.

26. The institution was located at 1–3, Armata Poporului Boulevard (presently Iuliu Maniu Boulevard), Bucharest.

27. For the university year 1966–1967, there was a massive increase in the number of places within the three faculties of Ștefan Gheorghiu Institution. For full time enrollment, there were 150 places for the first year of study distributed as such: 60 for the Faculty of Economy, 60 for the Faculty of Philosophy and Social-Political Sciences, and 30 for the Faculty of History. The candidates were recruited from the central apparatus, the regional and raion committees, the media, and ideological and educational institutions. These graduates would later become county Party secretaries. For details, see also *Propuneri cu privire la selecționarea candidaților pentru concursurile de admitere la Academia și Științe Social-Politice "Ștefan Gheorghiu,"* in ANIC, CC of the RPC Collection, Chancellery Section, file no. 84/1966, 12.

28. The diplomas—crucial in advancing one's status, also in one's future *cursus honorum*—had a column for evaluating the political training in the cadre. The options were between "good" and "very good."

29. Among other classes at the Ștefan Gheorghiu Academy of Social-Political Education, there were also classes of journalism and training for social sciences professors teaching at universities or unions. There was also a postgraduate program.

30. Socialist Republic of Romania

31. "Comunistul, om înaintat al societății noastre" in *În ajutorul propagandiștilor*, Year VII, no. 11/1967, 21.

32. In the 1980s, the only place where one could obtain the qualification of journalist was at the Faculty of Journalism of the Ștefan Gheorghiu Academy. All employees in the central and county press with other specializations were sent to the postgraduate courses of this faculty.

33. Over a third of the members and candidates entered the Party at the latter stage. For details, see Adam Burakowski, *Dictatura lui Nicolae Ceaușescu, 1965–1989, Geniul Carpaților (Dictatorship of Nicolae Ceaușescu, 1965–1989, Genius of the Carpathians)* (Iași: Polirom, 2011), 111.

34. Adam Burakowski, op.cit., 112.

35. In July 1972, at the RCP National Conference, the project for "norms of communist living and working and of Socialist ethic and equity" was approved—which was a set of written provisions for Party members whose conduct was supposed to be a model for society. For details, see Adam Burakowski, op.cit., 244.

36. *Stenograma ședinței de raportare ale instructorilor teritoriali din 1 martie 1968*, in ANIC, CC of the RCP Collection, Propaganda and Agitation Section, file no. 1/1968, 5.

37. In ANIC, CC of the RPC Collection, Propaganda and Agitation Section, file no. 58/1952, 1.

38. In ANIC, CC of the RCP Collection, Propaganda and Agitation Section, file no. 30/1952, 91–92.

39. Cristian Vasile, *Literatura și artele în România comunistă, 1948–1953* (Bucharest: Editura Humanitas), 55–56.

40. Serge Chakotin, *Rape of the Masses: The Psychology of Totalitarian Political Propaganda* (London: Routledge, 1940).

41. Ștefan Bosomitu, "Planificare-implementare-control. Apariția și dezvoltarea aparatului de propagandă comunist în România, 1944–1950," in *Structuri de partid și de stat în timpul regimului comunist*, Anuarul IICCR, vol. III (Iași: Editura Polirom, 2008), 20.

42. Ștefan Bosomitu, op.cit., 20. See also Jean-Marie Domenach, *Propaganda politică* (Bucharest: Editura Institutului European, 2004), 37–38.

43. Ștefan Bosomitu, op.cit., 20.

44. Idem, 20.

45. Ibid., 20.

46. in ANIC, CC of the RCP Collection, Propaganda and Agitation Section, file no. 16/1950, 34.

47. Idem, 35.

48. For privacy reasons, we only consider the activist's prototype cadre file to be of importance (entry B/982).

49. Ion Zainea, "Propagandiștii Partidului Comunist. Câteva portrete" in *Identități sociale, culturale, etnice și religioase* (eds.) Cosmin Budeancă, Florin Olteanu, IICCMER (Iași: Editura Polirom, 2015), 99–100.

50. "Pregătirea propagandiștilor-sarcină de mare răspundere," in *Scânteia* of July 12, 1951, 1.

51. Idem, 1.

52. Ibid., 1.

53. The teachers (especially from rural areas) and teachers in educational establishments were recruited into the propaganda apparatus and took place there according to a strict phased program that included: selection, training, distribution, and control.

54. *Propuneri de măsuri pentru îmbunătățirea propagandei de partid*, in ANIC, CC of the RCP Collection, Propaganda and Agitation Section, file no. 1/1961, 168.

55. Ioan Beu, *Perfecționarea continuă a pregătirii lectorilor și propagandiștilor* in *Propaganda de partid la nivelul sarcinilor actuale* (Bucharest: Editura Politică, 1967), 72.

56. "Cursurile pentru propagandiști," in *Munca de partid*, Year I, no. 1/1957, 38.

57. Gr. Cotovschi, "Rolul propagandistului în educarea comunistă a membrilor de partid," in *Lupta de clasă*, Series V, Year XXXII, no. 11, November 1952, 70–81.

58. Gr. Cotovschi, op.cit., 71.

59. *Stenograma ședinței cu tovarășii secretari și șefi de secție ai comitetelor regionale de partid, secretari cu probleme de propagandă ai comitetelor regionale a UTM și alți tovarăși care lucrează în domeniul propagandei și a culturii*, in ANIC, CC of the RCP Collection, Propaganda and Agitation Section, file no. 22/1961, 102.

60. Ștefan Partenie, "Răspunderile lectorilor și ale propagandiștilor," in *În ajutorul propagandiștilor*, Year VII, no. 10/1968, 13.

61. Ştefan Bogoi, "Pregătirea lectorilor şi propagandiştilor," in op.cit., Year VI, no. 1/1967, 14.

62. "Metodica muncii propagandistului," in *În ajutorul propagandistului*, Year VIII, no. 11/1971, 90.

63. Cristina Preutu, op.cit., 118.

64. At the same time, in addition to the specific bibliographies in the specialized magazines, there were also articles related to the role of the propagandist in other publications, such as *Lupta de clasă, Scânteia, Scânteia tineretului, Probleme de filosofie, Munca de partid*, and so forth.

65. *Informaţie cu privire la revista "În ajutorul propagandiştilor,"* in ANIC, CC of the RCP Collection, Propaganda and Agitation Section, file no. 7/1964, 21.

66. Cristina Preutu, op.cit., 118. For details on this, see "Metodica muncii propagandistului," in *În ajutorul propagandistului*, Year VIII, no. 11/1971, 90.

67. In actuality, some of the propagandists would send delegates to these meetings to represent them and to report back on what was discussed. Cristina Preutu, op.cit., 121. For details, see also *Sinteza problemelor reieşite din rapoartele instructorilor teritoriali*, in ANIC, CC of the RCP Collection, Propaganda and Agitation Section, file no. 4/1966, 17.

68. As a rule, the lesson was to outline those theoretical aspects that were most closely related to the Party organization's current tasks and needed to appear forceful in both shape and content. It was also supposed to unmask, with as much virulence as possible, bourgeois ideology and imperialistic theories; scale up revolutionary vigilance among the attendees; and teach them how to recognize their class enemies. A noted feature of such classes was the infusion of hatred toward any alternative other than the cause of Communism, which contrasted heavily with the cultivation of love and devotion toward the Socialist regime.

69. The seminar leader incited the students to criticize each other, and even to perform self-criticism in front of their colleagues, exposing their own gaps and shortcomings and, thus, benefiting from advice in improving their activity. Of course, nothing was said about the fact that this criticism and self-criticism worked only at the lower levels of the Party and not in the upper hierarchy. In other words, even among propagandists, the hierarchical criticism was only from top to bottom. For more details on this, see Gr. Cotovschi, op.cit., 77.

70. Cătălin Strat, "Tehnici de propagandă comunistă în România. II. 1961–1962," in *Arhivele totalitarismului*, Year VII, no. 24–25, 3–4/1999, 219.

71. *Despre arta agitatorului de a vorbi cu masele* (Bucharest: Editura Politică, 1960), 5.

72. *Referat cu privire la îmbunătăţirea muncii politice de masă* in ANIC, CC of the RCP Collection, Propaganda and Agitation Section, file no. 3/1963, 164.

73. Idem, 56.

74. Cristina Preutu, op.cit., 139.

75. For details on this, see *Lecţii pentru agitatori* (Cluj: Întreprinderea Poligrafică, 1960).

76. *Despre arta agitatorului de a vorbi cu masele* (Bucharest: Editura Politică, 1960), 6.

77. Alexandru Ştefan, "Rolul activ al agitatorului," in *Munca de Partid*, Year XVI, no. 1/1973, 54.

78. Eugen Denize, op.cit., 60–61.

79. Holidays such as May 1st, May 9th, August 23rd, November 7th, and December 30th.

80. The words and expressions of the propaganda slogans had to be meaningful, evocative, and expressive. It was also recommended that the verbs incite to action; indicative mood—person-centered; imperative mood—suggesting involvement, conditional mood—call to emotions; and infinitive—rendering continuity. It was not advisable to use neologisms or words that exceeded the students' understanding.

81. *Despre agitaţia vizuală* (Bucharest: Editura PMR, 1950), 17.

82. *Procesul verbal şi stenograma şedinţei Biroului Organizatoric din ziua de 22 martie 1952*, in AMR, microfilm fund, r.AS1–406, c.47–52.

83. The meeting addressed the fact that visual agitation is an important means of mobilizing and educating the masses and that, at the same time, it is an integral part of mass political agitation that "educates people in the spirit of love for the Romanian People's Republic, the Party, and the Soviet Union and which mobilizes the masses in the fight against the American and British imperialists." The successes of the visual agitation were also reviewed: "the number of political posters and their circulation increased, numerous photo-exhibitions, photo-newspapers were published and the dissemination of visual agitation materials improved. . . . its content is more combative," but the failures were not forgotten either, as there were considered to be "serious shortcomings that must be quickly liquidated" because "the visual agitation materials used by Party organizations such as portraits and panels were oftentimes at a low ideological and artistic level." For details on this, see *Procesul verbal şi stenograma şedinţei Biroului Organizatoric din ziua de 22 martie 1952*, in AMR, microfilm fund, r.AS1–406, c.47.

84. For details on this, see Alexandru Golianu's *Metodica studiului politic-ideologic. Criterii şi modalităţi ale organizării şi desfăşurării învăţământului de partid şi propagandei prin conferinţe* (Bucharest: Editura Politică, 1972), and *Metodica propagandei politice: studii, sinteze, experienţe* (coord) Gheorghe Aradavoaice (Bucharest: Editura Militară, 1987).

85. The Party no longer trusted anyone other than its own people and its own printing press, meaning that all political posters, slogans, and every single other visual propaganda material had to be put out by the Romanian Workers' Party Publishing House. Locally, the control of visual agitation was assigned to commissions that had the obligation of directing visual agitation anywhere in their range of action, which is to say in schools, lecture halls, and institutions. These commissions were simultaneously responsible for decorating for each and all public occasions, controlling and replacing, if the situation called for it, visual agitation material. In fact, articles in *Scânteia* gave excessive praise to this kind of propaganda. For details on this, see the editorial "Pentru ridicarea nivelului agitaţiei vizuale," in *Scânteia* of 18 May 1952, 1.

86. "Să dezvoltăm puternic agitaţia politică de masă," in *Scânteia* of 17 February 1949, 1.

87. Eugen Denize, op.cit., 66–67.

88. For more details on this, see *Lecţii pentru cursurile cu agitatorii* (Bucharest: Editura PMR, 1952), 6.

89. Cristina Preutu, op.cit., 143.

90. *Instrucţiuni cu privire la învăţământul de partid şi propaganda prin conferinţe*, in ANIC, CC of the RCP Collection, Propaganda and Agitation Section, file no. 20/1971, 12.

91. Cristina Preutu, op.cit., 122.

92. Nicu Dumitrescu, "Activitatea de pregătire a lectorilor" in *În ajutorul propagandiştilor*, Year VII, no. 10/1968, 36.

93. Cristina Preutu, op.cit., 131.

94. Based on archival documents, historian Cristina Preutu notes that in 1980 there were 613 recorded lecturers of the CC of the RCP: 264 teachers at Ştefan Gheorghiu Academy and other institutions of higher learning, 68 scientific researchers from the Academy of Social and Political Sciences and from other research facilities, and 45 press workers. For additional details on this, see ANIC, CC of the RCP Collection, Propaganda and Agitation Section, file no. 2/1979, 9.

95. ANIC, CC of the RCP fund, Organizational Section, file no. 30/1976, 20.

96. Nicu Dumitrescu, op.cit., 36.

97. Cristina Preutu, op.cit., 126.

98. *Informare* (Informative note), in ANIC, CC of the RCP Collection, Propaganda and Agitation Section, file no. 7/1972, 2.

99. *Stenograma şedinţei cu sectorul de agitaţie din Secţia de Propagandă şi Agitaţie a CC al PMR din ziua de 22 martie 1950* (Verbatim report of the meeting with the CC of the RWP Propaganda and Agitation Section on March 22, 1950), in AMR, microfilm fund, r.AS1–1517, c.1–6.

100. Idem, c.1.

101. *Stenograma Şedinţei de raportare a instructorilor teritoriali din 1 martie 1968* [A verbatim report of the reporting session for field instructors on March 1, 1969], in ANIC, CC of the RCP Collection, Propaganda and Agitation Section, file no. 1/1968, 5.

102. On February 8, 1972 there was a new meeting attended by Nicolae Ceauşescu and leaders of the Propaganda and Agitation Section with the purpose of reorganizing the Section, which had up until then functioned in accordance with regulations issued after 1952. The main issues facing the Section also went up for debate, with the more urgent one being precisely the lack of new regulations to reflect the current issues that were facing propaganda.

103. *Stenograma întâlnirii tovarăşului Nicolae Ceauşescu cu conducerea Secţiei de Propagandă a CC al PCR din data de 8 februarie 1972* (A Verbatim Report of Comrade Nicolae Ceauşescu's Meeting with the Propaganda Section of the CC of the RCP on February 8, 1972), in ANIC, CC of the RCP Collection, Propaganda and Agitation Section, file no. 11/1972, 2–5.

104. The Propaganda and Agitation Section had no financial autonomy before that year, and therefore, it lacked the means of support to function in mass political work. For details, see Cristina Preutu, op.cit., 72.

105. ANIC, CC of the RCP Collection, Propaganda and Agitation Section, file no. 11/1972, 5.

106. Cristina Preutu, op.cit., 76.

107. *Propuneri de măsuri pentru îmbunătăţirea propagandei de partid*, în ANIC, CC of the RCP Collection, Propaganda and Agitation Section, file no. 1/1961, 165.

108. ANIC, CC of the RCP Collection, Propaganda and Agitation Section, file no. 20/1971, 11.

109. *Stenograma şedinţei cu tovarăşii secretari şi şefi de secţie ai comitetelor regionale de partid, secretari cu probleme de propagandă ai comitetelor regionale şi alţi tovarăşi care lucrează în domeniul propagandei şi culturii* (Verbatim Report of the Meeting with Comrade Secretaries and Sectional Leaders of the Regional Party Committees, Propaganda Secretaries of the Regional Committees and Other Comrades Active in the Areas of Propaganda and Culture), în ANIC, CC of the RCP Collection, Propaganda and Agitation Section, file no. 22/1961, 102.

110. The magazine, *În ajutorul propagandistului*, made this observation: "in order to reach its objectives, Party propaganda needs more than reciters of texts, it needs lecturers and propagandists capable of free, competent, empassioned exposition of issues pertaining to Party policies, of making them well understood, of being able to answer any question that the audience may address." For more details, see the article "Ce împiedică realizarea unui studiu activ, interesant," in *În ajutorul propagandistului*, Issue 11/1968, 8.

111. For more details on regions, see Cristina Preutu, op.cit., 114.

112. Idem, 114.

113. "Introducere în practica anchetelor sociologice," in *Îndrumătorul cultural*, Year XXI, no. 4/1968, 36–37.

114. Idem, 125.

115. Cristina Preutu, op.cit., 124.

116. *Stenograma şedinţei cu instructorii teritoriali ai secţiei de propagandă şi agitaţie al CC al PCR din 5–6 august 1965*, in ANIC, CC of RCP Collection, Propaganda and Agitation Section, file no. 35/1965, 6.

Chapter 5

The Ideological Turn in Higher Education

Further Insights from the Romanian Case

We have already seen how, once the Communist Party took over Romania with the help of the Soviet Army at the end of the 1940s, the first step in the institutionalization of the new system was to go beyond the mere politicization. Political control over an organization or institution is one thing. Institutionalization of indoctrination is something different, taking things to a new and different level. Universities were at the forefront of this process. In Romania's case, the signal in this respect was the introduction of mandatory Marxism-Leninism courses and classes in the curriculum. In a 1948 meeting of the Propaganda and Agitation Section, Mihail Roller—quoted by the official publication *Lupta de Clasa* (*Class Warfare*)—asserted, "We must introduce the study of Marxism and Leninism in our universities. Indeed, some of them have already introduced it, but the way it is taught is very much wanting and compromises our very principles."[1] As a result, during the October 7, 1948, meeting of the Politburo, an official document called the "Structure of the university-level course on dialectical materialism and historical materialism for the academic year 1948–1949" was drafted.[2] The document had four sections: the first dedicated to dialectical materialism and the worldview of the Marxist-Leninist Party; the second concerned Marxist dialectics; the third section covered Marxist philosophical materialism and the forms of social consciousness; and the fourth focused on Socialism and Communism as one topic. After its introduction in the 1948–1949 university curriculum, the mandatory Marxism-Leninism course was constantly developed and extended. In its first year, it was taught at forty-four chairs (i.e., 133 full and associate professors and 223 assistant professors and lecturers teaching

29,324 students). In the next academic year (1949–1950), it was extended to 178 chairs of social sciences (i.e., 181 full and associate professors and 290 assistant professors and lecturers teaching 40,000 students).[3]

The same *Lupta de Clasă* article also described the objective of teaching Marxism-Leninism, namely to educate each and every higher education graduate into becoming "a conscious builder of Socialism." Disciplines such as natural sciences, engineering, and so forth, were also targeted, but frontline to these developments and directly impacted by the personal policy were, obviously, all the disciplines having something to do with social, cultural, and intellectual life. According to the new perspective, the teaching of the social sciences was meant to instill in the students "love for the Popular Republic of Romania and the Romanian Workers' Party, the great Soviet Union and its peoples, the great Communist Party, and the great leader of peoples, comrade Stalin."[4] Consequently, propagandist professors were assigned to all areas of higher education—the humanities (literary studies, philosophy, history), the sciences, or the arts (fine arts, film, music, theater)—as the curriculum provided mandatory scientific materialism courses in all educational cycles. But that, in turn, required large training programs of the much-needed professors of scientific materialism. The national structure described in the previous chapters was thus starting to emerge.

The frequent meetings of high-level Party officials to discuss the implementation of Marxism-Leninism in universities reflected the importance they attached to this initiative. From the very beginning, one of the key topics discussed was the problem of the level and performance of the ideological cadres. Their competence and their commitment to their responsibilities posed major challenges, as the universities constantly reported their shortcomings and their lack of training or awareness of the specific circumstances they had to adjust to in their approaches and methods. The complaints concerned mostly the social sciences. As the documents show, it was there that the greatest number of problems were found—either due to professors straying from the Party line or their disregard of the relevant publications. Marrying scientific materialism as a dogmatic ideology with scientific materialism as a scientific paradigm was not an easy task. Accomplishing that mission in the field of social sciences was a real challenge. We will return to the issue of social sciences later.

The range of activity of the ideological worker in higher education was vast. The mission was extended beyond standard academia. For instance, in addition to basic indoctrination and rewriting historical discourse, the Propaganda Section also aimed to reeducate the older generations of writers and—with the help of the ideological cadres—train the new generations of prose writers, disconnecting them from the past and national history tradition. The Mihai Eminescu School of Literature was intended to produce such novelists, but, as shown by archival documents, even at such an elite unit, the professors did not always meet the ideological requirements. On February 8, 1951, a meeting was held to analyze the School's activity, concluding that

> Despite of all the achievements, some serious shortcomings surfaced. The history of Romanian literature, one of the main curriculum subjects, was taught superficially, in an objectivist manner, and without passion. Some lectures even included hostile ideas. . . . The School's administration failed to adequately supervise the classes, as they deemed it a sufficient guarantee that said classes were taught by faculty members of the Chair of History of Romanian Literature at Parhon University.[5]

In the summer of 1952, instructors and Party activists, whose duty was to ensure the "ideological purity" of University of Bucharest undergraduates, were sent on site to check the truth of the statements in the undergraduates' mandatory autobiographies and in other records—yet another task of the "ideological worker." These verifications were conducted in the context of a so-called *deviation to the right* (i.e., one of the many episodes of real or imagined opposition to the Communist regime that troubled the life of the Faculty of Philosophy in Bucharest). The tensions were felt by both the undergraduates and the faculty.[6]

Later, during the 1956 student protests,[7] the activists assigned to education were instructed to prevent, discourage, denounce, unveil, and counteract "hostile manifestations," and they were called upon—along with Party activists—to surveil student gatherings. They were also assigned the task to nip in the bud any protest initiatives, making sure that young people's free time was occupied with various meetings and activities.[8] It is important to reemphasize that this vast range of activities and responsibilities required working systematically together with the State apparatus, the Communist Party, and the political police. That was not an accident but a feature of the system.

In this respect, a key for understanding the institutionalization of indoctrination was the national youth political organization, the Union of Working Youth (Uniunea Tineretului Muncitor—UTM),[9] which played a significant role in the politicizing of education at all levels. "The Party's main assistant in the effort to educate the youth in schools," the UTM was supposed to lead the youth toward "the spirit of love and commitment to the cause of the working class, the cause of building socialism, in the spirit of boundless love for and trust in the Soviet Union, the Homeland of triumphant socialism."[10] UTM[11] membership—which required a stringent process of vetting and was based strictly on referrals from senior Communists—was a fast track to the higher levels of the social ladder, as it came with opportunities for comfortable jobs in the administration, education, or the army. To become a UTM member,[12] the person had to be over fourteen years old, while the upper age limit varied over time. In 1989, any person under thirty could become a member of the Union of Communist Youth (UTC).[13]

A ceremony was held on being accepted, and the organization worked as the antechamber to Party membership. The number of UTM members grew gradually, from 20 percent in 1950 to the vast majority of young Romanians in the late 1980s.[14] The UTM leadership consisted of a Central Committee that elected the Bureau, the Secretariat, and the General Secretary. Mirroring the Party's pyramid organizational structure, UTM had organizations in every school and institution. In addition, it had its own school, the "Filimon Sârbu School," founded in 1949, with approximately one hundred graduates annually as well as an entire network of training courses or specializations within the Party schools. There, they trained cadres in the history of the CPSU,[15] Romanian Workers' Party (RWP) and world history, dialectical materialism, political economy, techniques of organization, and propaganda. The classes followed a fixed schedule, and the cadres attended lectures, clubs, meetings, and "coaching" sessions. Filimon Sârbu School was closed in 1958, for reasons of inefficiency, and the training of young cadres was assigned to the Ștefan Gheorghiu Academy.[16]

To give a sense of the significance of UTM, it is sufficient to note that some of those who headed the UTM/UTC included Ion Iliescu (1967–1971), Dan Marțian (1971–1972), Pantelimon Găvănescu (1979–1983), Nicu Ceaușescu (1983–1987), and Ioan Toma (1987–1989).[17] In time, the UTC became increasingly bureaucratic, as the fervor of the first Communist decade waned. Yet, within the structure of the Communist regime, UTM, later UTC, was a genuine lever for control and surveillance of young persons. Apart from their usual methods, including ideological agitation, organizing students to work on building sites, and paying homage to the leaders at rallies,[18] those who worked with students—especially high-ranking ones in the UTM—used a system of benefits and rewards that were very tempting for young people: jobs in the city after graduation, an apartment in a block of flats, and free trips. Therefore, it is hard to understand the magnitude and structure of the indoctrination operation if one focuses strictly on the ideological worker and their organizations. Once one studies them in operation, one must see them as part of an even larger and more complex structure in which the Youth Section of the Communist Party was pivotal.

THE SYSTEM REVEALED THROUGH ITS OPERATIONS: AMBITIONS AND LIMITS

Given the resources and manpower put behind the operation, it is surprising how many organizational and operational blunders and lacunae one may reveal through a cursory post-factum scrutiny. Let's take the evaluation function as an example. It is interesting that, seen in the light of the archives, the public and official assessments of the success of its institutions and operations seemed rather arbitrary and, in a sense, not very realistic. Such situations—which today we may recognize as textbook mistakes of organization and management—were far from isolated cases. For instance, as historian Cristian Vasile pointed out in his analysis, the number of students involved in the art brigades and cultural mass activities was used by the Central Committee of the RCP during their visits in the universities as a criterion in itself to assess the improvements in the educational process and, especially, the politico-educational work of the ideological cadres among the students.[19] In his book, Vasile quotes the findings of the committee that assessed the activity of Cluj-Napoca universities over a period of six weeks: "A large number of students participate in amateur art groups that perform in front of their fellow students and art lovers. We would like to mention here the rich cultural mass activities of the Student House of Culture, engaging a large number of university students."

One should not be misled by such naïve and propagandistic assessments for public purposes. A stream of pragmatism—sometimes taking brutal forms—was always present as a countervailing and, in most cases, dominating force. In the search for effective indoctrination, the regime created an entire line of publications targeting students. These publications offer a case in point, being arenas where the countervailing force collided. Created to be explicit propaganda instruments, such ventures repeatedly became vehicles for undermining the official line. The student press was recurrently a cause for concern for the nomenklatura and the high-ranking Party bureaucrats. In the summer of 1968, Paul Niculescu-Mizil urged the Party secretaries in charge of propaganda to make sure political issues were central to the youth's activity:

> Because, dear comrades, we do encounter some manifestations . . . let us call them [manifestations] of a-political, poor commitment to the cause. . . . Not long ago, I met with comrades working in the youth press, and it was with dissatisfaction that I found that our legitimate claim—which we clearly stated—that our newspapers for the youth should be much more active, engaging . . . was understood as a justification to turn, for instance, *Scânteia tineretului* into a (science and culture) magazine like *Magazin*.[20]

There was yet another reason for the Party leaders' dissatisfaction, namely the existence of a group of contributors who repeatedly expressed views and attitudes opposed to the official Party line. At the same time, among officials in the CC of the RCP, there was a perception that politically oriented newspaper articles had been replaced by nonconformist interviews.[21]

> Scânteia tineretului is the ultimate political newspaper; it is the newspaper of a political, revolutionary organization. Together with the comrades from the Viaţa studenţească, we compared this publication with student publications from capitalist states, only to conclude that the capitalist publications were much more political in content than our magazine Viaţa studenţească. . . . Regardless of its profile, each and every publication must participate in the debate on the major national and foreign politics issues placed on the agenda of our country.[22]

In addition to the sanctions against *Viaţa studenţească* and *Scânteia tineretului*, at the end of 1968, the editorial team at *Amfiteatru* magazine was simply disbanded.

In 1968, Leonte Răutu, member of the Secretariat of the Central Committee and later the Vice Prime Minister of Education, made it a point to praise the spirit of vigilance of the Press Directorate propagandists, while at the same time criticizing the ideological unit of the host university and its competence:

> Babeş-Bolyai University prepared the first issue of the University's student magazine (*Echinox*), announcing for this first programmatic issue three materials that claimed to reevaluate three figures. But all three of them had been prominent promoters of the (right wing) Legionary ideology in our country. This is inadmissible; it moreover points to a failure in choosing the supervisors of this magazine and in exercising control over them since, unfortunately, the publication of the magazine was prevented not by the County Committee, or the University Committee, or the UTC Committee, but by the Press Directorate representative.[23]

All of the above revealed one of the most interesting features of all these institutionalization efforts. They were never considered up to the task. They were never considered enough. They requested an ongoing reasserting and revamping effort on behalf of regime's authorities. For instance, in the early months of 1969, the Propaganda Section of the CC of the RCP and the Ministry of Education jointly held a series of meetings with faculty members from the social sciences departments of major Romanian universities: Bucharest, Iaşi, Cluj-Napoca, Timişoara, Târgu Mureş and Craiova.[24] The purpose of these meetings was to train the faculty members[25] and, consequently, to "improve" the way Marxism-Leninism was taught. The ultimate goal was "to instill the materialist worldview in the student."[26]

And thus, we see, more than 20 years after taking over the country, that such a basic task was still a major priority. The "New Man" did not seem to be able to emerge and function autonomously and required an ongoing effort of the apparatus. Ever after two decades of strict ideological enforcement and indoctrination, the results were still rather uncertain.

The previous chapters have shown how the very content and emphasis of propaganda changed overtime by trying to adjust in effective ways to circumstances and priorities. The de-Stalinization process that ensued throughout the Soviet Bloc countries after Khrushchev's report also had an echo and impact in Romania. In late October 1956, in several Romanian towns, and especially in university cities such as Bucharest, Cluj-Napoca, Iași, and Timișoara, the students organized actual protests. In Timișoara, where protests initially focused on the bad quality of food in the canteens, student protesters eventually radicalized their demands, pointing the finger at the curricula. The Romanian Hungarians in Timișoara—a city with a large Hungarian-speaking population—organized rallies in support of the ongoing anti-Communist revolution in Budapest at the time. To avoid a situation similar to that of Hungary, Romanian authorities, in addition to suppressing the movement, put pressure on the Union of the Working Youth (UTM) to hold several meetings to explain the events unfolding in Budapest to the students.[27]

Then there was the issue of competence and quality. Throughout the 1960s, academia continued to be dominated by the poorly trained promoters of Marxism-Leninism of the 1950s. The issue was a major concern and required the direct intervention of the top leadership of the Party. Ongoing efforts to fix that problem were made starting from the top of the political pyramid. In 1963, Athanase Joja, a Communist and Stalinist since the interwar years, was relieved of his position as president of the Romanian Academy and replaced by Ilie Murgulescu, a former scholarship student in Germany in the 1930s. In 1966, the position was assumed by to Miron Nicolescu, who held a PhD in mathematics from the Sorbonne and mastered the Western methods of doing scholarship research and training.[28]

The way the problem was seen by the decision makers may be illustrated by the following excerpts from two verbatim reports of meetings between the Party leadership and the representatives of the propagandists from fields of "research" and "culture and arts." Quoting from the verbatim report of the May 7, 1965, meeting between Party and State high officials and scientists, let us note that the Party and the State were represented at the highest possible level by Nicolae Ceaușescu, Chivu Stoica, Alexandru Bârlădeanu, Emil Bodnăraș, Leonte Răutu, Paul Niculescu-Mizil, Gheorghe Gaston Marin, and Gogu Rădulescu. The indoctrination and politization functions underlie the entire discussion: "Nicolae Ceaușescu: Esteemed comrades, . . . Our people expect from scientists to increase their contribution to the progress of the socialist construction. There is no greater pride for all of us than to raise up to the tasks assigned to us by our Party."[29]

A few days later, on May 19, 1965, another meeting was held, this time between Party and State high officials and major cultural and artistic personalities. Nicolae Ceaușescu, Chivu Stoica, Ion Gheorghe Maurer, Gheorghe Apostol, Emil Bodnăraș, Leonte Răutu, and Ștefan Voitec attended the meeting, representing the Party and the State, along with the heads of artistic associations and cultural institutions and faculty members from art universities. Propaganda and indoctrination are again, the central priority: "Comrade Nicolae Ceaușescu: As of late, a number of publications were created, with more to be established in the future. Meeting with other leaders of the Party yesterday, we thought and talked about creating a literary magazine addressing the youth and the students who have yet to join the ranks of professional writers."[30]

To make sure that the message of the Party was best conveyed in the universities with a high number of Hungarian- or German-speaking students, propagandist professors were encouraged to hold their lectures in those languages too. A report on the issues discussed in a meeting between the RCP leadership and intellectuals belonging to national minorities and on the solutions to some of the problems raised by the participants stated the following:

> Point 3—To increase the number of propaganda lectures in German and Hungarian . . . Point 11—To improve the teaching of the social sciences in higher education programs. Dialectical and historical materialism courses are to be offered also in Hungarian at Babeș-Bolyai University in Cluj-Napoca and other higher education institutions.[31]

In brief, the institutionalization of the propaganda and indoctrination was a never-ending story, always top-down, emerging from the highest levels of the Party–State, always in search of an optimal solution that continued to be elusive to the bitter end of the regime in 1989. The solutions emerging from these recurring high-level meetings were never fully satisfactory. New formulas, many of them absurd or amusing to us today, were tried at all levels. At one point, even merely changing the location of the activity was considered important. Mircea Flonta, freshly reappointed professor at Bucharest's Faculty of Philosophy, in the mid-1960s, recalls:

> In 1966–1967, political education was done differently in the departments of social sciences. Instead of being taught on site, in the university, people had to go to the municipal Party office. Once a month, on Mondays, if I remember correctly, lectures and discussions were held evenings and afternoons at the municipal Party office.[32]

Again and again, new challenges confronted the system in its never-ending tinkering, reforming, and adjusting to "the realities." According to historian Adam Burakowsky, the student protests on Christmas night 1968 had a decisive influence on the authorities' policy regarding students.[33] In the debate that followed, the analysis of the events of December 25, 1968, identified poor ideological training, which was found to be lacking in many respects, as the main culprit for the students' protests and dissatisfaction. Proposals were subsequently made to improve youth ideological training, but concerns about the effects of the liberalization granted in the mid-1960s loomed large in the Meeting of the Executive Committee on December 25. At the meeting, with the secretaries in charge of propaganda in late 1968, Paul Niculescu-Mizil stated:

> Unfortunately, we sometimes let things get out of hand . . . the Student House of Culture's program turned into a full-blown religious program, connected with the celebration of Christmas, and all this with the approvals of the Communist Youth Union organization and the student organization, with the knowledge of the Party organization there and of the leadership of the higher education institute, etc.[34]

This meeting was an occasion for criticism and self-criticism concerning the authorities' "lack of vigilance" and "poor ideological guidance" of "the student population." Nicolae Ceaușescu himself identified and criticized the main culprits: the secretary of the Central Committee of the Romanian Communist Party, Vasile Patilineț; the Mayor of Bucharest, Dumitru Popa; the Minister of Youth; and the higher officials of the Propaganda Section. The episode reveals how the institutional structure of responsibility is seen by the ultimate leader of the country and, at the same time, supports the thesis regarding the embeddedness and functional dependence of the propaganda institutions on the State and Party apparatus. The Christmas events also gave Leonte Răutu cause to remark that

> The efforts to provide students with ideological training are in most instances, though not all, plagued by many weaknesses. The Ministry of Education received harsh criticisms from the Party leadership and from our propaganda section in charge of education for the obvious deficiencies of our leadership in the ideological domain and the educational process. . . . These events reflect a series of shortcomings in our educational activity.

As one could see, leadership in the ideological domain was recurrently considered to have failed its mission. A strong pattern is thus emerging. As historian Cristian Vasile pointed out,[35] as a consequence of these events, the authorities adopted a set of stricter measures aiming to increase the importance of political guidance, increase ideological control, implement a restrictive reading of the education law or even amend it, and restrict student events. Surely, they were not afraid of the situation getting out of hand and turning into actual protests—as it had happened in Czechoslovakia—but they decided to preemptively tighten the political grip at all levels of education. Although not a major event in itself, the 1968 Christmas student incident prompted the leadership to take an even higher interest in the students' ideological training.[36]

In the aftermath of these events, a middle management cadre in the structure of the national propaganda apparatus in higher education reported:

> Adapting their methods to the requirements of working with the studious youth, the University of Craiova communist student's associations made outstanding progress in developing the students' socialist consciousness, helping them to internalize their patriotic duties, improving their politico-ideological education. . . . To this end, in addition to the discussions centered on the Party and State documents and political informative notes, with support from the chair and cabinet of social sciences, a major contribution was the advanced politico-ideological training designed by the Executive Committee of UASCR [Union of Romanian Communist Student Associations] to cater for each year and cohort of study, with a view to integrating the whole mass of students. The training focused, first and foremost, on the study of the works authored by the General Secretary of the Romanian Communist Party and on the Party's Program, and, second, on organizing clubs to discuss numerous current issues of national and international politics and ideology. Craiova students showed their politico-ideological proficiency, as well as their increased interest in the Party's politics and the prominent figure of its experienced leader, comrade Nicolae Ceaușescu.[37]

Thus, the evidence emerging from the archives backs up the notion that the institutionalization of indoctrination and propaganda in higher education was an open process, challenged at all junctions despite the formidable apparatus of monitoring, control, and repression used in its support. Human and material resources were poured into the process. New approaches and methods were tried. Old approaches were revamped. In all these, the problem of the "cadre" was always outstanding. Given these circumstances, the idea to convert almost as many professors as possible into scientific materialism indoctrination trainers had to come to the fore, sooner or later. That was, in fact, a recurring theme over the entire duration of the regime.

That being said, it is important to note that not all university professors incorporated or taught scientific materialism in their classes willingly. In other words, not all of them chose to be ideological workers—or to temporarily act as such, even if they submitted to the pressure. For instance, historian

Lucian Boia would write in his memoirs how he was forced to become part of the academic propaganda institution: "Regardless of the field of study, all the departments had to teach an Introduction to national history and the Party's history (aimed to educate students in the spirit of patriotism). I had no choice but to teach one of those courses. . . . I did my best to make it a decent one, avoiding to make ideological compromises as much as I could."[38] Needless to add, there were pure propagandists who made successful careers in universities, a fact that later complicated things when it came to disentangling genuine professors and propagandists.

THE SOCIAL SCIENCES ISSUE

We have already noted that at the core of the entire process was the vast domain of the social sciences. In fact, social sciences offer the most complicated and telling case in this respect. The pressure was huge. From two national conferences bringing together all the chairs of social sciences in 1967, the number went up to three such events two years later.[39] To their satisfaction, the political authorities found that the publishing activity of social science professors (increasingly perceived as essential pillars of the propaganda) had improved, as noted by the increased presence of their articles in the pages of central publications.[40] Yet, the same report also criticized both the methodology for teaching social sciences and the content taught, making it a point to emphasize the antithesis between the legacy of pre-1965 politics and the reformist aspirations of the Romanian Communist Party in 1968:

> The revolutionary nature of Marxist philosophy was overlooked, along with its transforming role, which is . . . fundamental to our Party's politics. Moreover, the conditions of today's capitalism . . . are insufficiently discussed, causing the persistence of confusions about today's society among the students . . . Discrepancies continue to exist between the demands of our developing socialist society and the activity of the Marxist-Leninist teaching staff, between the scientific, ideological and educational resources available to these chairs and their actual contribution to solving social, economic and political problems, as well as to the intellectual life of institutes and universities on the national ideological front. No real action was taken to instill an uninterrupted, strict combative spirit against any leftover religious ideas . . . to clear up any confusions that might persist in the students' minds.[41]

Unsurprisingly, the report's conclusion was that because of "insufficient dedication of the staff teaching Marxism-Leninism to shaping the civic character of future professionals . . . the chairs of social sciences must take adequate measures to improve their ideological and educational activities."[42] The objective was to increase the contribution of "the chairs of social sciences to explaining the scientific foundations of the Party's politics, helping students internalize the materialist-dialectical worldview, and training them to become active militants for socialist and communist ideals and to firmly reject idealistic, mystical and backward theories."[43]

Comparing the social sciences scientific content and curricula as taught in higher education institutions with the terminology in which the scientific activity was couched—"ideological front," "struggle of ideas," "active militantism," "ideological combat," "revolutionary nature," "uninterrupted, strict combative spirit"—historian Corina Pălășan concluded that the proclaimed "1968 reform" did not question the Marxist-Leninist dogma of the Romanian Communist Party and, in fact, was just a continuation and revamping of the traditional indoctrination and propaganda line.[44] This conclusion is reinforced by the restated official position regarding the mission of the Academy,[45] the universities, and the research institutes. That mission was, again, less about watching over the quality of the academic environment and more about making sure—via the cadres assigned to universities, of course—that everybody there complied with the ideology and fulfilled their "ideologizing" and militant role essential to the functioning of the Communist regime. The idea was that the professor/researcher served primarily as a propagandist under the direct control of the Party. This speaks about both the limits of the process of liberalization that Romania experienced in the late 1960s and the discrepancy between the rhetoric of liberalization and the rhetoric of the indoctrination and propaganda apparatus.

As mentioned earlier, the ideological workers in tertiary education were trained better than all the other propagandists in the education system. They would attend the best Party schools (out of which the Ștefan Gheorghiu Academy became the dominant force), and their activities would be regularly assessed and closely supervised by the highest offices in the state. At the same time, compared to other education institutions, universities were more likely to foster views that clashed with scientific materialism. Faced with occasional student protests, the university ideological cadres had to become much more finely attuned to the psychology of the group that they trained. Thus, in their training, the debates, seminars and symposiums replaced the field trips, visual propaganda, and mass festivities on which the cadres working in the secondary cycle (high schools) relied to build their approaches and tasks. The future propagandist cadres were recruited from among the students and graduates who showed a strong interest in the politics of the regime. The propagandist professor played a particularly important role in such cases, watching closely to identify which students had an inclination for politics, regardless of their field of study, not discriminating between the social sciences, medicine, sciences, or engineering.

In the context of our discussion, the fact that social sciences, broadly defined, and humanities represented such an important element in the regime's strategy is very telling. In his biography of Miron Constantinescu,[46] historian Ștefan Bosomitu included a substantial subchapter on the Academy of Social and Political Sciences (ASPS)[47] created in 1970 with the purpose of establishing "the main directions for development and the priorities in the social sciences" by "matching them more actively with the requirements of building socialism and understanding the social realities and present-day scientific progress."[48] On July 9, 1971, Nicolae Ceaușescu himself chaired the Protocol of the Central Committee of the Romanian Communist Party's Secretariat meeting concerning the improvement of politico-ideological and cultural-artistic activities, making the following proposals, which reveal the magnitude of the involvement of the Party in the field of social and political sciences:

> Point 5: Measures will be taken to strengthen the leadership of the Ministry of Education; to restructure the education and the social sciences by creating a separate sector, staffed with Party activists, under the direction of a deputy minister, to run the political and ideological training of both teaching staff and students, under the direct control of the Central Committee of the Romanian Communist Party. A dedicated collective will be set up to analyze how the social sciences are taught at all levels of education and, in a month's time, to submit proposals to improve the social sciences teaching plans and curricula and the structure of the staff teaching this discipline in the new academic year.
>
> Point 6: Measures will be taken to improve the structure of the Ștefan Gheorghiu Academy of Socio-Political Education and its teaching plans and curricula, as well as student recruitment criteria for the purpose of training the necessary cadres for the Party structures and the ideological field.[49]

The follow-up was swift. On July 16, 1971, the measures developed by the Executive Committee of the Central Committee of the Romanian Communist Party to implement the decisions for the strengthening of politico-ideological and cultural-educational activities are made public.

> In the course of July, measures will be taken to strengthen the leadership of the Ministry of Education; to restructure the education and social sciences directorates by creating a separate sector, staffed with Party activists, under the direction of a deputy minister, to run all the aspects of the political and ideological training of both teaching staff and students, under the direct control of the CC of the RCP.

In practical terms that meant that "a dedicated collective" had to be set up "to analyse how social sciences are taught at all levels of education and, in a month's time, to submit proposals to improve the social sciences teaching plans and curricula and the structure of the staff teaching this discipline in the new academic year." In doing that, those implementing the task had to make sure that Party activists will teach these disciplines. The magnitude of the task is glimpsed from the next directive: "Measures will be established to organize the political and ideological training of the entire teaching staff in the state education system, as well as a centre for training faculty members who teach social sciences (within the Ștefan Gheorghiu Academy)."[50]

The second half of 1971 marked yet another stage in the evolution of the Romanian Communist Party's ideological offensive. Again, the fields of social and political sciences were a major target. And again, we see the same patterns of mobilization and rhetoric targeting social sciences:

> The Ministry of Education will take the necessary steps to improve teaching plans and curricula, with a particular focus on improving the teaching of the social sciences . . . and social sciences teaching plans and curricula will be approved by the Secretariat of the CC of the RCP. At the same time, intense efforts will be made to educate the youth in the spirit of our materialist-dialectical philosophy.[51]

As one may expect in this context, some professionals in the field of the social sciences, propagandists, and, of course, the holders of various positions within the Academy of Social and Political Sciences publicly and enthusiastically endorsed the new ideological program, using unmistakably official rhetoric: "The July 1971 Program stipulates and emphasizes with revolutionary determination some of the main tasks that are naturally ours given our training, talent and profession, as we carry out our work in the field of our socialist education and culture and in the larger sphere of militant intelligence and of the Party's spirit."[52]

Historian Cristina Pălășan analyzed the role of the ideological cadres and the evolution of the social sciences in Iași County, from 1970 to 1971, in order to identify how important these sciences—along with the ideological workers assigned to them—were in the RCP's ideological project.[53] The CC of the RCP travelled to Iași—a major Romanian university center—to evaluate the situation on the ground. Their report concludes that "there are still many things to do to improve the ideological activity here." In an attempt to improve the ideological activity, the Iași[54] County Committee of the RCP organized training sessions for the teaching staff as well as theoretical seminars symposiums, a series of conferences on topics arising from the documents of the Tenth Congress of the RCP, and "discussion clubs in high schools on topics related to the social sciences."[55] At the same time, the distribution of printed media was significantly improved in several rural localities of Iași County, especially in high schools and primary schools.[56]

In his book dealing with change and adaptation in Communist and post-Communist Romania,[57] sociologist Cătălin Augustin Stoica reports an interview with a political sciences graduate regarding the ideological education in the 1970s:

> Party members went through political training. In the last decade, there was only one topic of discussion—the Party, the vital center. There were four meetings every month. A Party meeting, a trade union meeting, a political training meeting, and a meeting of the work collective. We would discuss Nicolae Ceaușescu and Elena Ceaușescu works.[58] The bibliography was made up exclusively of their works too.[59]

And yet, despite all these efforts, things never seemed to get aligned to the ways intended and desired by the authorities and the indoctrination apparatus. A 1973 report on the situation of the teaching of the social sciences in universities by the Propaganda and Agitation Section[60] (re)established the need for "action plans tailored to the needs of chairs and universities, outlines of new curricula for sociology, epistemology, aesthetics, ethics, Marxist axiology, history of philosophy, methodology, and logics of scientific knowledge." Things were once again in need of being shaken and jumpstarted. An attempt was made to diversify the content of courses by introducing subjects such as Socialist democracy, Socialism and religion, the relationship between tradition and progress, the struggle of ideas in contemporary philosophical, and sociopolitical thinking. For those students who had completed the compulsory Marxist-Leninist courses, debates on current RCP ideological issues were offered. Social sciences were again highlighted as venues for the renewed initiatives: "The chairs of social sciences must become the main high-level ideological hubs, the most active drivers of the political and ideological life of higher education institutions."[61]

We have seen that social sciences, broadly defined in Marxist terms, were the main territory of the indoctrination offensive in higher education. And we have also seen that scientific Socialism was the code word. The trick was to emphasize "scientific" and pretend that it all was about "science," suggesting that "Socialism" was just the natural outcome of the "scientific" approach. To doubt "Socialism" was to doubt "science."

Throughout the duration of the regime, one could see this strategy at work again and again. Its importance was reflected even in legislation. For instance, Art. 66 of the Education Law no. 28 of 1978 states that "Higher education must see to it that the students acquire knowledge of the greatest achievements of . . . scientific Socialism, as well as the materialist-dialectical and historical view of the world and life and the ideology of the Party's politics."[62]

Two consequences of these developments are noteworthy. The first was intellectual. More precisely, it was the impact on the function of critical thinking. Entire generations of students, and by implication of future intellectual elites, had to operate in the straitjacket of dogma and had to learn how to coexist and circumvent this condition. Generations of students have formed trying to avoid dogma or, if it was not possible, to coexist with it. Second, in addition to the intellectual dimension, on the institutional front, after 1971, "university professors were integrated in the Party nomenklatura." Shortly after that, the Romanian Academy began to be treated as an annex of the Propaganda and Agitation Section.[63] Needless to say, that was a move that had the consequence of further undermining the credibility of the entire academic community. The line separating science and scholarship from propaganda became even more blurred.[64]

As one may expect, all of the above were met with resistance. Various strategies were employed to avoid engaging Socialist ideology and Party documents and their "wooden language." For instance, at the Institute of Art History, the scholars assigned with political education "would start from ancient Greek democracy, which they analysed thoroughly, and somehow they would never make it to Marx."[65] There are multiple accounts that some of the faculty members in charge of ideological training would sometimes refuse to echo the voice of the regime, without, however, appearing hostile to it. Others simply made it into a routine task, devoid of any life of intellectual relevance.

A GLIMPSE AT THE CADRE FILES

One additional angle to help us to get a sense of how all of the above were instrumentalized is offered by a look at the Human Resources/Cadre departments through their archives. The Human Resources/Cadre departments were crucial in the institutionalization of Communist policy, and, as such, the archives offer a telling glimpse of how all these ongoing struggles of the regime to create a "New Man" and "a new society" were reflected in the lives of the cadres. At the same time, a glimpse at the lives of the cadres through the files offers a series of fresh insights. One striking aspect is the degree of bureaucratization and formalism of the process in all its aspects.

The University of Bucharest Archive (Human Resources collection) holds a number of cadre files belonging to several Bucharest faculty members from different departments. One could study and compare the files of professors working as ideological cadres.[66] The files contain fifty sheets and around twenty photographs, copies of documents, or bibliographical lists organized in the same manner as the standard cadre files described in the previous chapters. The autobiographies, personal data, recommendations, evaluation grades, pledge, reports, or, if the case may be, applications for passports for the purpose of attending international conferences all seem to have been recycled year after year and used the same "wooden language" wording with ever so slight changes in meaning or updates. All the faculty members' applications to attend international conferences were accompanied by passport applications and other documents for that purpose.

The sample cadre file presented below belonged to a propagandist employed at the University of Bucharest, the Cadres Section, as a professor at the Department of Philosophy within the Faculty of History-Philosophy.[67] His file includes his evaluations from 1960 through 1989, some of them titled "reports" but otherwise identical in structure; his personal data; data on his family (wife, children, parents, siblings, wife's parents, and siblings); one pledge; one oath; two autobiographies; and one characterization. He was graded "very good" every time by both the head of the History-Philosophy Department, who oversaw the evaluations, and the committee appointed for that purpose. The file included all of his characterizations and evaluations, spanning from the time when he was an assistant professor up until he became a full professor, many years later. Overall, the annual forms are almost identical, down to the wording, leading one to believe that they were filled out using the older ones as templates, with only the dates being changed. The file also included one pledge:

> I, . . . , in my full capacity of professor, employed with the University of Bucharest, hereby take it upon myself to fulfill my obligations under the contract-pledge to the best of my abilities, to actively militate for the continuous growth of socialist ownership and the rigorous enforcement of Party decisions and national laws throughout my activity. —signed on February 20, 1984.

The documents reveal a numbing bureaucratic routine at work. The evaluations are formulaic and, in fact, devoid of content:

> Given his prestigious teaching and research work, his participation in the ideological and propaganda efforts and in academic life, he stands out as one of our best philosophy professors and researchers and one of the preeminent activists on our ideological front. It is our recommendation that he should intensify his efforts to support the further training of our junior faculty members. (Evaluation of 1988).

By the end of the regime, things became so formulaic in nature that they reached plain comical absurdity:

> He is currently a member of the basic organization's bureau—Philosophy. He acts as a propagandist at the Municipal Party Cabinet. In this capacity, he attended numerous ideological debates and made presentations in a number of schools in Bucharest and elsewhere in the country. —Prepared on February 17, 1989.

The archival information on the private life of the higher education ideological workers is sparse. The few details concern their families and their moral conduct outside the classroom—an expectation that the Party had for all of the citizens, but even more so for those who were supposed to be role models. The ideological cadres would sometimes receive criticism for failing to toe the Party line, failing to observe higher-ups' instructions, or neglecting their duties as cadres.

The fact is that higher education propagandists were very much aware of the cost-benefit calculus associated with the position. They were treated with, if not respect, at least fear by their colleagues, and they would be on an "accelerated" tenure schedule, often enjoying material privileges in a pauperized society, especially after 1980. On the downside, however, the colleagues who did not agree with the Party politics did not hide their suspicion of, or even contempt for, them. Whether to be a propagandist professor was indeed a privilege is a relative matter, debatable from several angles. Those who sometimes gave up the position more likely did it for financial reasons, rather than acting out of conscience or other type of convictions. Some would have become propagandist professors to gain extra classes or promotions. Apart from privileges, it was also a question of image—the propagandist embodied the voice of the Party and its power within the school. Respected or not, beloved or blamed, approached with interest or contempt, the propagandist, given his or her very job description, could by no means be ignored.

The personal profile and the various typologies of those involved in the propaganda and indoctrination apparatus is a fascinating topic. What kind of people were attracted by this type of career? In what circumstances? What motivated them? Is there any pattern emerging once we overview a significant number of such profiles? Could we identify some commonalities in their profiles or socioeconomic circumstances that may explain their engagement in this field? Were there affective changes of mind in assessing and understanding the regime and their own contribution and relationship to the regime? In what circumstances did such changes take place? These and other similar questions are the beginning of a fascinating interrogation that would require a separate research project entirely.

Returning to the institutional side of things, our overview has revealed a process of ongoing institutional change and never-ending tribulations, never fully successful, even by the self-congratulatory standards used by the agents and leaders of the Communist Party. The institutionalization of indoctrination was never able to generate an internal operational self-motivating basis. It always trailed, in need of constant support from outside political and institutional forces. The might of the Communist Party and the security apparatus of the political police were always behind it—the first explicitly and the second tacitly working in the shadows. The resulting picture was very far from the official narrative or image of a "triumphant march" of Socialism toward the "new era" built for and around the "New Man." It was an excruciating muddling-through, a never-ending patching and improvising, while, at each juncture, the authorities were trying to contain a process that seemed to permanently escape their full control. And thus, the Romanian case may help us reveal important insights about both the efficacy and the limits of indoctrination in ideocratic regimes. The most important insight is how difficult it is to implement and maintain a program of indoctrination geared toward social change, even when one controls the entire apparatus of the modern state and ruthlessly runs it on totalitarian principles.

NOTES

1. Mihail Roller, "Pe drumul revoluției noastre culturale," *Lupta de clasă*, 5th series, issue no. 2, Oct–Dec 1948, 103.

2. *Stenograma ședinței discutării proiectului de program al Învățământului Superior din ziua de 7 octombrie 1949* (Verbatim report of the meeting to discuss the higher education draft curriculum of October 7, 1948) in AMR (Romanian Army Archives), microfilm records, roll no. AS1–1516, frame no. 1–25, as well as *Procesul verbal aș ședinței Biroului Politic cu Comisia pentru învățământul superior din data de 7 octombrie 1948* (Minutes of the Politburo meeting with the Higher Education Committee of October 7, 1948), in AMR, microfilm records, roll no. AS1–400, frame no. 1–4.

3. "Să îmbunătățim predarea marxism-leninismului în școlile superioare," *Lupta de clasă*, 5th series, XXX, issue no. 4, April, 1950, 45.

4. Idem., 54.

5. ANIC (Central National Historical Archive), Central Committee (CC) of the Romanian Communist Party (RCP) Collection, Propaganda and Agitation Section, file no. 6/1951, 17.

6. For details, see Cristian Vasile's work "Studentul, scriitorul și pedagogia infernală a regimului comunist. Cazul Alexandru Ivasiuc," *Revista istorica*, vol. XXIII, 1–2, 2012.

7. Many were detained after the 1956 student protests, in total a few thousand students, with dozens of them receiving sentences. This was also a time of numerous "unmasking" and "coaching" sessions led by UTM and RWP leaders and activists.

8. UTM activists participated in the detaining of student protesters in 1957, in Cluj-Napoca. For details, see ANIC, CC of the RCP Collection, Organizational Section, file no. 45/1956, 1–57.

9. Later Union of Communist Youth (Uniunea Tineretului Comunist—UTC).

10. Cornelia Filipaş, "Rolul UTM-ului în şcoli," *Lupta de clasă*, 5th series, XXX, 9–10, Sept–Oct 1950, 47–61.

11. In 1948, UTM leadership consisted of Gheorghe Florescu as general secretary and Petre Lupu, Pavel Lala, Drăgan Ilie, and Manea Anton as secretaries.

12. The UTM structure mirrored that of the RWP. UTM was under the direction of the Section of Party, Trade Union and Youth Leadership Organs of the Central Committee of the Romanian Workers' Party, later known as the Organizational Section. The supreme authority in the UTM was exercised by the Congress; between Congresses, the Union was headed by a Central Committee (with forty-five members in 1949), but actual authority was in fact exercised by an executive office (with eleven members) and the office's secretariat (five members) headed by a first secretary. In addition to the CC, there were several sections and commissions, while regional leadership was provided by county Party committees. A number of inspectors would check if the decisions were applied consistently throughout the country. For more details, see ANIC, CC of the RCP Collection, Organizational Section, file no. 23/1950, 2–55.

13. On February 20, 2019, the Museum of the Alexandru Ioan Cuza University in Iaşi organized an exhibition on the topic under the general title *Student în comunism* (Being a student in Communism).

14. In an article, Călin Hentea claimed that the UTC had over four million members in the 1980s. For details, see "Memoria cărţii poştale. Uteceul duce greul," *Ziarul financiar* of Sept 7, 2009.

15. Communist Party of the Soviet Union

16. ANIC, CC of the RCP Collection, Organizational Section, file no. 14/1956, 220–222.

17. *Viaţa studenţească* (starting with 1956) and *Amfiteatru* (since 1966) were also published under the aegis of the UTC.

18. Historian Cristina Diac evokes Ioan Toma, the last leader of the UTC, and some of his memories about the institution's management in its last years in the article "Ioan Toma, ultimul şef al UTC: Ceauşescu nu era mai incult ca Băsescu," *Jurnalul Naţional*, August 20, 2010.

19. For details, see Vasile, *Viaţa intelectuală şi artistică în primul deceniu al regimului Ceauşescu, 1965–1974* (Bucharest: Editura Humanitas, 2014), 136.

20. ANIC, CC of the RCP Collection, Propaganda and Agitation Section, file no. 21/1968, 184–85.

21. According to historian Cristian Vasile, these contributors included Ştefan Bănulescu, Ovidiu Papadima, Dan Deşliu, Iosif Sava, Radu Cosaşu, Şerban

Cioculescu, Petru Comarnescu, Grigore C. Moisil, Laurențiu Ulici, George Banu, and so forth. For details, see Cristian Vasile, op.cit., 137.

22. *Stenograma expunerii tovarășului Paul Niculescu-Mizil în fața secretarilor de partid responsabili cu probleme de propagandă, din data de 12 iulie 1968* (Verbatim report of comrade Paul Niculescu-Mizil's lecture to the Party secretaries in charge of propaganda of July 12, 1968). For details, see ANIC, CC of the RCP Collection, Propaganda and Agitation Section, file no. 21/1968, 15.

23. ANIC, CC of the RCP Collection, Propaganda and Agitation Section, file no. 21/1968, 80.

24. For details, see Ștefan Bosomitu, *Miron Constantinescu. O biografie* (Preface by Vladimir Tismăneanu) (Bucharest: Editura Humanitas, 2014), 320.

25. In 1969, under the direction of the Academy of the Socialist Republic of Romania, there were twenty-two social sciences and humanities research institutes. There were 1,250 employees working in these institutes and over 700 in the social sciences departments of universities throughout the country.

26. For details, see *Note of the Propaganda Section of the CC of the RCP* of May 22, 1969, ANIC, CC of the RCP Collection—Propaganda and Agitation Section, file no. 14/1969, 16–17.

27. To suppress the protests, the military was called upon to join forces with the Militia (the police); they arrested the more vehement student protesters. The authorities created a general commandment, whose sole purpose was to coordinate the suppression of the protests. The social ferment among Romanian students did not, however, take forms as radical as those in Hungary or Poland, making it easy to suppress in a matter of weeks. For details, see Adam Burakowsky, *Dictatura lui Nicolae Ceaușescu, 1965–1989, Geniul Carpaților* (Iași: Polirom, 2011), 44–49.

28. For details, see Adam Burakowsky, op.cit., 187.

29. *PCR și intelectualii, PCR și intelectualii în primii ani ai regimului Ceaușescu* (documentary edition) (Bucharest: National Archives of Romania, 2007), 2. For details, see ANIC, the CC of the RCP Collection—Chancery, file no. 63/1965, 2–29.

30. *PCR și intelectualii în primii ani ai regimului Ceaușescu* (documentary edition) (Bucharest: National Archives of Romania, 2007), 40. For details, see ANIC, the CC of the RCP Collection—Chancery, file no. 68/1965, 29.

31. *PCR și intelectualii în primii ani ai regimului Ceaușescu* (documentary edition) (Bucharest: National Archives of Romania, 2007), 190–92. For details, see ANIC, the CC of the RCP Collection—Organizational Section, file no. 47/1968, 1–53.

32. Cristian Vasile, op.cit., 150. Details are also available in the interview conducted by historian Cristian Vasile with philosophy professor Mircea Flonta on March 5, 2011.

33. According to the historian—quoting as his source an informative note by employees of the Popular Republic of Poland Embassy and the report prepared by Virgil Trofin for the Executive Committee of December 25—during the night of December 24–25, 1968, a large student protest took place on the streets of Bucharest, a spontaneous phenomenon that took the authorities by surprise. The initiators being theology students, they began by singing Christmas carols, but ended up chanting "Down with Ceaușescu!" A few hundred persons started from Cotroceni

neighborhood moving towards Piața Universității. When the large group reached Piața Romană, the authorities sent in activists to stop them. The protest ended in the early hours of December 25, without the intervention of the Militia or other enforcement agencies—despite the PRP Embassy's report claiming violent behavior by the students—as the activists' intervention was enough to convince the students to stop protesting. Outraged by the students' actions, Ceaușescu accused them of hooliganism. For more details, see Adam Burakowsky, op.cit., 190–91.

34. ANIC, CC of the RCP Collection, Propaganda and Agitation Section, file no. 28/1968, 54–55.

35. Cristian Vasile, op.cit., 80.

36. For details, see Adam Burakowsky, op.cit., 189–90, as well as *Stenograma Ședinței Comitetului Executiv al CC al PCR din 25 decembrie 1968* (Verbatim report of the Executive Committee of the CC of the RCP Meeting of December 25, 1968), ANIC, CC of the RCP Collection—Chancellery Section, file no. 216/1968, 7–12.

37. Ion Cetățeanu, "Mediul socio-cultural al Universității din Craiova," in Aculin Cazacu (ed.), *Dinamica socială a învățământului universitar—Studiu pe modelul Universității din Craiova* (Craiova: Editura Scrisul Românesc, 1973), 42–43.

38. Lucian Boia, *Cum am trecut prin comunism. Al doilea sfert de veac* (Bucharest: Editura Humanitas, 2019), 156–57.

39. ANIC, CC of the RCP Collection, Propaganda and Agitation Section, file no. 14/1969, 49.

40. The central publications were: *Lupta de clasă, Analele Institutului de studii istorice și social-politice de pe lângă CC al PCR, Revista învățământului superior*.

41. ANIC, CC of the RCP Collection, Propaganda and Agitation Section, file no. 14/1969, 43–44.

42. Idem, 47.

43. Idem, 7.

44. Corina Pălășan, "Organizarea științifică a societății sau științele sociale în România primilor ani ai regimului Ceaușescu," in *Structuri de partid și de stat în timpul regimului comunist*, Anuarul IICCR, vol. III, 2008, 132.

45. During the February 20, 1970, meeting to establish the Academy of Social and Political Sciences (Academia de Științe Social-Politice—ASSP), they agreed on the sections of the Academy and the heads of the sections as well as the highest management. Nicolae Ceaușescu, the general secretary of RCP, would be elected honorary president of the new Academy. For details, see "Constituirea ASSP a RSR," *România liberă*, February 21, 1970.

46. Ștefan Bosomitu, op.cit., 321–22.

47. In the autumn of 1969, a meeting was held bringing together researchers and professors across the field of social sciences; they decided to create a group (its members included: Paul Niculescu-Mizil, Dumitru Popescu, Miron Constantinescu, Miron Niculescu, and Constantin Daicoviciu) whose task was to find more members and together draft the memorandum of association of what was to become the Academy of Social and Political Sciences.

48. "Propuneri cu privire la îmbunătățirea îndrumării activității în domeniul științelor sociale și crearea Academiei de Științe Sociale," ANIC, the CC of the RCP

Collection—Propaganda and Agitation Section, file no. 14/1969, 23. For details, also see Ștefan Bosomitu, op.cit., 321

49. *PCR și intelectualii în primii ani ai regimului Ceaușescu* (documentary edition) (Bucharest: National Archives of Romania, 2007), 303–5. For details, see ANIC, the CC of the RCP Collection—Chancery, file no. 82/1971, 2–6.

50. National Archives of Romania, *PCR și intelectualii*, 306–312. For details, see ANIC, CC of the RCP Collection—Chancery, file no. 85/1971, 13–24.

51. "Propunerile de măsuri prezentate de tovarășul Nicolae Ceaușescu Comitetului Executiv al CC al PCR pentru îmbunătățirea activității politico-ideologice, de educare marxist-leninistă a membrilor de partid, a tuturor oamenilor muncii," *Scânteia*, July 7, 1971, points 6 and 7.

52. Mihai Dinu Ghiorghiu, "O elocventă dovadă a modului în care tovarășul Nicolae Ceaușescu sesizează cerințele fiecărei etape," *Scânteia*, July 9, 1971.

53. Corina Pălășan, op.cit., 144–45.

54. Regarding the University of Iași: the transition from the university as a toll for training elites to university completely annexed by the political regime (that means a discretionary social selection, propaganda and social control) will occur relatively easily in Soviet period. A series of recent studies have highlighted the facture between the founding values of the university and the education system of the Communist regime. For more details see: Florea Ioncioaia, Leonidas Rados (eds), *Fragmente de pe un câmp de luptă: studii în istoria universității* (Iași: Alexandru Ioan Cuza Publishing House, 2018), 50.

55. ANIC, the CC of the RCP Collection, Propaganda and Agitation Section, file no. 20/1973, 5.

56. The publications are: *Lupta de clasă, Lumea, Munca de partid*, and *În ajutorul propagandistului*.

57. Augustin Cătălin Stoica, *România continuă. Schimbare și adaptare în comunism și postcomunism* (Bucharest: Editura Humanitas, 2018), 113.

58. Nicolae and Elena Ceaușescu.

59. Augustin Cătălin Stoica, op.cit., 113.

60. "Referat cu privire la predarea disciplinelor de Marxism-Leninism în învățământul superior," see ANIC, the CC of the RCP Collection, Propaganda and Agitation Section, file no. 42/1973, 55.

61. Idem, 38–42.

62. Art. 66 of the Education Law no. 28 of 1978.

63. For more details, see Cosmin Popa, *Intelectualii lui Ceaușescu și Academia de Științe Sociale și Politice (1970–1989)* (Bucharest: Editura Litera, 2018), 122.

64. As for recruiting students to train them as cadres from the mid-1970s onwards, quoting professor Ioan Mihăilescu, historian Cristian Vasile wrote about an anti-intellectual trend among those in power as a reaction to the students' intellectual arrogance. See also CristianVasile, op.cit., 181.

65. Idem, 181.

66. University of Bucharest Archive, Human Resources Department collection, file no. 3464.

67. Idem, file no. 3470.

PART III

Evolving Frameworks of Analysis and Emerging Research Agendas

The first part of the book introduced the most significant ways in which the phenomenon of indoctrination has been approached in the relevant literature by looking at the rationality and motivation behind the institutional and organizational arrangements defining its institutionalization. In the second part of the book, we complemented that perspective with an incursion into the rich historical data of a real-life case—Communist Romania between 1948 and 1989. The case revealed, first and foremost, important insights about both the efficacy and the limits of indoctrination systems and ideocratic regimes. The most important insight was how difficult it is to implement and maintain a politically and ideologically "correct" line, even when one controls the entire State apparatus, operating on totalitarian principles. At the same time, the case made evident that in dealing with the real-life situations, we were dealing with a large-scale organizational phenomenon of complex linkages and relationships, a cluster of organizational and institutional elements that, in conjunction, characterized the institutionalization process of interest to us. Hence, a renewed sense emerges that focuses on the need to approach the phenomena in a way that captures the organizational complexity and dynamic continuity in addition to and beyond the approaches focused on the functional logic, whether it is ideas-driven or interests-driven. The initial insights brought forth by the case have thus led us to novel venues, inviting a more systematic and better-grounded effort in our investigation.

The third part of the book makes a couple of tentative steps in the direction of engaging these venues. First, it takes a set of key observations coming from the case study and brings to them a framing inspired by an already existing literature pertaining to the field of organizational sociology. With the help of this literature, we introduce an additional explanatory level of the institutionalization processes associated with propaganda and indoctrination. The conclusions reached by this exercise illuminate in an even firmer way the relevance of the theme and the importance of its investigation. Based on that, several possible research agendas are outlined, some of them on comparative lines—exploring the external validity of the insights reached by our investigation—and some exploring the internal validity of the explanatory frameworks employed in our discussion of the case study. What is at stake, it is claimed by the argument advanced in the last chapter of the book, is far from trivial and not of a meager historical relevance. The phenomena associated with propaganda and indoctrination are an ongoing (and perhaps increasing) threat in the contemporary technological, ideological, and institutional settings; hence, a robust and intensive research agenda aiming at their study is more than warranted.

Chapter 6

A Failure of Institutionalization

A Key Insight from the Case Study and the Challenges of its External Validity

So far, the definition of institutionalization used in our discussion was a basic and intuitive one (i.e., a process following the logic of the creation and administration of a system of organization via formal rules defined by a view toward a set of organizational objectives or functions). The insights generated by the previous chapters put us in the position to advance our understanding of the institutionalization process thus defined. However, at the same time, the limits of the functionalist framing—typical for the basic approach advanced in the literature that inspired the first part of the book— become more evident once placed in the light of the case study. Two aspects are important in our attempt to take the discussion to the next analytic and interpretive level. First, there is a need to construct an approach that forms a middle way between, on the one hand, the level of generality of the functionalist theoretical frameworks presented in the first part of the book and, on the other hand, the historical and empirical observations and narratives that were the bulk of the second part of the book. Second, the need to try to frame things using a more substantive view of institutionalization, a view that goes beyond the basic means-ends logic of social functions and functionalism.

A SYSTEMIC AND SOCIOLOGICAL PERSPECTIVE

The Romanian case has indicated the need to further conceptualize the phenomenon of interest as a "system" and to think about its evolution as a dynamic phenomenon having its own lifecycle. The reality is that this is precisely how we have treated the issue under investigation from the very beginning. We have considered the indoctrination system at the national level as a relatively coherent system, or at least sufficiently coherent or integrated to be treated methodologically and analytically as such. At this stage, we make that assumption explicit and move it from the background to the foreground as part of a strategy of articulating some of its descriptive, explanatory, and interpretive implications.

Obviously, we know that this is not as simple of a task as it may seem at first sight. One recognizes that, once conceptualized this way, the "system's" boundaries are always fuzzy and dynamic, and there is a certain degree of imprecision set up in the approach. Yet, at the same time, one recognizes that there is sufficient precision and clarity to be able to start constructing an approach around this conceptualization that unites both the general theoretical framing and the empirical and historical content on which the case is focused into a working system of analysis.

As we have seen in Romania, the arrangements of indoctrination and propaganda had a vast range of activities, functions, and responsibilities that came in diverse organizational forms. They had both manifest and latent functions. Even more important, they required working together with the state apparatus, the Communist Party, the political police, and other administrative and professional organizations. The indoctrination was part and parcel of a compounded phenomenon of multiple institutional arrangements and organizational forms. That complex and multifaceted nature was not an accident, but a feature. Understanding "the system" means trying to see all these elements in connection and illuminating their relationships.

Recognizing that the institutionalization of indoctrination and the institution of the "ideological commissar" were part and parcel of this institutional and political ecology allows us to set the stage for building up an additional dimension to our understanding of the institutionalization process. Seeing the phenomenon as embedded in a larger social context of a systemic nature offers the possibility of an approach that is better-grounded sociologically. This way of conceptualizing gives more substance to what we have identified as a middle ground, composite approach. We will return to these systemic linkages later. Now, we need to turn away from the external systemic embeddedness aspects and toward the internal organizational processes. Our case study has alerted us to the fact that we need to articulate, in this respect, an additional approach that incorporates but goes beyond the basic logic of social functions and functionalism.

In a sense, it should not be a surprise that one of the pioneers of the sociological study of the organizational side of the Communist phenomenon, Philip Selznick, offers what is possibly the most promising approach to our topic. Selznick is well known for his foundational contribution to our understanding of the organizational, administrative, and institutional side of Communism via the study of the Communist Party as an organizational instrument. However, it is a fascinating and ironic turn of intellectual history that we have found the resources to deal with our problem not in his classic work on the Communist Party (*The Organizational Weapon: A Study of Bolshevik Strategy and Tactics*)[1] but in his contribution to organizational sociology, and especially in two of his such works: *Leadership in Administration: A Sociological Interpretation*[2] and *TVA and the Grass Roots: A Study in the Sociology of Formal Organization.*[3] In these two works, Selznick advances the elements of a particular conceptualization and analysis of institutionalization that is both convergent with our observations and, at the same time, a very good framework for our analytical tasks. Before introducing it, let us note that it has to be seen, without a doubt, as part of a larger picture outlined in his landmark study on the Communist organizational strategy of the Bolshevik type of parties and the "front" organizations manipulated by them. So, the relevance of the *Organizational Weapon* remains critical for our topic.

Selznick's work is, in this respect, focused on what we have identified (in chapter 2) as the first stage (or operating mode) of the Communist Party and its offensive against the status quo: the ways in which Communists seek to gain control over crucial groups and organizations in their endeavor to control modern society. Selznick shows that, at this first stage, the Communist strategy and tactics are not so much to indoctrinate the masses or to take control of the government in the traditional revolutionary style. Instead, the objective is to control the functioning units in a society—groups such as labor unions, youth groups, and the unemployed. In other words, it is to gradually establish influence bases in society "which will offer in turn means of moving progressively to greater conquests of power until the control of the social apparatus of a society is secured."[4] These observations are important because they help emphasize the radical differences between, on the one hand, Communism as a revolutionary phenomenon and, on the other hand, Communism in power. We thus could determine both the lines of continuity and those of discontinuity between the two stages or avatars of Communism in action.

Our claim is that although Selznick did not address the second stage of Communism—the takeover of the developments associated with the regime's administration once in full control—his work offers the resources to understand some aspects of this stage in which it is the ruling power. More specifically, it helps us to get a better view of the institutionalization processes associated with the ideocratic apparatus that any Communist regime has to put in place.

Selznick starts with some familiar insights that one may recognize behind our own discussion, either derived from the literature used in part I or based on the intuitions framing our narrative and descriptive observations in part II. Selznick noted that organizations are defined by their functions or their manifest goals. As such, they have a strong element of instrumental rationality intrinsically built into their structure. The organization is "a technical instrument," "an exercise in engineering" for "mobilizing human energies and directing them toward a set of aims." In this respect, "the most striking and obvious thing" about an organization is "its formal system of rules and objectives." An organization is something that functions based on an officially approved pattern that sets out "how the work of the organization is to be carried on, whether it be producing steel, winning votes, teaching children, or saving souls."[5]

At the same time, and here comes the major point of interest to us, the formal or official design "never completely accounts for what the participants do." It is always supplemented by what is called the "informal structure," which arises "as the individual brings into play his own personality, his special problems and interests. Formal relations co-ordinate roles or specialized activities, not persons."[6] In the end, the organization is also a group of human beings, not just a pattern of social order based on rules. But the informal structure and the personalization bring an entire new domain of social facts and processes with them to the process of organization. It is precisely this set of social facts and processes that is essential for our approach to the institutionalization taking place with respect to the organizational forms of indoctrination and propaganda.

The structure of Selznick's argument is again dovetailing smoothly with the underlying logic of our investigation so far. As one may recall, the first part of our book was actually organized around a discussion pivoting on the functional bases of organizations. If one takes the ideological mission of creating the "New Man" as being a manifest function, then we have already identified a first level structure of institutional rationality shaping the pattern of that type of organization. But then, in a second step, we have also identified a different level of functions and a distinctive corresponding rationalization principle. The initial discussion of the phenomenon on the ideological line went quickly from the first level rationality of ideological functions to a second level focused on strategic consideration of power and resources control. So, we have been heading toward a discussion of the strategic employment of propaganda organizations and the roles that they may have, above and beyond those induced by the pure ideological function. We have seen how our understanding of the evolution of the systems of propaganda and indoctrination always had to go on the lines of these two basic levels. We have articulated, from the very beginning, a perspective that captured these double institutional dynamics. That was the setting within which the case study brought to the light a richer set of observations and, with them, the awareness of the need to engage with other facets of organization from alternative angles.

More specifically, the case study has drawn attention to the existence of a set of social facts and processes confirming Selznick's simple observation that "the most important thing about organizations is that, though they are tools, each nevertheless has a life of its own."[7] The discussion of the Romanian case, as we have already seen, gravitated naturally toward the idea of a life cycle. While looking at the historical and archival evidence, the approach was structured almost unwittingly by a narrative of the rise and fall of a complex social system, defined by a multitude of endogenous and exogenous social processes. We have seen, based on historical evidence and archival sources, how the Romanian propaganda in education, active from the beginning until the end of the regime, transformed and calibrated its main functions over time under the influence of the historical, social, and political context. Imported from the USSR, it had different priorities and functions at different points in time, from shaping the "New Man" and building the "multilaterally developed socialist society" to the nationalist "protochronism" of late Romanian Communism.

We had the opportunity to note the interplay of factors that went beyond the dynamics of the basic functional rationalities. Again, Selznick's work validates the relevance of our observations. Selznick has noted repeatedly in his organizational sociology investigations the fact that functions may change within levels and between levels throughout the life cycle of an organization. Moreover, he noted that these dynamics may well be the key factor in both the performance and the resilience of an organization. Hence, reading the case study through these lenses makes sense.

In its institutional form, the Romanian national system of social organization of indoctrination was born with the establishment of the Agitation and Propaganda Section. Originally the Agitation and Propaganda Department, later renamed the Agitation and Propaganda Section, the organization was both an intrinsic part and a symptom of the Communist regime's evolution. The birth of the organization led to the creation of an entire horizontal and vertical network, connecting the various ministries that had a role (or direct interest) in the education system (e.g., Ministry of Education, Ministry of Internal Affairs) as well as in the creation of a monocentric system consisting of a center of decision making dominating the rest of the organizations in the system. In terms of the structure, there were only two main levels: the head office (an entity with decision-making power) and the branches spread out in the country that were in charge of implementing the decisions. The head office tightly coordinated the activity of the branches and local offices, and it also saw to it that the decisions made by the top leadership of the Party were put into practice.

These features were a structural constant. However, the structure had different operational codes over time, as it had to operate under different parameters and with different interpretations of a fluctuating set of functions or roles. To mirror the changes in the allocation of power, as well as to adapt to their own internal dynamics and challenges—some formal, some informal—the propaganda institutions and organizational units were continuously reshaped, specialized, and recalibrated over time. While in the 1950s, the emphasis was on agitation and control, starting with the mid-1960s, a shift was felt in both society and the education system as propaganda started to focus more on its socializing and educational roles than on agitation, control, and mobilization. Moreover, compared to the 1950s activist/agitator, the propaganda worker toward the end of the regime had to operate in a different environment.[8] As the previous chapters have extensively shown, the Agitation and Propaganda Department of the CC of the RWP was created in the times of Zhdanovism as a prime agent in the social engineering project aiming to generate the "New Man" according to the materialist-dialectical ideology. Yet, it later became one of the key instruments in the turn taken by the regime toward National Communism.

The branching structure of the Section meant that there was an extension of it in every ministry, and hence, adjustments had to take place at each reorganization. A succession of changes in the regime's branding, leaders, and even in how it managed the relations between the structures that constituted the Communist state were reflected in the periodical reorganization of the Department and the network it coordinated. Gheorghiu-Dej was directly involved in the roles propaganda played in the system; as for Ceaușescu, not only did he rely on developing and fine tuning the institution, but he also consistently took active measures to reinforce the role and the training of the propagandist. These changes in functions, or in the emphasis or interpretation of roles and functions, were thus always associated with concrete changes that affected the structure of the system as well as the careers and the lives of those operating within the system. For instance, when the regime first ascended to power, the "agitators" were in high demand. Toward the end of the Communist rule, new categories of ideological workers emerged, such as the "lecturers," who were specially trained to convey much more finely tuned messages and whose higher status was in greater demand than the "agitators."

To sum up, looking at the functional and structural changes over the life cycle of the organizational phenomenon of interest has helped us to get a better, more nuanced sense of the fate of the institutionalization of indoctrination and propaganda in the architecture and management of the Romanian Communist regime. In the process, we have noted that the dynamics of organization were not driven solely by functional rationality and rational behavior, be of the first level (that is to say, ideological) or second level (that is to say, strategic and political). Again, our discussion has converged with Selznick's organizational sociology thesis, according to which organizational procedures and rules that are designed or emerge as means to achieve functional success are more often than not accompanied by alternative or complementary social processes. The multitude of functions and social processes that clustered around and inside the indoctrination organization made sure that developments on these lines were a statistical certainty. Individuals have multiple commitments and social goals, and they behave as such even when they are operating in a highly dedicated Communist organization; that applies even to the most devoted cadres of the Communist propaganda apparatus. The main point is that all of the above induce a series of developments that may take the organization even further away from the path of its pure functional, organizational rationality.

All of the above have major implications, in the sense that individuals—even when they are part of highly messianic organizational missions—do not act purely based on the scripts and expectations of their formal roles. Conflicts, dilemmas, and trade-offs take place, and a space is created for the emergence and manifestation of organizational behavior not fully aligned with the formal organizational blueprint. A living association, wrote Selznick, "blends technical aims and procedures with personal desires and group interests." In order to maintain the organization and the objectives, "there is a need to accommodate internal interests and adapt to outside forces."[9] Therefore, to further understand the nature of institutionalization, one needs to look at one of the most important features of organizations: the tendency for structures and processes to be affected by and become "infused with value beyond the technical requirements at hand"[10] as they operate in a given social, institutional, and cultural environment. To repeat: this is precisely how our intuitive approach has proceeded in the second part of the book. Let us now further specify these intuitions using as a vehicle Selznick's work.

INSTITUTIONALIZATION IN A NEW KEY

In exploring the Romanian case, we have started with the discussion of the central national institutional instrument for implementing the indoctrination function as defined under the leadership of the Communist Party: The Agitation and Propaganda Department (later renamed Section). Then, we have focused on the agent (the ideological worker, propagandist) and their role and operation principles. Once that was done, we were in the position to take a closer look at the strenuous dynamics set into motion by both the agent and institutional arrangements operating in the evolving circumstances of the Communist regime during the second part of the twentieth century. We have seen that the organization of indoctrination and propaganda and the activities of the ideological worker in the education system (and more specifically in the university) had to tackle multiple responsibilities and challenges. We have seen that the emerging image was one of a dynamic process of ongoing institutional change and adjustment, never fully successful. What one could see was not the official narrative or image of a "triumphant march," but rather an ongoing muddling-through, a never-ending patching and improvising, while at each juncture the authorities were trying to contain a process that seemed to recurringly escape their full control. We have also seen how the evolutions we have identified in the Romanian case study require additional explanatory efforts.

And this is where a crucial conceptual distinction borrowed from Selznick is to be introduced. Selznick brings to the fore a way of defining institutionalization that takes the analysis to a new level. Both in his work on the sociology of formal organization and in his work on the sociology of leadership, Selznick defines institutionalization as a process that happens to an organization over time, reflecting the organization's own distinctive history, the specificities of the people who have been in it, the groups it embodies, the vested interests they have created, and the way it has adapted to its environment. Institutionalization, in this sense of the term, begins when people start to value "the social machinery beyond its instrumental technical role." That, he notes, is largely a function of "the way in which it fulfills personal or group needs." Individuals "become attached to an organization or a way of doing things as persons rather than as technicians." A new type of relationship develops between the social actor and the organization: "From the standpoint of the committed person, the organization is changed from an expendable tool into a valued source of personal satisfaction."[11]

An important corollary is that as this process moves along, an organization's structures tend to take on new functions and meanings that are unrelated to the reasons they were created or adopted in the first place. Our initial definition of institutionalization, as applied to our topic in the first part of the book, was more or less referring to the national-level organization of a social function via politically engineered institutional arrangements. Selznick introduces an important nuance. For him, institutionalization is something that comes after—and builds on—the organization stage and the structures thus created. This is the sense in which organizations become "institutionalized." Under this understanding, institutionalization is a result of a fusion of individual identities, personal preferences, and strategies with organizational structures. Once this more "sociological" dimension is identified, the notion of institutionalization gains a new extension, as the basic organizational functions and structures are just a starting point. Once populated with social actors, an organizational structure slowly takes a life of its own. It becomes institutionalized. Our own overview of the Romanian case has given us multiple clues regarding this phenomenon. The closer we get to the historical data and archival resources, the clearer the nature and significance of this process becomes.

Approaching things from this angle requires a shift toward the sociological dimension. First of all, in order to further clarify the problem of institutionalization under this second definition, we need to pay closer attention to the social actors directly involved and their setting. For instance, we need to give full attention to the fact that the national system of indoctrination managed to create a special social group of people that had their social identities and their careers tied to their places and roles in the system. They were, undoubtedly, in this respect, a creation of the Communist regime. The regime—whether they liked it or not—defined their social life and structured their relationships with the rest of the society.

That raises a very important set of questions that has been always latent in the background of our discussion. First, who were these people after all? What was their social background? Did their social background make a difference for their attitudes, behavior, and performance? What was, more precisely, their relationship to the organizational structure that defined their social identities and social roles as a social category? How were the organizational stringencies of the indoctrination apparatus shaping their relationships to the other social roles these social actors had and to their social milieu in general? How did they navigate the trade-offs and tensions of attachment and identity between their, on the one hand, functioning as propaganda commissars or agents of the ruling Party and, on the other hand, functioning in other social roles and social commitments? These are some of the first key questions brought to the fore by this second level, more substantive and sociologically oriented definition of institutionalization.

Our overview of the Romanian case has shown that the number of ideological workers was large enough to justify an interest in their sociological features and their status as a social group or social category. However, when it comes to the educational system, there is no way to accurately determine how many there were. In some cases, the archival documents mention the number of propaganda agents in one region, but they do not include a breakdown for education. Our estimate of the number of propagandists in education is based on a rough assessment focused on the number of educational institutions. With one primary school and one kindergarten in each locality, ten high schools, at the very least, in each municipality, and one university for each region,[12] we can reach a very basic and very conservative estimate by multiplying that by a very conservative factor of two. But we need to keep in mind that the large educational institutions (high schools and universities) assigned one propagandist per department, and they also offered a special course named *Political Information/Political Education*, for which several instructors were assigned. Also, more often than not, there were no records stipulating the educator's additional capacity as propagandist—except for those of them who would file a request to opt out of working as propagandists because of the low pay, hence, giving us a track record regarding them.

Those difficulties are amplified by the fluctuations over time. Given that the sharpest growth in the number of Party members occurred from 1963 to 1964,[13] this translated into a hike in the number of propagandists too. But starting with 1972, propaganda was amplified on new parameters, seeking to co-opt the largest number of citizens possible to actively participate in the system. That further compounded the difficulties in estimating the total number of those involved. Then, there is the additional problem of the overlapping roles of the ideological workers operating in several organizations and in several functions at the same time. So, all in all, the magnitude of the phenomenon has to be assessed within very wide margins. Depending on how one counts, between 100,000 and 500,000 Romanians were involved, at any time, in direct or indirect full-time or part-time propaganda and indoctrination activities as agents. That makes roughly two or three persons in one hundred that were either induced or forced to operate as a propaganda agent in a specific functional role in the system.

As to their social origin, the situation—though not straightforward—is relatively easier to be figured out. On the one hand, there were educators of the old generation who rallied with the regime and agreed to support it ideologically after being either coerced or incentivized with career opportunities. They were the ones who were neither born in poverty nor lacked education. In any case, in most circumstances they did not do it because they sincerely adhered to the Communist ideals. However, they did not represent the majority, as, with very few exceptions, the education system had to be "purged" of the "old bourgeoisie" hence they were a minority. On the other hand, there were the propagandists trained in the Communist regime's schools or at their workplace who had a "healthy social origin."[14] As revealed by the majority of the files of education propaganda workers, they came from modest backgrounds, many of them from peasant families. The basis for their future careers as professional propagandists was, in fact, their membership in the Communist Party. This is both the most common and the most relevant category. Trained in special schools, regularly assessed based on ideological and loyalty criteria, and assigned to educational institutions across the country (from village kindergartens to universities), the ideological workers were a social group that was undoubtedly the creation of the Communist regime. The propaganda corps was a category of the Communist apparatus, a profession and a social status group whose "healthy social origin" was—at the least in theory—its main sociologically distinctive feature.

As a creation of the Communist regime, they were dependent on the regime, and, at least in theory, they were supposed to defend it, as their status, income source, and career all depended on the regime's survival and the viability of the ideocratic system it aimed to put in place. This is the social group on whose shoulders the burden of institutionalizing indoctrination and propaganda was falling. To understand the evolutions and avatars of the regime, one needs to always keep in mind that the formal organizational structure in place had to be operated through these *people*. And once we see things in this light, one could revisit one of the most salient observations of our inquiry having to do with the failure of the system, a failure that—we have indicated—could be established by a simple comparison between the social and economic reality and the self-imposed manifest ideological goals of the regime. And in this respect, the role that the propaganda and indoctrination apparatus had was crucial. Therefore, the questions are these: What was the nature of the ongoing dysfunctionality of the propaganda and indoctrination apparatus? How can we explain its ultimate failure as well its role in the general failure of the regime?

INSTITUTIONALIZATION AS AN EXPLANATORY FACTOR

Our contention is that Selznick's notion of institutionalization may offer a possible answer to these questions. His approach to the aspect of organizational phenomena that he identified under the notion may reveal an intriguing pathology of the Communist regime's institutional apparatus. The observation is that in Romania's case, the process of institutionalization, under this definition (that focuses on the meta-organizational and sociological aspects), did not happen. Or, more precisely, that it happened in deficient and dysfunctional ways. Let's recall that Selznick introduced a distinction between "organization" (the formal social machinery aiming at specific functions and goals) and the emergent phenomenon of "institutionalization," through which organization takes new functions via social actors who are starting to use its structures (including for additional purposes) and growing those structures into new dimensions coevolving with them.

That being said, what Selznick calls "institutionalization" may go in two major directions. The first is one in which the emergent process is aligned or convergent with the goals of the formal organization. In this case, it is not undermining the formal organizational structure and its objectives. It may not support it, but at least it is not undermining it. The second is divergent and even dysfunctional in its relationship to those formal goals and structures. In the Romanian case, by all accounts, it looked like the second direction was prevalent. Hence, the focus of the discussion has to shift toward an effort of understanding why that was the case. Why the second direction and not the first one?

Answering the question of why a convergent, constructive, and reinforcing institutionalization did not happen in the case of the organization of the Communist Romania propaganda requires a multicausal explanation, and it is, without any doubt, a project in itself. That doesn't mean, however, that at this point we cannot offer a conjecture. One possible clue may be found in the relationship the propaganda organizations (and the institutional structure of propaganda in general) had with other institutions and organizations of the Communist system, more specifically: the Romanian Communist Party, the political police, the Securitate,[15] and the nomenklatura. In brief, they were part of a larger system inducing a broader logic and rationality that had a life of its own, overriding the endogenous logic of the indoctrination organizations that operated as limited functional units within this larger system. We are now returning to the systemic aspect evoked at the beginning of the chapter.

As extensively discussed, the propaganda workers were on the front line in their relationship with the targeted Romanian population. But at the same time, they were, obviously, a part of the apparatus of the Communist state. They were a part of a complex system in which they had to interact in a multitude of roles and functions with the rest of the society. And the problem was that the interactions generated incentives, identities, and aspirations that clashed profoundly with the motivation and mission of the organizational units that ideological workers were a part of. That reality created both organizational and individual problems for the activists/ideological workers. As members of the Romanian society forced on the path of an ideocratic project, they had one of the most important tasks in creating the "New Man" for the "new system." But the old system—that is to say a typical society—was more resilient than the Marxist ideology was expecting and predicting it to be.

Without a doubt, some of the propagandists fully believed that the Communist regime was a just one. At the same time, however, we have reasons to conclude that, over time, in the propagandists' own perceptions, the credibility of the propaganda eroded up to a critical threshold. The sinking living standards, pauperization, and radical censorship of the late 1980s took their toll on the propaganda's power of persuasion and the propagandists' enthusiasm and motivation. That, in turn, eroded the credibility of the regime in radical ways, leading to a perception of the whole social construction of Communism as implausible. People accepted the signals sent by the propaganda institution out of a generalized fear pervading the society, a feeling of uncertainty and terror mostly induced by the Securitate on the lines discussed in chapter 2. In a country marked by severe shortages and political repression, the propaganda activities were casting the events in a cartoon-like, surreal light. To be an agent of indoctrination in these circumstances was not easy, even with a true believer's commitment to the Communist dogmas.

But the most sensitive aspect in this context is even more specific. The persons and groups, writes Selznick, who are part of such organizational systems "are not content to be treated as manipulable or expendable." More precisely,

> Rules apply to foremen and machinists, to clerks, sergeants, and vice-presidents, yet no durable organization is able to hold human experience to these formally defined roles. In real life, men tend to interact as many-faceted persons, adjusting to the daily round in ways that spill over the neat boundaries set by their assigned roles.[16]

To put it in the context of our discussion, people do not see themselves as mere instruments of organizational structures, even if those organizations may be defined in relationship with missions that claim to have historical magnitudes, such as to create a "new society" or a "New Man." The ideological workers were not exceptions to the rule that people acting in organizations "have their own needs for self-protection and self-fulfillment—needs that may either sustain the formal system or undermine it." These needs, aspirations, and relations, warned Selznick, "may be directed in constructive ways toward desired ends or they may become recalcitrant sources of frustration. One objective of sound management practice is to direct and control these internal social pressures."[17]

These general observations are more than relevant for our case. A closer look at the position and functioning of the ideological workers in the circumstances of the Romanian society reveals, first of all, that they were in a very uneasy position with the rest of the society, as they were supposed to indoctrinate and manipulate the beliefs and perceptions of a targeted population of countrymen with whom they had to share almost all aspects of life in circumstances in which the gap between the propaganda and reality was glaring.[18] At the same time, however, they had an uncomfortable relationship with the nomenklatura and the rest of the apparatus of the Communist state. In conjunction, these factors created a very tense and uncomfortable operating environment. In brief, the Communist system was unable to stabilize and manage the basic social environment of the propaganda workers in a constructive way. But this is exactly what the Communist regime was supposed to offer to this social group in order to contain and control social pressures and avoid frustrating, confusing, and demobilizing its members. It is most telling that this failure of the regime was in relation to one of its core groups, a social category that was supposed to be essential for its ideocratic and totalitarian designs. If one is unable to motivate, capacitate, and make an effective use of this social category, the ideocratic regime has a serious problem.

To get a better sense of the contours and magnitude of this problem, all one has to do is place things into the broader architecture and context of the

Communist state and society. One of the keys is the relationship between the ideological workers and the power structures of the Communist system. This relationship, starting from their recruitment and continuing to their training and the responsibilities assigned to them, followed a blueprint that, although amended ostensibly over time, remained largely unchanged in its essence. Centralization was essential, as decisions were taken at the top for the lower tier, going from the central office to the territorial offices. The career of the propagandist included several milestones: recruitment of the future cadre (who had to not only have a "healthy social origin" but also, at least in theory, had to prove a talent for persuasion and a higher level of ideological knowledge); training (in the form of courses at the central or territorial offices); assignment (to an educational unit); and assessment (through regular inspections and reports). All of these were based on the principles of a hierarchical monocentric system. The activity of the propagandists—whether they operated in education or other areas—was monitored and assessed by the Propaganda and Agitation Section. The Propaganda Section was built as a seemingly simple structure, according to the official records, but it was very complex in practice. In addition to educating, controlling, and surveilling, another important role of it was to recruit and deploy the cadres under its direction and to guide their trajectories through both professional and personal life. To make a long story short, the life of a propaganda worker was, without a doubt, a nexus of control and monitoring.

The Section closely watched how propaganda workers understood and applied the Party's decisions and guidelines in practice, reporting to the local Party Committee on all of these aspects. At the same time, the Section would regularly send out activists to disseminate information about the experiences of other Party organizations with propaganda among the structures under the direction of the Propaganda and Agitation Section. The activists were expected to explain the activities of the Section, its divisions, and the Party schools and courses, and then communicate their findings and comments to the *raion*,[19] county, or town-level Party committees. Upon their return, the activists would report to the Section about their findings during the assignment. Another method of control—and an obligation for the local propaganda agents—was to regularly call on the propaganda secretaries of *raion*-or town-level Party Committees to report on the local state of affairs or to train them. At the same time, the Section would receive complaints from its territorial structures about attitudes hostile to the "Party line," the propagandists in charge having an obligation to analyze them and indicate the best action to take. A file was created for each propagandist to be updated and regularly assessed using the reports, promotions, warnings, or periodical assessments submitted by the structure he or she worked for. Every now and then, the Section would convene meetings with the secretaries and the local propaganda officials to train them how to best implement the central policies.

Since the propagandist was required to gather information in local educational units (schools, colleges) to be communicated to the political leaders, it can be said that, despite a rather strict hierarchical structure, in practice, the information flowed both ways: from the top to the bottom and back. However, while that ensured full control of the center/top of the hierarchy, it did not translate into a sufficient degree of freedom of initiative for the front line or field worker. Thus, the responsibilities of the ideological worker within the system unfolded on both the horizontal, as in the requirement to work together with the other local educational institutions (i.e., schools, high schools, kindergartens, libraries, cultural centers), and on the vertical coming from all levels: county secretaries, heads of sections, editors-in-chief of various publications, and so forth. In all cases, the propagandist had to be on the front line. Therefore, it is not an exaggeration to say that the propaganda worker, or more specifically, the propaganda role as defined in the context of the Communist system, was a nexus of control and monitoring.

The burdens and harassment of constant monitoring and control were, in the end, crucial. As operational constraints, they frustrated and reduced the effectiveness of the agents on the ground. The trade-off between the stringencies of following a "Party line" and the efficacy of the ideological worker operating in specific circumstances with specific tasks was evident. Also evident was the impact on the commitment, loyalty, and enthusiasm, which were all undermined by these general parameters under which the propaganda worker was supposed to perform. The closer one gets to understanding the real structure of power of the Communist system, the clearer the reality becomes that the propagandists (activists, ideologists, propagandists, agitators, or lecturers) were not a real elite under the political science definition. They had no real decision-making power. Their (epistemic) authority was essentially derivative. They were rather those who put into practice the decisions, mere agents of the power, or cogs in the system.

At the same time, that privilege of being part of the power system did not come without costs. It meant, for instance, a stricter and more taxing monitoring. As mentioned, a propagandist's family background was thoroughly checked by the Securitate. They were all carefully selected to have a "healthy social origin." It was not only those recruited in the Party schools but also the teaching staff, the lecturers, and the assistant professors were also thoroughly checked. In performing the checks, the Securitate would use methods like phone tapping and opening private mail. To determine whether there were Securitate informers among the propagandists is not within the scope of this study. However, in the large universities, especially those where international students were enrolled, the Securitate officers were undoubtedly in touch with the propagandist faculty members. Working as a propagandist did not rule out being forced to work as a Securitate informer.

The cadres files of the propagandists working in education indicate that they were regularly investigated and assessed, particularly whenever they applied for promotions in their careers or, in the case of university professors, when they wished to participate in international conferences (and, hence, they needed to get approved for receiving a passport). According to the archival records, the officers in the structures within the Ministry of Internal Affairs were assigned to check (and make copies of) the propagandists' cadres files. Further, each step in their careers as university professors and propagandists were recorded in a dossier that consisted—among others—of a number of reports and evaluations, some of them under the signatures of the dean, the representative of the local Party Committee, the head of the trade-union group, or the director or the chair of their department. The relationship between the professors working as propagandists and the state structures within the Ministry of Internal Affairs, including the latter's intelligence and political police services, was—without a doubt—one of de facto subordination.

The implications of all of the above for the morale, dedication, commitment, and self-esteem of the ideological worker having to operate under such conditions should be obvious. In light of the above, we get a better sense of how the phenomenon identified by Selznick under the label of "institutionalization" comes to play a role in our story. The process, when it comes to the organization of propaganda and indoctrination by the Romanian Communist regime, was set up in a manner that was doomed, sooner or later, to have problems in matching with the formal organizational goals and patterns. Selznick has drawn our attention to the fact that an organization over its life cycle will naturally adjust and adapt based on individual actions, contextual elements, and environmental pressures. In this case, one would expect that the constant and methodical surveillance and control, as well as the tense interface with the rest of the Romanian society, had a major impact on both the operations and the institutionalization of the organizations having to do with propaganda and indoctrination.

We have seen how in the Romanian case, the performance of the propaganda apparatus was often affected by the day-to-day management problems that went unsolved, while its long-term operations were hindered by the frequent changes and power struggles within the Party leadership or the fluctuating attitudes toward Moscow. There is no doubt that the Propaganda and Agitation Section, for instance, was plagued by poor management—this was in fact the reason for the 1972 reorganization of the Section, which clarified the responsibilities assigned to it and the extent of its authority. From the verbatim report of a meeting, we learn that the agitators did not know whether their work was supposed to be individual, collective, or organized by brigades or where their responsibility ended. At the same time, given that propaganda work was, in many cases, individualized work and that they were even encouraged to adopt a personal style, the central authorities found that the propaganda messages that the ideological workers disseminated throughout the country were rather inconsistent, even distorted at times. The efforts of regularizing, not to speak of fine tuning, the messages had failed repeatedly. On the "human resources" side, the records also show that the system struggled because of the ideological workers' dissatisfaction with their compensation. We have observed how many of them, struggling on their promotion and career path, would sometimes give up the ideological work and go back to being simply teachers/professors.

But in addition to these basic managerial dysfunctions, one major outcome of the failure to institutionalize, in the Selznick meaning of the term, was that it further increased the deviation of the organization from the expected trajectory, as defined by its manifest function. That undoubtedly undermined or restricted its capability to achieve the very basic initial functions and maintain the effectiveness of organizational patterns. In our own exploration of the Romanian case, we have seen at work a natural history of an organization that was never able to get beyond a certain point in its functional institutionalization. Hence, the never-ending efforts to restart, redefine, and revamp a propaganda and indoctrination system that was always found to be deficient in one aspect or another. But if our analysis is correct, the solution to the problem resided neither within those specific organizational units dedicated to the indoctrination tasks nor with the minor adjustments in their management or their human resources policies. The real problem was larger. It resided in the regime and in the overall institutional and governance system of the Communist state, as applied to the Romanian society.

If our interpretation is sound, then we may conclude by saying that the Communist regime managed to create and run the organizational side of things while setting up the basis of an indoctrination system. Yet, it never managed to move things in the direction of a functional institutionalization of the propaganda and indoctrination machine. It never managed to embed its ideological apparatus into the structure of society, and it never managed to create the internal cohesion and socialization necessary for a healthy organizational development. The reason was not accidental or contextual. It was structural: a culture of control, surveillance, suspicion, double talk, and manipulation. A hierarchical system in which the propaganda workers' initiative, enthusiasm, and loyalty were constantly stifled; a social context of muted hostility and contempt. In such circumstances, one is structurally unable to develop the informal, personal, internal structure of motivation. It is impossible to create a basis for "institutionalization," as defined from Selznick's perspectives. Sooner or later, that indoctrination function becomes routinized, formulaic, and a parody to itself. The lessons and the implications of these observations are a fascinating topic for a separate research project.

THE EXTERNAL VALIDITY CHALLENGE

In light of the insights gained so far, the key question is this: In what measure is the Romanian case generalizable? In other words: What is the relevance of this case (and for that matter of other similar cases) for our understanding of the institutionalization of propaganda and indoctrination, in general? Are the inexorable developments toward failure, that we have described and documented in the Romanian case, intrinsic to any effort toward indoctrination and propaganda institutionalization? In other words, is there something universal in human nature or societies that generate the institutional and social reactions that lead to the social and institutional failure of such efforts? Or is this development something having to do with the specific Romanian case? Are the Romanian case and the other cases, as known in Eastern Europe, for instance, just one possible type of development, a trajectory relevant only for the circumstances, both historical and cultural, determining those specific experiments that took place under the ideocratic designs of the Soviet Communism?

There is also an even more interesting question: Have we, in fact, identified a structural feature of such systems? Are we confronted with a fascinating internal contradiction of ideocratic and totalitarian systems? That is to say, the fact that in the structure of such systems, the need for monitoring, control, and top-down authoritarian management (all intrinsic to such systems) comes to clash with and undermine the very organization and functioning of the propaganda and indoctrination institutions. These structures are supposed to perform a key function that is, by definition, central and emblematic for the very nature of the ideological-ideocratic society in general, but the very system is setting them up for failure. The failure in this respect is undoubtedly a systemic failure. But then, would a polycentric system of propaganda and indoctrination have succeeded when a monocentric system has failed?

To put it differently, the question is one of the universality or generalization of certain case studies of "natural experiments" in the large-scale indoctrination and institutionalization of ideology. In what measure are the lessons and insights of case studies like the Romanian one generalizable? And what is the particular domain of their generalizability? What are the conditions that may lead to more successful institutionalization of indoctrination? Is it possible to identify or to imagine cases that may circumvent the structural problems we have identified in our tentative investigation? What are the features that facilitate a successful indoctrination and propaganda organization and institutionalization? And what are the social, psychological, institutional, and economic barriers they may encounter?

These are fascinating questions whose deeper dimensions and implications have been brought to the fore by our case study and the exploratory engagement with the insights emerging from it. Dealing with them and with the other questions and research venues that have emerged as salient in our inquiry is the task of the next steps in the development of a research agenda that is fascinating and—as we are going to argue in the next chapter—very topical and consequential.

NOTES

1. Philip Selznick, *The Organizational Weapon: A Study of Bolshevik Strategy and Tactics* (New York: McGraw-Hill Book Company, 1952), 350.

2. Philip Selznick, *Leadership in Administration: A Sociological Interpretation* (Berkeley: University of California Press, 1984).

3. Philip Selznick, *TVA and the Grass Roots: A Study of Politics and Organization*, Vol. 3 (Berkeley: University of California Press, 1980).

4. The foundation for this line of effort is the formation of the Communist Party as a combat Party consisting of an elite of "reliable agents who are thoroughly indoctrinated, skillfully trained and rigidly disciplined." . . . Such a type of Party operated as the instrument employed to utilize and direct, for party ends, the potential energy resident in the mass of people. The mass is conceived not as an amorphous and diffused aggregate but as consisting of specialized groups and organizations, which are favorably located and which are or may be sources of power. Such groups and institutions become the targets for the power seeking efforts of the communists. . . . Only a few of the strategies need be mentioned here: the formation of small, concealed cadres in the target groups; their mutual efforts to gain official positions; the discrediting of officials and inner groups who stand in their way; the readiness to espouse vigorously the objectives of the target organizations as a means of moving into power; entering into united fronts in such manner as to make impossible demands and then throw on other groups the onus for the breakdown of the united front; the carrying on of conspiratorial activity behind and beyond the facade of the legitimate tasks of official positions. . . . In an ultimate sense, the Communists seek to develop progressively a network of power and control inside of established groups and institutions and, thus, to be in a position at the propitious time to displace constitutional authority in a given society. See also Herbert Blumer, "Review of The Organizational Weapon: A Study of Bolshevik Strategy and Tactics by Philip Selznick," in *American Sociological Review* 17 (1952): 630–31.

5. Philip Selznick, *Leadership in Administration: A Sociological Interpretation* (Berkeley: University of California Press, 1984), 5

6. Philip Selznick, op.cit., 8.

7. Philip Selznick, *TVA and the Grass Roots: A Study of Politics and Organization*, Vol. 3 (Berkeley: University of California Press, 1980).

8. The relation between teaching and propaganda is an interesting indicator. Some professors were asked to give up teaching in favor of working full-time as propagandists. Some propagandists wanted to return to teaching. The "revolving door" in this case is a very interesting phenomenon.

9. Philip Selznick, *TVA and the Grass Roots: A Study in the Sociology of Formal Organization* (Berkeley: University of California Press, 1953), 16–17.

10. Idem, 17.

11. Philip Selznick, *Leadership in Administration: A Sociological Interpretation* (Berkeley: University of California Press, 1984), 17.

12. Bucharest, Cluj-Napoca, Iași, Timișoara, and Târgu Mureș were the large universities. Apart from them, other cities that had their own universities were Craiova, Galați, Constanța, Ploiești, and Sibiu.

13. Compared to 1962, the number of Party members and candidates among the peasants practically doubled. This new situation made it possible to establish a large number of new Party organizations in localities that had none before.

14. A "healthy origin" referred to the family background, which must not include priests, landowners, relatives living abroad, and so forth.

15. The Securitate was the intelligence service subordinated to the Romanian Communist Ministry of Internal Affairs, responsible for maintaining a state of terror and repression. The Investigation Department of the Securitate had agents and informers infiltrated on each level of the Party structures and the society, reporting on any activities or views opposing the regime. When it was first established in 1948, the Securitate was named the General Directorate for the Security of the People (GDSP).

16. Philip Selznick, op.cit., 137–38.

17. Idem, 8.

18. The propagandists, especially those working in higher education, were aware of the advantages that their job offered them. They effortlessly obtained tenure and often enjoyed material advantages in a society ruled by scarcity, at least from the 1980s on. As already noted, whether being a propagandist professor was a privilege isn't debatable from several angles. After the fall of the Communist regime, the propagandist had lost his or her function in the state and society. Moreover, as an agent of the old regime, the propagandist had become subject to public blaming. It should be noted that, despite it being requested by many, a law of lustration was never adopted in Romania. As a result, in the post-1989 world, the propagandists, including those operating in education, were dictated by their conscience. The majority converted to being voices of the new power structure, adapting their discourse to the realities of post-Communism and, at the same time, making efforts to preserve the client-patron (hierarchical) system that had produced them. As for any symbolic gestures to acknowledge their complicity with the Communist regime, there were none. They only acknowledged their complicity when their political police dossiers were made public, and even then, they claimed that they had been coerced by the system and had done it against their will.

19. From 1950 to 1968, the *raion* was an administrative unit, just below the region level, in accordance with the Soviet model. After the 1968 reform, the *raion* was replaced by *județ* (county), the pre-Communist administrative unit.

Chapter 7

Research Directions in the Study of Indoctrination and Its Institutionalization

The contributions to the study of the institutionalization of indoctrination reflected in the previous chapters had an exploratory nature. Each chapter has tried, in its own way, to give an overview and explore particular perspectives and approaches to the phenomena of interest, or better said, to the cluster of phenomena associated with the ways a particular type of political system (what we have labeled as an "ideocratic" system) organizes and institutionalizes its ideological functions. As noted in the introductory chapter, at stake is something rather ambitious: these exploratory investigations were meant as an exercise in preparing us to better engage analytically and empirically with the problem of indoctrination and its institutionalization. How do we conceptualize and theorize about the social organization of ideology? How should we think systematically—in theoretically and empirically informed ways—about the institutionalization of indoctrination and propaganda? How should we approach the social organization of ideology in regimes or systems that make the stringent organizing and legitimization principles of their very existence out of an ideological historical mission? The chapters of the book have outlined several converging and complementary venues toward responding to these and similar questions.

The book has started by looking at the relevant scholarly literature, focusing on several salient ways in which that literature has confronted the tasks implied by these questions. It has presented these views while it further elaborated and calibrated some of them. In this respect, it has concentrated on three related conceptual schemes: The first was centered on the potential offered by the notion of "ideocracy." The second was centered on the much more familiar concept of "totalitarianism." Both were united at a third level by the problem of the role of the "models of man" in the theories and the practice of governance systems. The result was a fresh contribution to the taxonomy of political systems. It offered a constructive approach to the nature and the role of the institutions of propaganda and indoctrination in the architecture of these systems, putting them in a potentially very fruitful analytical and comparative light. In this respect, one of the most distinct contributions of our research effort came from the fact that it made a first step in the direction of placing the problem of indoctrination and its institutionalization in the broader context of the studies of alternative political systems and comparative institutional analysis.

That move creates the prospects of a double strategy: On the one hand, the researcher may use the study of the institutionalization of indoctrination as an entry point and as a window toward the structure, operation, and dynamics of a political system. On the other hand, the researcher may understand the institutionalization of indoctrination in light of it being a part of a larger system having its own dynamics and then build the explanatory and interpretive approaches, emphasizing its embeddedness and linkages. But even more important, placing the institutional aspects of the ideological functions in the context of the public choice and institutionalist analytical framework on the lines defined, for instance, by Bernholz's work, is a contribution that has more than just a taxonomic and static analysis relevance. Contributions on such lines may serve as an approach in which propaganda and indoctrination organizations (and, in general, the institutionalization of these activities) become important elements in the analysis of the transition from open systems to totalitarianism—and the other way around—from totalitarianism to open societies.

The other approach to propaganda and indoctrination outlined in the first part of the book had to do with the logic of functionalism and functional analysis, broadly defined. The structure of motivation behind the institutional and organizational forces at work in various social settings is central to this approach. The interpretive and explanatory argument is based on identifying the functions that institutional arrangements have in relation to the needs and objectives of the social actors and the social system. We have seen how the assumptions regarding the motivating factors that set into motion the processes associated with indoctrination, propaganda, and censorship have been used in the existing literature as main drivers of conceptualization and analysis. In this respect, the first part of the book looked at the two major types of approaches: the ideology and belief-systems-based perspectives and the perspectives based on strategic rationality. In conjunction, they create the possibility of an analytical engagement that is not trapped in circular explanations in terms of ideas and beliefs or in deterministic materialist speculation, but which introduces incentives and political and organizational elements into the picture institutions. As such, they offer a model of how to equip our theoretical thinking in the efforts to decipher and explain the social and historical features or patterns associated with indoctrination and its social organization.

The second part of the book moved to the other end of the range of possible approaches: the historical case study, in which the emphasis is not so much on the conceptual and theoretical apparatus, but rather on a real-life case circumscribed in time and space that becomes the unit of observation and the center of interest. The idea behind this approach has been that we could advance our understanding of the problem of institutionalization of ideology by looking in depth at specific cases and trying to get as many valid insights as possible about the phenomena of interest by illuminating and exploring their multiple facets in their historical, social, and cultural settings. With this end in view, we have engaged in an overview of the historical elements and patterns of the institutionalization of indoctrination in the Romanian context of the Communist regime. Thus, we have tried to capture—through a series of factual observation based on historical data—a sense of the complexities and multiple dimensions of the institutions and the process of indoctrination in a real-life Communist system. At the same time, we have tried to uncover the operating dynamics of the successes and failures of this natural experiment in institutionalizing an ideological program.

Read in conjunction, the first two parts of the book have offered the reader complementary perspectives, each approaching the phenomenon of interest from different angles. At the same time, they have created the possibility to illuminate the gaps in our understanding and provide the missing conceptual tools that we may need in order to deal with the topic in appropriate analytic and interpretive ways. Getting familiarized with the case while operating on the background shaped by the functionalist conceptual frameworks has helped us to identify a series of possible ways of going beyond and complementing these typical functionalist frameworks.

Therefore, building on the ground covered in the first two parts of the book, the third part has started to explore new venues of engaging the problem. As such, it illustrates the type of effort needed to articulate an approach that incorporates insights from the first two sections while dealing explicitly with the challenge of advancing additional forms of conceptualization and interpretation, a challenge that has been brought to the fore by the problems raised in this case study. In this respect, the previous chapter has tried to illustrate how one could start to put together a way of dealing with the institutionalization process as an organizational phenomenon using the perspective and the tools of organizational sociology. We have seen how a more sociologically nuanced conceptualization of institutionalization brings to the fore the possibility of novel interpretations and explanations.

When it comes to more a precise look at a future research agenda, one possible direction has to be an extension, in a more methodical manner of the investigation, of the Romanian case itself. The reality is that, at the end of this project, our sense is that the richness of the Romanian case has been barely touched in our exploratory study. The complexity of the case and the variety of insights that have been revealed in this preliminary investigation are just the result of a surface engagement. A vast potential of insights—both about Romania as it went through its Communist experience and about the potentially more general patterns underlying the phenomenon of the institutionalization of indoctrination—lie yet untapped in the wealth of Romanian primary and secondary sources. Our investigation has merely charted the territory, so to speak—indeed, it was tentative and exploratory. A lot of work in this respect is ahead of us. A vast range of themes and topics needs to be further documented and investigated, and there are numerous archives and historical records to be tapped. Further research may move in both the quantitative direction (better estimates of the magnitude, resources, scope, and impact associated with the maintenance and operation of the institutional apparatus) and the qualitative direction (in-depth case studies of propagandists' profiles and career tracks, propaganda units and organizational structures, propaganda and indoctrinations campaigns, or policies and institutional designs implemented throughout the duration of the regime).

Another possible direction has to do—obviously—with the broader theoretical and analytical side. As we have seen, using Selznick's notion of "institutionalization" has opened up for us an entire new dimension of interpretations and explanations. The strategy of taking a working concept or model that has a track record in a well-established discipline—such as sociology, institutional theory, or public choice—and applying that concept or model to the phenomena related to propaganda and indoctrination has proven its value. One is encouraged to further engage in this type of research strategy. In this respect, one finds an embarrassment of riches in the technical literature dealing with socialization, social stratification, and the political sociology elite theories as well as in the interdisciplinary literature exploring the relationship between beliefs systems and institutional structures and their social change.

The above reference to the institutional theory sets the stage for a smooth transition to the identification of a possible direction of research that is inspired precisely by the aforementioned strategy of applying more complex theoretical frameworks and models to the theme and the problems of interest. It is a research track that first incorporates, but then goes beyond, the approaches evoked, used, or elaborated in the book so far. Two such different theoretical constructs stand out, each very enticing for its own reasons.

The first is the application of the Institutional Analysis and Development (IAD) Framework created by the 2009 Nobel Prize in Economic Sciences laureate, Elinor Ostrom, and her team of researchers. The IAD Framework is a natural candidate for a major analytical and interpretive tool for any type of institutional arrangements and institutional processes. For those interested in the institutional aspect of ideology and beliefs systems, the IAD Framework is one of the most salient and promising instruments available in the technical literature relevant for such a research agenda.

The IAD Framework provides a language for describing the institutional configurations of various social systems and integrating insights on how institutions impact and shape incentives and—consequently—individuals' behavior.[1] The framework is based on an analytical-combinatorial formula. The focus in on the social space where individuals "interact, exchange goods and services, engage in appropriation and provision activities, solve problems, or fight" and is determined by a set of factors, pivotal among which are the rules organizing interindividual relationships, the attributes of a physical world, and the nature of the community within which the arena is located.[2] Its application involves three steps: (1) identifying and mapping the action arena (the action situation and the actors); (2) identifying factors that determine the action arena (the rules, social norms, attributes of a physical world, and community); (3) performing an analytical scenario building exercise reviewing how (1) and (2), once put together, generate patterns of interaction and outcomes over multiple action arenas.[3] As such, it is apt to function as a mapping instrument that is able to chart any institutional domain of interest and as a heuristic to identify structures and situations that define that institutional domain in ways that facilitate a solid theoretically grounded interdisciplinary stance and a high degree of intercomparability.[4]

One could easily see how this type of approach could be applied in the case of the institutional settings of propaganda and indoctrination activities and arenas. The action situations in which a propaganda or indoctrination process is taking place could be mapped and the social actors that are supposed to operate in those settings could be described using the various attributes that are relevant for the case. The factors determining that action arena (be they of an organizational, institutional, cultural, political, or strategic nature) could be constructively sorted out and organized using this framework. The theoretical apparatus associated with institutional theory could then take the stylized facts and use them in the task of interpretation, analysis, or hypothesis development. The result would be a constructive step forward toward a more systematic approach. For instance, once the departments, units, and offices of national institutions are modeled as action arenas, they are amenable to a series of research designs with a proven track record to be used as they become sources of inspiration.

The second theoretical construct we would like to present as an example of the type of theoretical tools of potential interest for our agenda is in reference to Timur Kuran's work on preference falsification. Timur Kuran has developed a penetrating analysis of the dynamics of the climate of opinion in conditions of heavy censorship, propaganda, and political ideological repression. In a series of publications, he has developed a powerful technical approach to the relationship between the climate of opinion, the personal belief systems, the private policy preferences, and the preferences expressed publicly.[5] Kuran's model of preference falsification "illuminates not only why a policy that few people support privately may command an overwhelming public endorsement, but also why, once this policy is in place, the degree of private opposition will diminish."[6] At the same time, his work explains why regimes that are based on foundations that incorporate preference falsification may unravel easily in very surprising ways. One could already recognize a theme and a pattern that we have encountered in our own investigation of the Romanian case.

Kuran builds his analysis around a simple model in which (a) there are two alternative positions on a public policy issue—for instance, support for a Communist regime or opposition to it—and (b) the assumption that the personal, private preferences between these alternatives are the result of a typical, rational, self-interested calculus: people favor whichever alternative will personally benefit them most. The interesting dynamics of Kuran's story, explains Robert Frank, who is another author whose ideas may inspire the future research agenda on ideology and indoctrination, "emerges from the dependence of reputational utility on the distribution of people who favor the two alternatives." The dynamics illuminated by the model follow straightforwardly: "As more and more people favor one position publicly, the reputational cost of favoring the alternative position rises, and vice versa." Hence, "if p denotes the proportion of the population that publicly opposes the regime, each individual may be seen as having a threshold value of p above which he, too, will oppose the regime. Under these circumstances, Kuran explains, it is no mystery that seemingly small changes can wreak social havoc."[7]

The promise of a project that connects the phenomenon of institutionalization of indoctrination, on the one hand, with the phenomena of preference falsification, on the other hand, is not hard to imagine. One could study the interrelationships between the two, not only as an institutionalist exercise in theory building to be supported by empirical evidence, but also as an empirical case study of the manifestations of these linkages in a very concrete case (like, for instance, the Romanian case) that uses a research design in which the heuristics of the study are guided by this compounded framework. A compounded Ostrom-Kuran theoretical apparatus could thus help to forge

Research Directions in the Study of Indoctrination and Its Institutionalization 153

an approach that connects the institutional and organizational process to the dynamics of public opinion. For instance, the problem of "thresholds" may emerge as pivotal, both in terms of building "preference falsification" regimes and in terms of unraveling them. If one adds the Selznick angle on institutionalization to these, forging all of them in the context of the Bernholz-inspired taxonomical conceptualization of liberal political systems, the potential of these compounded research venues becomes truly captivating.

Seen in conjunction, the chapters of this book and the potential research directions outlined above have revealed some of the key features of the phenomena associated with the institutionalization of indoctrination and propaganda. At the same time, they have illuminated fertile and constructive venues for a robust research program. Underlying all of the above is a rather ambitious research horizon: a comparative analysis of ideocratic totalitarianism that includes its manifestations in forms and circumstances distinct from the standard, well known cases of National Socialism, Communism, and Fascism that are typically used as illustrations in the literature. Looking ahead, there are two possible major research paths that emerge as salient.

The first possible direction is to extend the discussion and analysis by looking at a larger pool of historical cases of ideocratic-totalitarian-bent regimes. In his work, Bernholz bolstered his interpretation with a survey of the empirical evidence.[8] In his inventory of the relevant historical cases that are closest to the ideal type implied by his models of the totalitarianism-ideocracy continuum, he identified and listed mature ideocracies regimes such as those of Saudi Arabia, Iran (or in the past, the Jesuit State in Paraguay or Massachusetts Puritans), while the list of totalitarian systems comprised the cases of Soviet Union, China, Nazi Germany, Cambodia, North Korea, Eastern Europe, Cuba, and the Islamic State. Following this line of broad comparative analysis could be a fruitful direction, indeed. That being said, the next immediate step in comparative analysis may be a more focalized one: the case of Eastern Europe Communist countries. One could be even more specific and put a comparative focus on higher education systems. Thus, a comparative study of the political ideological indoctrination mechanisms and organizations created or consolidated in universities and research centers and the way they operated in in Communism may be a very promising topic for the next steps of the research agenda.

That being said, there is a second direction, suggesting a similarly challenging and, perhaps, an even more intriguing approach. A striking question is whether the presence of any of the traits associated with ideocracy in a liberal democratic (or simply nonauthoritarian) system denotes the existence of a potential trend toward totalitarianism. That is a crucial question for comparative analysis, as it suggests the possibility that a social or political system may move in a totalitarian direction in a sequence of stages, starting from different sectors of the society in small and partial steps to gradually extend to the level of taking over the entire system. That observation, correlated to the remark that there are some intrinsic connections between these traits that reinforce each other, makes for a fascinating set of conjectures. Thus, we may see a fresh research agenda emerging that looks at totalitarianism not only in systemic, national-level (state-level) regimes but also in more localized and personalized organizational or sectorial forms within various social and historical circumstances. By understanding the past of such social and institutional experiments, we get a better understanding of the present and become better equipped for the future.

Two final observations, first made by Friedrich and Brzezinski, may be vital in connecting a deeper sense of what is at stake in this potential line of research.[9] First, we have seen how Friedrich and Brzezinski drew our attention, as noted in the first part of our book, to the fact that totalitarianism is intertwined with technology and technological progress. Progress in communication technologies or developments of an institutional-technology nature (such as those related to bureaucratization, rationalization, and the span of authority management) facilitate and are instrumental to the objective of total control. The objective of imposing an ideology defined by absolute value is henceforth facilitated. The goal to remodel the consciousness of human beings seems more enticing and feasible. The first decade of the twenty-first century was the stage of a remarkable evolution in this respect. The task to better investigate and understand these developments is a priority.

The second observation that has a huge promise for comparative analysis was also evoked in the first section of the book—Friedrich and Brzezinski have pointed out to our attention a very peculiar phenomenon. The curious fact is that the ways totalitarianism defines itself for the public—and even in the mind of its own agents—have been strongly shaped by the vocabulary and sensitivities of modern liberal democracy. Friedrich and Brzezinski warned that we are getting to a moment when totalitarianism is increasingly presented by its own supporters as a natural extension of democracy. It is advocated as the true form of democracy, either the fulfillment or the transcendence of Western liberal democracy. That has important repercussions, as the entire vocabulary of liberal democracy may be taken over and its semantics altered as this process is unfolding. When that happens, the "vulnerability of democracy"—as Vincent Ostrom[10] put it—becomes glaring and manifest. Institutional mutations of an informal nature start to alter the structure and function of the formal ones, while preference falsification may become rampant. In brief, two phenomena strongly associated with totalitarianism are thus facilitated. How these all may play in conjunction with the momentous developments induced by the information technology and artificial intelligence revolutions emerges as one of the most significant and consequential research agendas in contemporary political, moral, and social sciences.

NOTES

1. Michael D. McGinnis, "An Introduction to IAD and the Language of the Ostrom Workshop: A Simple Guide to a Complex Framework," in *Policy Studies Journal*, 39, no. 1 (2011): 169–83. L. L. Kiser & E. Ostrom, "Synthesis of Institutional Approaches," in *Polycentric Games and Institutions: Readings from the Workshop in Political Theory and Policy Analysis* (Ann Arbor: University of Michigan Press, 2000), 56.

2. E. Ostrom, R. Gardner, and J. Walker, *Rules, Games, and Common-Pool Resources* (Ann Arbor: University of Michigan Press, 1994).

3. Elinor Ostrom, "Background on the Institutional Analysis and Development Framework," in *Policy Studies Journal*, 39, no. 1 (2011): 7–27.

4. The goal is to have a unified framework composed of the *same set of elements* for all cases explored that could be applicable to any social space investigated. The institutional and analysis procedure tries to conceptually capture the basic form of an *action arena*, composed of an *action situation* involving *participants* who have preferences, information-processing capabilities, selection criteria, and resources. Social actors decide among diverse actions in light of the information they possess, and those actions are linked to potential outcomes and the costs and benefits assigned to actions and outcomes. See Michael D. McGinnis, "An Introduction to IAD and the Language of the Ostrom Workshop: A Simple Guide to a Complex Framework," in *Policy Studies Journal*, 39, no. 1 (2011): 169–83.

5. Timur Kuran, *Private Truths, Public Lies* (Cambridge, MA: Harvard University Press, 1997) and Timur Kuran, "Preference Falsification, Policy Continuity and Collective Conservatism," in *The Economic Journal*, 97, no. 387 (1987): 642–65 and Timur Kuran, "The Inevitability of Future Revolutionary Surprises," in *American Journal of Sociology*, 100, no. 6 (1995): 1528–51, and also see Timur Kuran, "Sparks and Prairie Fires: A Theory of Unanticipated Political Revolution," in *Public Choice*, 61, no. 1 (1989): 41–74.

6. "The arguments," explains Kuran, "rest on distinctions between private and public preferences and between private and public beliefs. The first distinction explains why societies retain policies they might have abandoned if not for the pull of the past. The two together explain why adopted policies condition people's perceptions and wants. The model uncovers a tendency for beliefs and preferences to become homogenized. Such outcomes may be sought intentionally by some. But they are ultimately caused by multitudes of individual decisions made without an awareness of where they will lead. . . . In recognizing that people depend on each other for their beliefs about how the world works, the model confers to the process of belief formation an important role in the collective decision process." See for details Timur Kuran,

"Preference Falsification, Policy Continuity and Collective Conservatism," in *The Economic Journal*, 97, no. 387 (1987): 642–65.

7. Robert H. Frank, "The Political Economy of Preference Falsification: Timur Kuran's Private Truths, Public Lies," in *Journal of Economic Literature*, 34, no. 1 (1996): 115–23.

8. P. Bernholz, "Ideocracy and Totalitarianism: A Formal Analysis Incorporating Ideology," in *Public Choice*, 108, no. 1 (2001): 33–75, and Peter Bernholz, "The Theory of Totalitarianism and Mature Ideocracy, Part I: Evolution and Development," in: *Totalitarianism, Terrorism and Supreme Values* (New York: Springer, Cham, 2017), 23–26 and see also Peter Bernholz, "Mature Ideocracies," in: *Totalitarianism, Terrorism and Supreme Values* (New York: Springer, Cham, 2017), 39–45.

9. Carl J. Friedrich and Zbigniew K. Brzezinski, *Totalitarian Dictatorship and Autocracy* (Cambridge, MA: Harvard University Press, 1956), 26–28.

10. Vincent Ostrom, *The Meaning of Democracy and the Vulnerability of Democracies: A Response to Tocqueville's Challenge* (Ann Arbor: University of Michigan Press, 1997).

Bibliography

Amfiteatru (*Amphitheater*)—since 1966.
Angenot, Marc, *La propagande socialiste: six essais d'analyse du discours*, Montréal: Editions Balzac, 1997.
ANIC, the CC of the RCP Collection—*Central National Historical Archive, Central Committee (CC) of the Romanian Communist Party (RCP)* (Arhivele Naționale Istorice Centrale, fond Comitetul Central al Partidului Comunist Român)
ANIC, the CC of the RCP Collection, Chancellery Section, file no. 58/1948, 57; 71.
ANIC, the CC of the RCP Collection, Chancellery Section, file no. 63/1965, 2–29.
ANIC, the CC of the RCP Collection, Chancellery Section, file no. 68/1965, 29.
ANIC, the CC of the RCP Collection, Chancellery Section, file no. 82/1971, 2–6.
ANIC, the CC of the RCP Collection, Chancellery Section, file no. 85/1971, 13–24.
ANIC, the CC of the RCP Collection, Organizational Section, file no. 23/1950, 2–55.
ANIC, the CC of the RCP Collection, Organizational Section, file no. 14/1956, 220–22.
ANIC, the CC of the RCP Collection, Organizational Section, file no. 45/1956, 1–57.
ANIC, the CC of the RCP Collection, Organizational Section, file no. 47/ 1968, 1–53.
ANIC, the CC of the RCP Collection, Organizational Section, file no. 30/1976, 20.
ANIC, the CC of the RCP Collection, Propaganda and Agitation Section, file no. 49/1948, 1.
ANIC, the CC of the RCP Collection, Propaganda and Agitation Section, file no. 45/1949, 45.
ANIC, the CC of the RCP Collection, Propaganda and Agitation Section, file no. 16/1950, 34.
ANIC, the CC of the RCP Collection, Propaganda and Agitation Section, file no. 6/1951, 17.
ANIC, the CC of the RCP Collection, Propaganda and Agitation Section, file no. 30/1952, 91–92.
ANIC, the CC of the RCP Collection, Propaganda and Agitation Section, file no. 58/1952, 1.
ANIC, the CC of the RCP Collection, Propaganda and Agitation Section, file no. 10/1960, 65.

ANIC, the CC of the RCP Collection, Propaganda and Agitation Section, file no. 46/1965, 8.
ANIC, the CC of the RCP Collection, Propaganda and Agitation Section, file no. 10/1967, 43.
ANIC, the CC of the RCP Collection, Propaganda and Agitation Section, file no. 21/1968, 80; 184–85.
ANIC, the CC of the RCP Collection, Propaganda and Agitation Section, file no. 28/1968, 54–55.
ANIC, the CC of the RCP Collection, Propaganda and Agitation Section, file no. 14/1969, 39; 43–44; 49.
ANIC, the CC of the RCP Collection, Propaganda and Agitation Section, file no. 20/1971, 11.
ANIC, the CC of the RCP Collection, Propaganda and Agitation Section, file no. 20/1973, 5.
ANIC, the CC of the RCP Collection, Propaganda and Agitation Section, file no. 2/1979, 9.
Aradavoaice, Gheorghe (ccord.), *Metodica propagandei politice: studii, sinteze, experiențe* (*Method of Political Propaganda: Studies, Summaries, Experiences*), Bucharest: Editura Militară, 1987.
Arendt, Hannah, *La nature du totalitarisme*, Paris: Payot, 1990.
Aron, Raymond, *The Opium of the Intellectuals*, trans. Terence Kilmartin, New York: W. W. Norton & Company. Inc, 1962.
Bălănescu, Flori, unpublished manuscript.
Bernholz, P., "Ideocracy and Totalitarianism: A Formal Analysis Incorporating Ideology" in *Public Choice*, 108, no. 1 (2001): 33–75.
Bernholz, Peter, *Totalitarianism, Terrorism and Supreme Values*, New York: Springer International Publishing, 2017.
Betea, Lavinia, *Maurer și lumea de ieri. Mărturii despre stalinizarea României* (*Maurer and the World of Yesterday. Confessions about the Stalinization of Romania*), Arad: Editura Fundației Ioan Slavici, 1995.
Betea, Lavinia, *Psihologia politică. Individ, lider, mulțime în regimul comunist* (*Political Psychology: Individual, Leader, Masses in the Communist Regime*), Iași: Editura Polirom, 2001.
Bîtfoi, Dorin-Liviu, *Așa s-a născut omul nou—În România anilor '50* (*Thus Was the New Man Born—In 1950s Romania*), Bucharest: Editura Compania, 2012.
Blumer, Herbert, "Review of The Organizational Weapon: A Study of Bolshevik Strategy and Tactics by Philip Selznick," in *American Sociological Review* 17 (1952): 630–31.
Bogoi, Ștefan, "Pregătirea lectorilor și propagandiștilor" ("Training of Lecturers and Propagandists"), in *În ajutorul propagandiștilor* (*Support for the Propagandists*), Year VI, No.1/1967, 14.
Boia, Lucian, "Un mit Gheorghiu-Dej?" ("A Gheorghiu-Dej Myth?"), in *Miturile comunismului românesc* (*The Myths of Romanian Communism*), vol. 2, Bucharest: Editura Universității București, 1995, 173–82.

Boia, Lucian, *Cum am trecut prin comunism. Al doilea sfert de veac* (*How We Went through Communism: Second Quarter Century*), Bucharest: Editura Humanitas, 2019.

Bosomitu, Ştefan, "Planificare-implementare-control. Apariţia şi dezvoltarea aparatului de propagandă comunist în România, 1944–1950" ("Planning-Implementation-Control: The Emergence and Development of the Communist Propaganda Apparatus in Romania, 1944–1950") in *Structuri de partid şi de stat în timpul regimului comunist* (*Party and State Structures during the Communist Regime*), Anuarul IICCR, vol. III, Iaşi: Editura Polirom, 2008, 20.

Bosomitu, Ştefan, *Miron Constantinescu. O biografie* (*Miron Constantinescu. A Biography*), preface by Vladimir Tismăneanu, Bucharest: Editura Humanitas, 2014.

Brooks, Jeffrey, *International Review of Social History*, 55, no. 3 (2010): 529–30.

Brucan, Silviu, *Generaţia irosită* (*Wasted Generation*), Bucharest: Editura Univers-Calistrat Hogaş, 1992.

Burakowsky, Adam, *Dictatura lui Nicolae Ceauşescu, 1965–1989, Geniul Carpaţilor* (*Dictatorship of Nicolae Ceauşescu, 1965–1989, Genius of the Carpathians*), Iaşi: Polirom, 2011.

Buzatu, Gheorghe, *Românii în arhivele Kremlinului* (*Romanians in the Kremlin archives*), Bucharest: Editura Univers Enciclopedic, 1996.

Carnetul agitatorului (*The Aggitator's Notebook*).

Cassinelli, C. W., "Totalitarianism, Ideology, and Propaganda," in *The Journal of Politics*, 22, no. 1 (1960): 68–95.

Cathala, Henri-Pierre, *Epoca dezinformării* (*Age of Disinformation*), trans. by Nicolae Bărbulescu, Bucharest: Editura Militară, 1991.

Cetăţeanu, Ion, "Mediul socio-cultural al Universităţii din Craiova" ("The Socio-Cultural Environment of the University of Craiova"), in Aculin Cazacu (ed.), *Dinamica socială a învăţământului universitar—Studiu pe modelul Universităţii din Craiova* (*Social Dynamics of University Education—Study on the Model of the University of Craiova*), Craiova: Editura Scrisul Românesc, 1973, 42–43.

Chakotin, Serge, *Rape of the Masses: The Psychology of Totalitarian Political Propaganda*, London: Routledge, 1940.

Che Guevara, Ernesto, *Oeuvres 1957–1967*, vol. 2, Paris: François Maspero, 1971.

Cheng, Yinghong, *Creating the "New Man": From Enlightenment Ideals to Socialist Realities*, Honolulu: University of Hawai'i Press, 2009.

Cioroianu, Adrian, *Camarazii utopiei. Destine individuale şi de grup din ilegalitatea comunistă* (Comrades of Utopia: Individual and Group Destinies from Communist Illegality), Bucharest: Editura Universităţii din Bucureşti, 2017.

Cioroianu, Adrian, *Pe umerii lui Marx. O introducere în istoria comunismului românesc* (*On Marx's Shoulders: An Introduction to the History of Romanian Communism*), Bucharest: Curtea Veche Publishing, 2005.

Congresul PMR, Bucureşti, 21–23 februarie 1948 (*PMR Congress, Bucharest, 21–23 February 1948*), Bucharest: Editura PMR, 1948.

Conquest, R. *Reflections on a Ravaged Century*, New York: W. W. Norton & Company, 2001.

Constantiniu, Florin, "Geneza nomenclaturii comuniste" ("The Genesis of the Communist Nomenclature"), in *Dosarele istoriei (History Files)*, no. 4 (1996): 2.

Cotovschi, Gr., "Rolul propagandistului în educarea comunistă a membrilor de partid" ("The Role of the Propagandist in the Communist Education of Party Members"), in *Lupta de clasă (Class Fight)*, Series V, Year XXXII, no. 11 (November 1952): 70–81.

Cravata Roşie (The Ted Tie) (1953–1967).

Cunningham, S. B., *The Idea of Propaganda: A Reconstruction.* Greenwood Publishing Group, 2002.

Cutezătorii (The Brave) (1967–1989).

Deletant, Dennis, *Communist Terror in Romania: Gheorghiu-Dej and the Police State, 1948–65*, London: C. Hurst & Co. Publishers, 1999.

Deletant, Dennis, *România sub regimul communist (Romania Under the Communist Regime)*, Bucharest: Editura Fundaţia Academia Civică, 1997.

Denize, Eugen and Cezar Mâţă, *România comunistă. Statul şi propaganda (Communist Romania: State and Propaganda)*, Târgovişte: Editura Cetatea de Scaun, 2005.

Denize, Eugen, *Propaganda comunistă în România—1948–1953 (Communist Propaganda in Romania—1948–1953)*, Târgovişte: Editura Cetatea de Scaun, 2011.

Despre agitaţia vizuală (About the Visual Agitation), Bucharest: Editura PMR, 1950.

Despre arta agitatorului de a vorbi cu masele (About the Agitator's Art of Talking to the Masses), Bucharest: Editura Politică, 1960.

Diac, Cristina, "Ioan Toma, ultimul şef al UTC: Ceauşescu nu era mai incult ca Băsescu" ("Ioan Toma, Last Head of UTC: Ceauşescu Was No More Uneducated than Basescu"), in *Jurnalul Naţional (National Journal)*, August 20, 2010.

Domenach, J. M., "Leninist Propaganda" in *Public Opinion Quarterly*, 152 (1951): 265–73.

Domenach, Jean-Marie, "Leninist Propaganda," in *The Public Opinion Quarterly* 15, no. 2 (1951): 272.

Domenach, Jean-Marie, *Propaganda politică (Political Propaganda)*, Bucharest: Editura Institutului European, 2004.

Dumitrescu, Nicu, "Activitatea de pregătire a lectorilor" ("Lecturer training activity"), in *În ajutorul propagandiştilor (Support for the Propagandists)*, Year VII, no. 10/1968, 36.

Ellul, Jacques, *Histoire de la propaganda*, Paris: Presses Universitaires de France, 1967.

Ellul, Jacques, *Propaganda: The Formation of Men's Attitudes*, New York: Vintage Books, 1973.

Expunere făcută de tovarăşul Leonte Răutu despre sarcinile muncii de propagandă şi agitaţie (Comrade Răutu's Memorandum on the Responsibilities of Propaganda and Agitation Work), in ANIC, the CC of the RCP Collection, Propaganda and Agitation Section, file no. 10/1960, 65.

Expunere făcută de tovarăşul Leonte Răutu despre sarcinile muncii de propagandă şi agitaţie (Comrade Leonte Răutu's Memorandum on the Duties of the Propaganda and Agitation Work), in ANIC, the CC of the RCP Collection, Propaganda and Agitation Section, file no. 14/1969, 39.

Ficeac, Bogdan, *Cenzura comunistă și formarea omului nou* (*Communist Censorship and the Formation of the New Man*), Bucharest: Editura Nemira, 1999.

Ficeac, Bogdan, *Tehnici de manipulare* (*Manipulation's Techniques*), Bucharest: Editura Nemira, 1996.

Filipaș, Cornelia, "Rolul UTM-ului în școli" ("The Role of UTM in Schools"), *Lupta de clasă* (*Class Fight*), 5th series, XXX, 9–10 (Sept–Oct 1950): 47–61.

Fireside, H., *Soviet Psychoprisons,* New York: Norton, 1979.

Frank, Robert H., "The Political Economy of Preference Falsification: Timur Kuran's Private Truths, Public Lies," in *Journal of Economic Literature*, 34, no. 1 (1996): 115–23.

Friedrich, Carl J. and Zbigniew Brzezinski, *Totalitarian Dictatorship and Autocracy*, Cambridge, MA: Harvard University Press, 1956.

Frunză, Victor, *Istoria stalinismului în România* (*History of Stalinism in Romania*), Bucharest: Editura Humanitas, 1990.

Ghiorghiu, Mihai, Dinu, "O elocventă dovadă a modului în care tovarășul Nicolae Ceaușescu sesizează cerințele fiecărei etape" ("An Eloquent Proof of How Comrade Nicolae Ceaușescu Understands the Requirements of Each Stage"), in *Scânteia* (*The Spark*), July 9, 1971.

Gleason, Abbott, *Totalitarianism: The Inner History of the Cold War*, Oxford: Oxford University Press, 1997.

Golianu, Alexandru, *Metodica studiului politic-ideologic. Criterii și modalități ale organizării și desfășurării învățământului de partid și propagandei prin conferințe* (*Method of Political-Ideological Study: Criteria and Modalities for the Organization and Conduct of Party Education and Propaganda through Conferences*), Bucharest: Editura Politică, 1972.

Guriev, Sergei, and Daniel Treisman, "How Modern Dictators Survive: An Informational Theory of the New Authoritarianism," no. w21136, in *National Bureau of Economic Research*, 2015.

Harold D. Lasswell and Nathan Leites, *Language of Politics. Studies in Quantitative Semantics*, Cambridge, MA: M.I.T. Press, 1965.

Heller, Michel, *La machine et les rouages. La formation de l'homme sovietique,* Paris: Calmann-Lévy, 1985.

Henein, Georges, *Petite Encyclopédie Politique,* Paris: Le Seuil, 1969.

Hentea, Călin, *Propagandă fără frontiere* (*Propaganda without Borders*), Bucharest: Editura Nemira, 2002.

Hentea, Călin, "Memoria cărții poștale. Uteceul duce greul" ("Postcard memory. The UTC carries the brunt"), in Ziarul *financiar (Financial Newspaper),* of Sept 7, 2009.

Hollander, P., "Creating the 'New Man': From Enlightenment Ideals to Socialist Realities," *Slavic Review*, 701 (2011): 205–6.

Hollander, Paul, *Slavic Review* 70, no. 1 (2011): 205–6.

Hume, David, "On the Independence of Parliament" (1742) in *Essays Moral, Political, and Literary*, ed. Eugene F. Miller, Indianapolis: Liberty Fund, 1985, 98.

Ilie, Oana, *Propagandă politică. Tipologii și arii de manifestare (1945–1958)* (*Political Propaganda: Typologies and Areas of Manifestation, 1945–1958*), Târgoviște: Editura Cetatea de Scaun, 2014.

În ajutorul propagandiștilor (*Support for the Propagandists*).

Informare (*Informative note*), in ANIC, the CC of the RCP Collection, Propaganda and Agitation Section, file no. 7/1972, 2.

Informare cu privire la măsurile luate pentru organizarea vacanței de iarnă a pionierilor și elevilor din învățământ (*Note on the Measure Taken to Organize the Pioneer's and Other Students' Winter Break*), in ANIC, the CC of the RCP Collection, Propaganda and Agitation Section, file no. 20/1967, 59.

Informare din data de 22 mai, 1969 (*Informative Note of the 22 May 1969*), in ANIC, the CC of the RCP Collection, Propaganda and Agitation Section, file no. 14/1969, 16–17.

Informație cu privire la revista "În ajutorul propagandiștilor" (*Information on the Magazine "Resources for Propagandists"*), in ANIC, the CC of the RCP Collection, Propaganda and Agitation Section, file no. 7/1964, 21.

Instrucțiuni cu privire la învățământul de partid și propaganda prin conferințe (*Instructions on Party Education and Propaganda through Cnferences*), in ANIC, the CC of the RCP Collection, Propaganda and Agitation Section, file no. 20/1971, 12.

Instructorul de pionieri (*The Pioneer's Instructor*) (1951–1958).

Învățământul politico-ideologic de partid 1975–1979. Probleme orientative și bibliografii pentru cursuri și seminarii (*Political-Ideological Party Education 1975–1979: Guidance and Bibliography Issues for Courses and Seminars*), Bucharest: Editura Politică, 1975.

Ioncioaia, Florea, Rados, Leonidas (eds), *Fragmente de pe un câmp de luptă: studii în istoria universității* (*Fragments from a Battlefield: Studies in the History of the University*), Iași: Alexandru Ioan Cuza Publishing House, 2018.

Ionescu-Gură, Nicoleta, "Modernizarea PMR-ului după modelul PC al URSS și crearea nomenclaturii CC al PMR în Republica Populară Română (1949–1950)," ("Modernization of the PMR Following the PC Model of the USSR and the Creation of the CC Nomenclature of the PMR in the People's Republic Romanian (1949–1950)" in *Totalitarism și rezistență, teroare și represiune în România comunistă* (*Totalitarianism and Resistance, Terror and Repression in Communist Romania*), ed. Gheorghe Onișoru, Bucharest: Editura CNSAS, 2001 216–50.

Ionescu-Gură, Nicoleta, *Nomenclatura CC al PMR* (*The Nomenclature of the CC of the PMR*), Bucharest: Editura Humanitas, 2006.

Jeane, J., "Dictatorships and Double Standards," *Commentary Magazine*, November, 1979.

Kirkpatrick, J., *Dictatorships and Double Standards: Rationalism and Reason in Politics*, New York: Simon and Schuster, 1982.

Kiser L., and E. Ostrom, O., "Synthesis of Institutional Approaches," in *Polycentric Games and Institutions: Readings from the Workshop in Political Theory and Policy Analysis*, Ann Arbor: University of Michigan Press, 2000, 56.

Koopmans, Tjalling, C. and Jojn Michel Montias, "On the Description and Comparison of Economic Systems," in *Comparison of Economic Systems: Theoretical and Methodological Approaches,* ed. by A. Eckstein. Berkeley: University of California Press, 1971, 27–78.

Koutaissoff, E., "Soviet Education and the New Man," in *Soviet Studies,* 5, no. 2 (1953): 103–37.

Kuran, Timur, "Preference Falsification, Policy Continuity and Collective Conservatism," in *The Economic Journal,* 97, no. 387 (1987): 642–65.

Kuran, Timur, "The Inevitability of Future Revolutionary Surprises," in *American Journal of Sociology,* 100, no. 6 (1995): 1528–51.

Kuran, Timur, *Private Truths, Public Lies: The Social Consequences of Preference Falsification,* Cambridge, MA: Harvard University Press, 1997.

Kuran, Timur, "Sparks and Prairie Fires: A Theory of Unanticipated Political Revolution" in *Public Choice,* 61, no. 1 (1989): 41–74.

Le Bon, Gustave, *Psihologia maselor (Psychology of the Masses),* Bucharest: Editura Științifică, 1991.

Le Bon, Gustave, *Psihologie politică (Political Psychology),* trans. Simona Pelin, Prahova: Antet Press, 2002.

Lecții pentru agitatori (Lessons for Agitators), Cluj: Întreprinderea Poligrafică, 1960.

Lecții pentru cursurile cu agitatorii (Lessons for the Courses with the Agitators), Bucharest: Editura PMR, 1952.

Lenin, V., *Three Sources and Three Essentials of Marxism,* 1913.

Lifton, R. J., *Thought Reform and the Psychology of Totalism: A Study of "Brainwashing" in China,* Chapel Hill: UNC Press Books, 2012.

Lupta de clasă (Class Struggle).

Makarenko, A. S., *Problems of Soviet School Education,* Moscow: Progress Publishers, 1965.

Makarenko, S., "Pedagogi Pozhimayut Plechami," written in 1927, in *Izbrannye Pedagogicheskiye Sochinenia,* 1949, vol. 4, quoted by E. Koutaissoff, 134.

Marin, Manuela, *Originea și evoluția cultului personalității lui Nicolae Ceaușescu (Origin and Evolution of Nicolae Ceaușescu's Cult of Personality),* Alba-Iulia: Editura Altip, 2008.

Măsuri de aplicare a hotărârilor privind întărirea activității politico-ideologice și cultural-educative (Measures to Apply the Decisions on the Strengthening of the Political-Ideological and Cultural-Educational work), in ANIC, the CC of the RCP Collection, Chancellery Section, file no. 85/1971, 19.

McGinnis, Michael, D., "An Introduction to IAD and the Language of the Ostrom Workshop: A Simple Guide to a Complex Framework," in *Policy Studies Journal,* 39, no. 1 (2011): 169–83.

Mihăilescu, Dan, C., "Acrobatul cu plasa roșie" ("The Acrobat with the Red Net"), *Evenimentul zilei (Event of the Day),* January 23, 2009, accessed August 27, 2014, https://evz.ro/dan-c-mihailescu-acrobatul-cu-plasa-rosie-836777.html.

Mihalache, Andi, Adrian Cioflâncă, *In media res. Studii de istorie culturală (In Media Res: Cultural History Studies),* Iași: Editura Universității Alexandru Ioan Cuza, 2007.

Mocanu, Maria Radu, *Cenzura comunistă—Documente* (*Communist Censorship—Documents*), Bucharest: Editura Albatros, 2001.

Munca de partid (*Party Work*).

Notă-probleme ce urmează a fi rezolvate în munca politică de masă (*Note—Issues Related to Mass Political Work to be Solved*), in ANIC, the CC of the RCP Collection, Propaganda and Agitation Section, file no. 3/1965, 109.

Ostrom, E., Walker, Gardner, J., *Rules, Games, and Common-Pool Resources*, Ann Arbor: University of Michigan Press, 1994.

Ostrom, Elinor, "Background on the Institutional Analysis and Development Framework," in *Policy Studies Journal*, 39, no. 1 (2011): 7–27.

Ostrom, Elinor, *Governing the Commons: The Evolution of Institutions for Collective Action*, Cambridge: Cambridge University Press, 1990.

Ostrom, Vincent, *The Meaning of Democracy and the Vulnerability of Democracies: A Response to Tocqueville's Challenge*, Ann Arbor: University of Michigan Press, 1997.

Pălășan, Corina, "Organizarea științifică a societății sau științele sociale în România primilor ani ai regimului Ceaușescu," ("Scientific Organization of Society or Social Sciences in Romania of the First Years of the Ceaușescu Regime"), in *Structuri de partid și de stat în timpul regimului comunist*, Iași: Editura Polirom, Anuarul IICCR, vol. III, 2008, 132.

Partenie, Ștefan, "Răspunderile lectorilor și ale propagandiștilor" ("Responsibilities of Lecturers and Propagandists"), in *În ajutorul propagandiștilor* (*Support for the Propagandists*), Year VII, no. 10/1968, 13.

PCR și intelectualii în primii ani ai regimului Ceaușescu (*PCR and Intellectuals in the Early Years of the Ceaușescu's Regime*), documentary edition, Bucharest: National Archives of Romania, 2007.

Petcu, Marian, *Puterea și cenzura. O istorie a cenzurii* (*Power and Censorship: A History of Censorship*), Iași: Editura Polirom, 1999.

Pionierul (The Pioneer)—beginning with 1949.

Pipes, R., "Human Nature and the Fall of Communism," in *Bulletin of the American Academy of Arts and Sciences*, 4, no. 94 (1996): 38–53.

Plenara CC al PCR din 22–25 aprilie 1968 (The Plenary Session of the CC of the RCP of April 22–25, 1968), Bucharest: Editura Politică, 1968.

Popa, Cosmin, *Intelectualii lui Ceaușescu și Academia de Științe Sociale și Politice (1970–1989)* (*Ceaușescu's Intellectuals and the Academy of Social and Political Sciences (1970–1989)*, Bucharest: Editura Litera, 2018.

Preutu, Cristina, *Propaganda politică în România socialistă. Practici instituționale și tehnici de comunicare 1965–1974* (*Political Propaganda in Socialist Romania: Institutional Practices and Communication Techniques 1965–1974*), Iași: Editura Universității Alexandru Ioan Cuza, 2017.

Procesul verbal al ședinței Biroului Direcției de Propagandă și Agitație al CC al PMR din 15 mai 1948 (*The Report of the Meeting of the Bureau of the of Propaganda and Agitation Direction of the CC of the PMR of 15 May 1948*), in AMR, microfilm fund, roll no. AS1-1516, frame no. 1.

Procesul verbal al şedinţei Biroului Politic cu Comisia pentru învăţământul superior din data de 7 octombrie 1948 (*The Report of the Politburo Meeting with the Higher Education Committee of 7 October 1948*), in AMR, microfilm fund, roll no. AS1-400, frame no. 1–4.

Procesul verbal al Şedinţei Biroului Secţiei Centrale de Educaţie Politică din 2 februarie 1948 (*The Report of the Meeting of the Bureau of the Central Section for Political Education of February 2, 1948*), in AMR, Arhivele Militare Române (Romanian Army Archives), microfilm fund, roll no. AS1-1516, frame no. 1.

Procesul verbal şi stenograma şedinţei Biroului organizatoric din ziua de 29 iunie 1950 (*The Report and the Stenogram of the Meeting of the Organising Office of 29 June 1950*), in AMR, microfilm fund, roll no.AS1-405, frame no. 16–42.

Procesul verbal şi stenograma şedinţei Biroului Organizatoric din ziua de 22 martie 1952 (*The Report and the Stenogram of the Meeting of the Organising Office of 22 March 1952*), in AMR, microfilm fund, roll no. AS1-406, frame no. 47–52.

Procesul verbal şi stenograma şedinţei Biroului Politic din data de 26 ianuarie 1953 (*Minutes and Verbatim Report of the Meeting of the Politburo of 26 January 1953*), in AMR, microfilm fund, roll no. AS1-407, frame no. 30.

Propuneri cu privire la îmbunătăţirea îndrumării activităţii în domeniul ştiinţelor sociale şi crearea Academiei de Ştiinţe Sociale (*Proposals on Improving the Guidance of Work in the Field of Social Sciences and the Creation of the Academy of Social Sciences*), in ANIC, the CC of the RCP Collection, Propaganda and Agitation Section, file no. 14/1969, 23.

Propuneri cu privire la selecţionarea candidaţilor pentru concursurile de admitere la Academia de Ştiinţe Social-Politice "Ştefan Gheorghiu" (*Proposals for the Selection of Candidates for the Entrance Competitions to the Academy of Social-Political Sciences "Stefan Gheorghiu"*), in ANIC, the CC of the RPC Collection, Chancellery Section, file no. 84/1966, 12.

Propuneri de măsuri pentru îmbunătăţirea propagandei de partid (*Proposals for Measures to Improve Party Propaganda*), in ANIC, the CC of the RCP Collection, Propaganda and Agitation Section, file no. 1/1961, 175; 165–68.

Protocol nr. 11 al şedinţei Secretariatului CC al PCR din ziua de 29 noiembrie 1976 (*Protocol No. 11 of the Meeting of the CC of the RCP Secretariat of November 29, 1976*), in ANIC, the CC of the RCP Collection, Chancellery Section, file no. 110/1976, 2.

Protocolul nr.18 al şedinţei Comitetului Executiv din ziua de 6 iulie 1971 (*Protocol No. 18 of the Executive Committee Meeting of July 6, 1971*), in ANIC, the CC of the RCP Collection, Chancellery Section, file no. 76/1971, 52.

Quentin, Paul, *La propagande politique. Une techinque nouvelle*, Paris: Librairie Plon, 1943.

Radu, Sorin, *Învăţământul de partid şi şcolile de cadre în România comunistă. Context naţional şi regional* (*Party Education and Cadre Schools in Communist Romania: National and Regional Context*), Iaşi: Editura Universităţii Alexandru Ioan Cuza, 2014.

Recomandări cu privire la organizarea şi desfăşurarea învăţământului de partid în anul şcolar 1966–1967 (*Recommendations on the Structure and the Process of*

Party Education in the Academic Year 1966–1967), in ANIC, the CC of the RCP Collection, Chancellery Section, file no. 106/1966, 31.

Referat cu privire la îmbunătățirea muncii politice de masă (*Report on Improving Mass Political Work*), in ANIC, the CC of the RCP Collection, Propaganda and Agitation Section, file no. 3/1963, 164.

Referat cu privire la îmbunătățirea muncii politice de masă (*Report on Improving Mass Political Work*), in ANIC, the CC of the RCP Collection, Propaganda and Agitation Section, file no. 3/1965, 158.

Referat cu privire la predarea disciplinelor de marxism-leninism în învățământul superior (*Report on the Teaching of Marxism-Leninism Subjects in Higher Education*), in ANIC, the CC of the RCP Collection, Propaganda and Agitation Section, file no. 42/1973, 55.

Revista *Arici Pogonici* (*Prickly Hedgehog*) (1957–1980).

Roller, Mihail, "Pe drumul revoluției noastre culturale" ("On the Road to our Cultural Revolution"), *Lupta de clasă* (*Class Fight*), 5th series, no. 2, Oct–Dec 1948, 103.

Rosefielde, S., *Red Holocaust,* New York: Routledge, 2009.

Sântimbreanu, Mircea, *Să stăm de vorbă fără catalog* (*Let us Talk without the Class Roster*), Bucharest: Editura Politică, 1976.

Scânteia Pionierului (*Pioneer's Spark*) (1953–1967).

Schema Secției de propagandă (*Organizational Chart of the Propaganda Section*), in ANIC, the CC of the RCP Collection, Chancellery Section, file no. 110/1976, 87–185.

Schema secției de propagandă și agitație (*The Organization Chart of the Propaganda and Agitation Section*), in ANIC, the CC of the RCP Collection, Propaganda and Agitation Section, file no. 46/1965, 8.

Seawright, Jason, and John Gerring, "Case Selection Techniques in Case Study Research: A Menu of Qualitative and Quantitative Options," in *Political Research Quarterly* 61, no. 2 (2008): 294–308.

Ședința Biroului Organizatoric din 12 mai 1950 (*Meeting of the Organising Office of 12 May 1950*), in AMR, microfilm fund, roll no. AS1-405, frame no. 44–85.

Selznick, Philip, *Leadership in Administration: A Sociological Interpretation*, Berkeley: University of California Press, 1984.

Selznick, Philip, *TVA and the Grass Roots: A Study of Politics and Organization*, Vol. 3, Berkeley: University of California Press, 1980.

Selznick, Philip, *The Organizational Weapon: A Study of Bolshevik Strategy and Tactics*, Vol. 18, New Orleans: Quid Pro Books, 2014.

Sinteza problemelor reieșite din rapoartele instructorilor teritoriali (*Summary of Problems Emerged from Territorial Instructors' Reports*), in ANIC, the CC of the RCP Collection, Propaganda and Agitation Section, file no. 4/1966, 17.

Ștefan, Alexandru, "Rolul activ al agitatorului" ("The Active Role of the Agitator"), in *Munca de Partid* (*Party Work*), Year XVI, no. 1/1973, 54.

Stenograma expunerii tovarășului Paul Niculescu-Mizil în fața secretarilor de partid responsabili cu probleme de propagandă, din data de 12 iulie 1968 (*Stenogram of the Report of Comrade Paul Niculescu-Mizil's Lecture to the Party Secretaries in*

Charge of Propaganda of July 12, 1968), in ANIC, the CC of the RCP Collection, Propaganda and Agitation Section, file no. 21/1968, 15.

Stenograma întâlnirii tovarășului Nicolae Ceaușescu cu conducerea Secției de Propagandă a CC al PCR din data de 8 februarie 1972 (*Stenogram of the Report of Comrade Nicolae Ceaușescu's Meeting with the Propaganda Section of the CC of the RCP on 8 February 1972*), in ANIC, the CC of the RCP Collection, Propaganda and Agitation Section, file no. 11/1972, 2–5.

Stenograma Ședinței Comitetului Executiv al CC al PCR din 25 decembrie 1968 (*Stenogram of the Executive Committee of the CC of the RCP Meeting of December 25, 1968*), in ANIC, the CC of the RCP Collection, Chancellery Section, file no. 216/1968, 7–12.

Stenograma ședinței cu instructorii teritoriali ai Secției de Propagandă și Agitație al CC al PCR din 5-6 august 1965 (*Stenogram of the Meeting with the Territorial Instructors of the Propaganda and Agitation Section of the CC of the RCP of 5-6 August 1965*), in ANIC, the CC of RCP Collection, Propaganda and Agitation Section, file no. 35/1965, 6.

Stenograma ședinței cu sectorul de agitație din Secția de Propagandă și Agitație a CC al PMR din ziua de 22 martie 1950 (*Stenogram of the Meeting with the CC of the PMR Propaganda and Agitation Section on 22 March 1950*), in AMR, microfilm fund, r.AS1-1517, frame no. 1–6.

Stenograma ședinței cu tovarășii secretari și șefi de secție ai comitetelor regionale de partid, secretari cu probleme de propagandă ai comitetelor regionale și alți tovarăși care lucrează în domeniul propagandei și culturii (*Stenogram of the Meeting with Comrade Secretaries and Sectional Leaders of the Regional Party Committees, Propaganda Secretaries of the Regional Committees and Other Comrades Active in the Areas of Propaganda and Culture*), in ANIC, the CC of the RCP Collection, Propaganda and Agitation Section, file no. 22/1961, 102.

Stenograma ședinței de raportare ale instructorilor teritoriali din 1 martie 1968 (*Stenogram of the Meeting of Territorial Instructors of 1 March 1968*), in ANIC, the CC of the RCP Collection, Propaganda and Agitation Section, file no. 1/1968, 5.

Stenograma ședinței discutării proiectului de program al Învățământului Superior din ziua de 7 octombrie 1949 (*Stenogram of the Meeting Discussing the Draft of the Higher Education Curriculum of 7 October 1949*), in AMR, microfilm fund, roll no. AS1-1516, frame no. 1–25.

Stenograma Ședinței Secretariatului CC al PCR din ziua de 18 octombrie 1977 (*Stenogram of the Secretariat of the CC of the RCP's Meeting of October 18, 1977*), in ANIC, the CC of the PCR Collection, Propaganda and Agitation Section, file no. 10/1967, 23.

Stoica, Augustin Cătălin, *România continuă. Schimbare și adaptare în comunism și postcomunism* (*Romania Continuous: Change and Adaptation in Communism and Postcommunism*), Bucharest: Editura Humanitas, 2018.

Strat, Cătălin, "Tehnici de propagandă comunistă în România" ("Communist Propaganda Techniques in Romania"), II. 1961–1962," in *Arhivele totalitarismului* (*Archives of Totalitarianism*), Year VII, No. 24–25, 3–4/1999, 219.

Svolik, Milan W., *The Politics of Authoritarian Rule*, Cambridge: Cambridge University Press, 2012.

Tămaș, Sergiu, *Dicționar politic. Instituțiile democrației și cultura civică* (*Political Dictionary: Institutions of Democracy and Civic Culture*), Bucharest: Editura Academiei Române, 1993.

Tânărul Leninist (*The Young Leninist*) (1951–1974).

Tănase, Stelian, *Elite și societate. Guvernarea Gheorghiu-Dej, 1948–1965* (*Elite and Society: Gheorghiu-Dej Government, 1948–1965*), Bucharest: Editura Humanitas, 1998.

Tănăsescu, Antoaneta, "Un Făt-Frumos de laborator, un Făt-Frumos de tip nou: 'omul nou'" ("A Prince Charming Obrained in the Lab, a New Type of Prince Charming: The New Man"), in *Miturile comunismului românesc* (*Myths of Romanian Communism*), ed. Lucian Boia, Bucharest: Editura Universității din București, 1995, 18.

Taylor, P. M., *Munitions of the Mind: A History of Propaganda from the Ancient World to the Present Era, Manchester:* Manchester University Press, 2013.

Thompson, Oliver, *Easily Led: A History of Propaganda*, London: Sutton Publishing, 1999.

Tismăneanu, Vladimir and Cristian Vasile, *Perfectul acrobat. Leonte Răutu, măștile răului* (*The Perfect Acrobat: Leonte Răutu, the Masks of Evil*), Bucharest: Editura Humanitas, 2008.

Tismăneanu, Vladimir, "The Ambiguity of Romanian National Communism," *Telos*, no. 60 (1984): 65–79

Tismăneanu, Vladimir, "Un posedat ideologic. Cine a fost Mihail Roller?" ("An Ideological Maniac: Who Was Mihail Roller?"), *Vladimir Tismăneanu's Blog*, accessed June 17, 2019, https://tismaneanu.wordpress.com/2011/04/04/un-tartor-ideologic-cine-a-fost-mihail-roller/.

Tismaneanu, Vladimir, *Fantasies of Salvation: Democracy, Nationalism and Myth în Post-Communist Europe*, Princeton, NJ: Princeton University Press, 1998.

Tismăneanu, Vladimir, *Fantoma lui Gheorghiu-Dej* (*Ghost of Gheorghiu-Dej*), Bucharest: Editura Univers, 1995 and the expanded 2nd ed., Bucharest: Editura Humanitas, 2008.

Tismaneanu, Vladimir, *Promises of 1968: Crisis, Illusion and Utopia*, Budapest: Central European University Press, 2010.

Tismaneanu, Vladimir, *Reinventing Politics*, Detroit: Free Press, 2000.

Tismaneanu, Vladimir, *Stalinism for All Seasons*, Berkeley: University of California Press, 2003.

Tismăneanu, Vladimir, *Stalinism pentru eternitate. O istorie politică a comunismului românesc* (*Stalinism for All Seasons: A Political History of Romanian Communism*), Iași: Editura Polirom, 2005.

Tismaneanu, Vladimir, *The Devil în History: Communism, Fascism and Some Lessons of the Twentieth Century*, Berkeley: University of California Press, 2012.

Troncotă, Tiberiu, *România comunistă, propagandă și cenzură* (*Communist Romania, Propaganda and Censorship*), Bucharest: Editura Tritonic, 2006.

University of Bucharest Archive, Human Resources Department Collection (Arhiva Universității din București, Departamentul de resurse umane), file no. 3464.

Vasile, Cristian, *Politici culturale comuniste în timpul regimului lui Gheorghiu-Dej*, Bucharest: Editura Humanitas, 2011.

Vasile, Cristian, "Educație și ideologie în România, 1948–1953" ("Education and Ideology in Romanian, 1948–1953"), in *Revista istorică* (*Historical Magazine*), XV, no. 5–6 (2004), 128.

Vasile, Cristian, "Studentul, scriitorul și pedagogia infernală a regimului comunist. Cazul Alexandru Ivasiuc" ("The Student, Writer and Infernal Pedagogy of the Communist Regime: The Case of Alexandru Ivasiuc"), *Revista istorica* (*Historical Magazine*), vol. XXIII, 1–2, 2012.

Vasile, Cristian, *Literatura și artele în România comunistă, 1948–1953* (*Literature and the Arts in Communist Romania, 1948–1953*), Bucharest: Editura Humanitas, 2010.

Vasile, Cristian, *Viața intelectuală și artistică în primul deceniu al regimului Ceaușescu, 1965–1974* (*Intellectual and Artistic Life in the First Decade of the Ceaușescu Regime, 1965–1974*), Bucharest: Editura Humanitas, 2014.

Viața studențească (*Student Life*)—starting with 1956.

Voicu, Marian, *Matrioșka mincinoșilor, fake news, manipulare, populism* (*Matrioska Liars, Fake News, Manipulation, Populism*), Bucharest: Editura Humanitas, 2018.

Volokoff, Vladimir, *Tratat de dezinformare: de la Calul Troian la internet* (*Disinformation Treaty: From the Trojan Horse to the Internet*), Bucharest: Editura Antet, 1999.

Wintrobe, Ronald, "The Tinpot and the Totalitarian: An Economic Theory of Dictatorship," in *The American Political Science Review*, 84, no. 3 (Sep. 1990): 849–72.

www.evz.ro

www.slavicreview.com

www.tismaneanu.wordpress.com

Zainea, Ion, "Propagandiștii Partidului Comunist. Câteva portrete" ("Communist Party Propagandists: A Few Portraits"), in *Identități sociale, culturale, etnice și religioase (Social, Cultural, Ethnic and Religious Identities)* (eds.) Cosmin Budeancă, Florin Olteanu, IICCMER, Iași: Editura Polirom, 2015, 99–100.

Zinoviev, Alexander, *Homo sovieticus*, trans. Charles Janson, London: Gollancz, 1985.

"Să îmbunătățim predarea marxism-leninismului în școlile superioare" ("To Improve the Teaching of Marxism-Leninism in Higher Schools"), *Lupta de clasă* (*Class Fight*), 5th series, XXX, issue no. 4, April 1950, 45.

"What Was National Stalinism," in *Oxford Handbook of Postwar European History*, ed. Dan Stone, Oxford: Oxford University Press, 2012, 462–80.

"*Biroului Politic al PMR a decis transformarea școlii de lectori A.A. Jdanov într-o școală superioară de științe sociale cu durata de 2 ani*" ("The Political Bureau of the PMR Decided to Transform the School of Lecturers A. A. Jdanov into a Higher School of Social Sciences"), in *Scânteia* (*The Spark*), July 22, 1949,. 1.

"Metodica muncii propagandistului" ("Method of the Propagandist's Work"), in *În ajutorul propagandistului* (*Support for the Propagandists*), Year VIII, no. 11/1971, 90.

"Pentru ridicarea nivelului agitației vizuale" ("To Raise the Level of Visual Agitation"), in *Scânteia* (*The Spark*), of May 18, 1952, 1.

"Comunistul, om înaintat al societății noastre" ("Communist, the Advanced Man of Our Society"), in *În ajutorul propagandiștilor* (*Support for the Propagandists*), Year VII, no. 11/1967, 21.

"Cursurile pentru propagandiști" ("The Courses for Propagandists"), in *Munca de partid (Party Work)*, Year I, no. 1/1957, 38.

"Deschiderea primului Cabinet de Partid de consultanță marxist-leninistă" ("Opening of the First Marxist-Leninist Advisory Party Cabinet"), in *Scânteia* (*The Spark*), din February 15, 1949, 1.

"Introducere în practica anchetelor sociologice" ("Introduction to the Practice of Sociological Surveys"), in *Îndrumătorul cultural (The Cultural Guide)*, Year XXI, Issue 4/1968, 36–37.

"Pregătirea propagandiștilor—sarcină de mare răspundere" ("Training of Propagandists—Task of Great Responsibility"), in *Scânteia* (*The Spark*), of July 12, 1951, 1.

"Să dezvoltăm puternic agitația politică de masă" ("Let's Strongly Develop the Mass Political Agitation"), in *Scânteia* (*The Spark*), of February 17, 1949, 1.

Index

activist(s), 12, 23, 25, 37, 49, 52–53, 63n42, 68, 70, 73, 75, 77–79, 84, 88, 101, 111–12, 115, 118, 120, 136, 138–39
agitator(s), 32, 35–37, 47, 49, 52–54, 64n52, 69, 75, 77, 81–82, 84, 86–87, 130, 139, 140
authority, 3, 14, 23–24, 28, 34, 55, 63n37, 71, 118n12, 139–40, 143n4, 154

Bernholz, Peter, 4–5, 11–12, 16, 18n31, 148, 153, 156n8
Bolshevik(s), 20, 32, 34, 79, 127, 143n4
Brzezinski, Zbigniew, 13–15, 18n31, 154
bureaucracy, 59n12, 67
   bureaucratic, 46, 102–3, 115
   bureaucratization, 14, 114, 154

Cassinelli, C. W., 23–25
Ceaușescu, Nicolae, xv, 54, 56–57, 65nn68–69, 71–72, 83–85, 87, 91n17, 96n102, 102, 105–8, 111, 113, 118n18, 120n33, 120n45, 130
censorship, 29–30, 60n17, 136, 148, 152
Chișinevschi, Iosif, 48, 51–53, 60n21
class struggle, 11, 33, 43n2, 50, 55, 61n24, 68, 74

Constantinescu, Miron, 48, 91n17, 111, 120n47

dictatorship, xv, 13–14, 28, 38n25, 39, 47, 65n68, 92n33
doctrine(s), 3–4, 10, 15, 22–26, 30, 47, 50, 54–55, 63n49
Domenach, Jean-Marie, 32–36, 39n48

economy, xiii, 7, 13, 27, 53, 70–71, 80, 92n27, 102
experiment(s), 9–10, 12, 17n8, 20, 142, 149, 154

freedom, xv, 59n11, 60n17, 139
Friedrich, Carl, 13–15, 18n31, 154

Gerring, John, xv, xviiin7
Gheorghiu-Dej, Gheorghe, 52, 54–55, 63n49, 64nn60–61, 69, 79, 86, 90n2, 130
governance, x, xii, 3–9, 12, 17n8, 19, 21–22, 31–32, 37, 141, 148
   governance system, xii, 3–4, 7, 9, 17n8, 19, 31, 37, 141, 148
Guriev, Sergei, 28–30, 39n29

Hollander, Paul, 10–11, 19–20, 37
Hume, David, 10, 17n8

ideocracy, 3–7, 10, 12, 18n31, 31, 46, 147, 153, 156n8
implementation, 6, 11, 19, 53, 62n37, 85, 100
intellectual(s), 1, 15, 24, 36–37, 39n46, 47, 50, 55, 60n17, 62n28, 71–72, 75, 79, 88, 92n25, 100, 106, 109, 114, 121n64, 127
internationalism, 47, 55, 57–58n3

Koopmans, Tjalling, C., 7, 17n7
Koutaissoff, Elisabeth, xiv, 21
Kuran, Timur, 152, 155n5

legitimacy, 3, 49–50, 58n3
  legitimization, 9, 50, 68, 147
Lenin, 10–11, 21, 32–36, 39n46, 82
Leninism, 10, 25, 50, 52, 55, 70, 73, 81, 99–100, 104–5, 109, 119, 121n60

manipulation, 19, 23–24, 27, 51, 55, 58n3, 59n11, 141
Marx, Karl, 10–11, 32, 114
Marxism, 10, 17, 24–25, 31, 33, 50, 52, 55, 70, 73, 79, 81, 99–100, 104–5, 109, 117, 121, 163
  Marxism-Leninism, 50, 52, 55, 70, 73, 81, 99–100, 104–5, 109
materialism, 11, 50, 52, 70, 91n25, 99–100, 102, 106, 108, 110
Montias, Jojn Michel, 7, 17

nationalism, 45, 47, 54–55, 57, 74
New Man, 9–12, 19–23, 25–26, 38n5, 41, 46, 49–50, 57–59, 59n10, 59n12, 68, 105, 114, 117, 128–30, 136–37
Nomenklatura, 48, 52–53, 65n69, 67–68, 87, 89n1, 90n2, 103, 114, 136–37

organization, 6, 14, 21, 31–34, 54, 80, 83, 99, 102–3, 107, 125, 128–32, 135–37, 140–43
  organization of ideology, ix, xiv, xvi, 147
  organization of indoctrination, xii–xiv, 131
Ostrom, Elinor, xiv, 151–52, 155n4

Party (Communist), x–xi, xiv, xvi–xvii, 11–15, 20, 22–24, 26, 28–29, 32–37, 39n51, 42, 45, 47–63, 63n42, 63n49, 67–88, 90–92, 95n83, 95n85, 97n110, 99–119, 126–27, 129, 131, 133–34, 136, 138–40, 143–44
policy (public), 8, 21, 55, 57, 72, 74, 80, 84, 100, 107, 114, 152, 155n5n6
political economy, xiii, 27, 70, 80, 102
political system(s), ix–xii, xiv–xv, 3–4, 7, 9, 12–13, 17n8, 37, 59n11, 64n61, 85, 147–48, 153
press, 37, 49, 52–54, 59n8, 63n42, 65n69, 70, 77, 82, 86, 91n15, 92n32, 95n85, 96n94, 103–4
public choice, 19, 27–28, 41, 148, 150, 155n5

Răutu, Leonte, 48, 51–53, 60n22, 63n49, 70–72, 91n17, 104–7
reform(s), 46, 53–54, 69, 74, 89, 110, 145n19
  reforming, 107
  reformist, 109
reorganization, 58, 74, 87, 140
repression, 27, 29–30, 38, 45, 48–49, 55, 108, 136, 144n15, 152
revolution, 10–11, 21, 30–36, 38n7, 50–51, 61–62, 72, 80, 94n68, 104–5, 109–10, 112, 127, 155n5
  revolutionary, 10–11, 21, 33–36, 61n28, n62, 72, 80, 94n68, 104, 109–10, 112, 127, 155n5
Roller, Mihail, 52–53, 91n15, 99
Romanian Communist Party (RPC)
  Bureau of, 49, 51, 69, 73, 77, 79–80, 84, 102, 116
  Central Committee (of the RCP), 42, 47–49, 51–52, 61n22, 62n37, 63nn48–49, 69, 71, 74,

76, 83, 85–86, 102, 104, 107, 111, 118n12
Congress, 48, 51, 54, 56, 61n24, 64n59, 65n69, 69, 85, 112, 118n12

school(s), xi, 22, 37, 46–47, 50, 52, 54, 59n8, 62n34, 69–77, 79, 81–85, 90n2, 91n18, 91n25, 95n85, 100–102, 110, 112–13, 116, 133–34, 138–39
securitate, 45, 48, 136, 139–40, 144n15
  political police, xi, 48, 101, 117, 126, 136, 140, 144n18
Selznick, Philip, 126–32, 135, 137, 140–43n4, 150, 153
social engineering, 9, 21, 30, 49, 130
Socialism, xii, 9, 11–12, 19, 22, 26, 29, 34, 42, 45, 48, 50–51, 56–58n1, 60n12, 65nn73–74, 72, 78, 82–83, 85, 90n6, 92n35, 94n68, 106, 108–10, 112–15, 119n25, 129
  Socialist society, 45, 48, 56, 85, 129
  Socialist (construction of) 78, 106
sociology, xvii, 113, 123, 127, 129–30, 132, 149
  sociology of formal organization, 132
  sociology theory, 150
Soviet, 12, 20, 23, 34, 36, 45, 47, 48, 55, 59n8, 64, 64n59, 64n61, 67, 79, 121n54, 142
  Soviet Army, 47, 99
  Soviet Bloc, 105
  Soviet blueprint, 69, 91n25
  Soviet citizen, 25–26
  Soviet educator, 58n4
  Soviet ideologue, 91n13

Soviet leaders, 21, 46–47, 55
Soviet model, 47–48, 145n19
Soviet Union, 5, 41, 54–55, 59n10, 91n19, 95n83, 100–101, 118n15, 153
Sovietization, 46, 54–55, 64n58
Stalin, xiv, 23, 47, 54, 59, 64n61, 82, 86, 100
Stalinism, xv, 55, 58n2, 60n15, 64n58, 64n60, 65n68
Stalinist, xiv, 47, 54, 64n61, 105
Stalinization, 47, 64n58, 105
strategy, xiv–xv, xvii, 29, 31, 37, 41, 47, 49–50, 59n11, 111, 113, 126–27, 143n4, 148, 150

tactics, 31, 127, 143n4
theory, 1, 5, 29, 38n25, 57–58, 58n4, 80, 85, 134, 138, 150, 152
  organizational theory, xiii
  institutional theory, xvii, 151
  theory of Marxism-Leninism, 25
Tismaneanu, Vladimir, 10, 17n11, 43, 58n3, 60n22, 64n58, 64n60, 119
Toma, Sorin, 50, 52
totalitarianism, 3–6, 12–16, 23–24, 31–32, 46, 147–48, 153–54, 156n8
tradition, 9–10, 28, 45, 49, 101, 113
  traditional, 5, 7, 48, 57, 110, 127
transition, 18n31, 21, 26, 65n68, 121n54, 148, 150

university, 42, 71–73, 75, 82, 84, 99, 101, 103–6, 108, 110, 112, 114, 118n13, 121n54, 131, 133, 140
University of Bucharest, 42, 74, 91n15, 91n25, 92n27, 101, 105, 114–15

About the Authors

Paul Dragos Aligica received his PhD in political science from Indiana University Bloomington in 2004. He is a professor at the University of Bucharest and a senior research fellow in the F. A. Hayek Program for Advanced Study in Philosophy, Politics and Economics at the Mercatus Center, George Mason University. He is the author and coauthor of ten books and numerous academic articles on political theory, institutional analysis, Eastern European political economy, and post-Socialist transition. Aligica has written for a wide variety of academic journals, including *American Political Science Review*, *Revue française d'economie*, *Society*, *East European Economics,* and *Communist and Post-Communist Studies*. His publications include *The Neoliberal Revolution in Eastern Europe: Economic Ideas in the Transition from Communism,* with Anthony Evans (2008), *Institutional Diversity and Political Economy* (2014) and *Public Entrepreneurship, Citizenship, and Self-Governance* (2018).

Simona Preda received her PhD in History from the University of Bucharest in 2011, and MA in history of ideas from the University of Bucharest in 2006). She is the author and coauthor of five books on Romanian history in the context of modernization of Eastern Europe and on Communist education and propaganda, including *All the Way Forward!* (2016) and *Romanian Homeland, Country of Heroes* (2014). Her articles on ideology and indoctrination in the Romanian education system, on textbooks during Communism, and on Stalin's image in the children literature were published in both scholarly journals (such as *The National Archives Review, The Romanian Academy Library Review* and *Studies of Contemporary History*) and in the popular press. Preda has also been a screenwriter for historical documentaries such as *Queen Mother Elena* and *"All the Way!" Communist Propaganda for Children*, in collaboration with the Romanian National Television, The Centre for Memorial Studies and Identity, and the National Archives of Romania.

www.ingramcontent.com/pod-product-compliance
Lightning Source LLC
Chambersburg PA
CBHW021355300426
44114CB00012B/1245